FETAL ALCOHOL SYNDROME
———— AND ————
FETAL ALCOHOL EFFECTS

FETAL ALCOHOL SYNDROME
——— AND ———
FETAL ALCOHOL EFFECTS

Ernest L. Abel

Research Institute on Alcoholism
Buffalo, New York

PLENUM PRESS • NEW YORK AND LONDON

Library of Congress Cataloging in Publication Data

Abel, Ernest L., 1943–
   Fetal alcohol syndrome and fetal alcohol effects.
   Includes bibliographical references and index.
   1. Fetal alcohol syndrome. 2. Fetus—Effect of drugs on. I. Title. [DNLM: 1. Fetal
alcohol syndrome. 2. Alcohol drinking—In pregnancy. 3. Alcoholic beverages—
Adverse effects. 4. Fetus—Drug effects. WQ 211 A139f]
RG629.F45A34   1984   618.3′68   83-26898
ISBN 0-306-41427-9

© 1984 Ernest L. Abel
Plenum Press is a Division of
Plenum Publishing Corporation
233 Spring Street, New York, N.Y. 10013

Preface

I have written this book because I felt there was a need to bring together in one place the vast amount of research that has been published in the past 10 years concerning alcohol's effects on the conceptus. My hope is that this book will be of value to the many clinicians, basic research scientists, social workers, and others who are interested in this important issue.

The number of such publications continues to grow each year, and it was a very difficult task to review even a proportion of them completely. While I have cited many of these research studies, only those that in my very subjective opinion warranted extended coverage were discussed. In this regard, much of my ask was facilitated by the many excellent reviews that have already been written. To those whose important contributions have not been discussed or cited, I offer my sincere apologies. Omission of these publications in most cases reflects my own personal interests or awareness, rather than merit.

In the writing of a book such as this, there are a number of people to whom a special thanks is owing. These are Hebe Greizerstein, Carrie Randall, Edward Riley, and Robert Sokol, for reading various chapters of the manuscript and suggesting improvements. Any remaining errors or biased opinions are mine, not theirs. I also thank Carrie Randall, Robert Sokol, Phillip Spiegel, Kathy Sulik and James West for providing photographs for the text. Diane Augustino, librarian of the Research Institute on Alcoholism, was, as always, of immense help in locating research publications that might otherwise have been unobtainable.

Contents

CHAPTER 1

Is Fetal Alcohol Syndrome a New Discovery?

Whenever a common substance is suddenly found to be a health hazard, and especially a possible cause of birth defects, many people begin to wonder why it took so long for such a hazard to be discovered.

Alcohol is no exception to this general rule.

When the fetal alcohol syndrome was first brought to international attention in 1973 by Jones and Smith,[1,2] many authors, including Jones and Smith themselves, claimed that awareness of alcohol's potential to cause birth defects was nothing new. Jones and Smith[2] cited some ancient Greek authors and a Carthaginian law that seemed to indicate that the dangers of drinking during pregnancy were clearly perceived in the ancient world. Other authors subsequently noted what they believed to be further evidence of such awareness during the course of history.

This chapter examines the various epochs in the alleged history of the "fetal alcohol syndrome." I use the word *alleged* intentionally since I believe that a critical examination of the evidence will show that nearly all the statements investing the ancient and medieval past with precognition of this disorder are wrong. Most are simply repetitions of what has been written before, thus perpetuating the error. In those instances when there does seem to be an awareness of "fetal alcohol effects" in the ancient and medieval world, the emphasis is almost entirely on the father. Moreover, these comments are not based on empirical evidence but are deductive—arising from alcohol's observable effects on sperm production and libido. It is not until the late 19th century that a general appreciation of the link between drinking during pregnancy and "fetal alcohol effects" appears.

Even so, why did it take so long for the medical profession and the general public to become aware of the potential dangers of drinking during pregnancy?

1

The answer, is that the evidence prior to Jones and Smith was far from convincing, and in some cases it was interpreted as showing that fetal alcohol damage was generally a good thing for mankind as a whole!

The Biblical and Postbiblical Eras

The biblical passage that is most often cited as proof that the ancient Hebrews were aware of alcohol's injurious effects on the fetus is Judges 13:3–4. This is an excerpt from the saga of Samson in which an angel appears to the hero's mother before she is pregnant and cautions:

> Behold now, thou art barren, and bearest not: but
> thou shalt conceive, and bear a son.
> Now therefore beware, I pray thee, and drink not
> wine nor strong drink, and eat not any unclean
> thing.[3]

The reason for this injunction is not that the storyteller was aware of alcohol's potential to produce spontaneous abortion or birth anomalies. Rather it is because Samson is foreordained to live the austere life of a Nazirite, as stated in the next verse (Judg. 13:5)[3]:

> . . . for the child shall be a Nazirite unto God from
> the womb. . .

The Nazirite vow, as described in the book of Numbers (6:2–6)[3] prohibited those who took it from all intoxicants, from cutting their hair, and from touching dead bodies.

There is no interpretation or commentary of the passage in Judges 13:3–4 in the Talmud or any other commentary indicating that this passage is to be considered in any way other than that binding Samson as a Nazirite. The reason his mother is enjoined from taking alcohol is that Samson was to be a Nazirite from the moment of his conception ("from the womb"). While this passage indicates a possible awareness that alcohol could pass from the mother's body to the conceptus, it does not presage any awareness that such passage could be damaging to the conceptus.

Feldman, in his book, *The Jewish Child*,[4] cites two Talmudic passages (Sabbath 80b and Moed Katon 9b) that he interpreted as possibly showing that paternal drinking could lead to hirsutism in children. The passage from the tractate Sabbath (80b),[5] however, states only that Rabbi Bibi had a daughter that he treated with a depilatory. Rabbi Nachman says that he didn't have to do so to his daughters and explains: "As for R. Bibi who drank strong liquor, his daughter required pasting over; [but] as for us, who do not drink strong liquor, our daughters do not require such treatment." In tractate Moed Katon (9b),[5] the same anecdote is mentioned as follows: "Said R. Nahman: 'R. Bebai drinks beer, therefore his daughters needed unguents; [but as] we do not drink beer, our daughters need no unguents." In the footnote to this passage, the commentator cites the biblical scholar Rashi, who explained that beer produces obesity and growth of hair.

Although one might interpret these two passages in agreement with Feldman, there does not seem to be much support for such a view. Possibly Rabbi Nachman means only that his family doesn't drink beer or wine at all. As a result, his daughters don't get fat or hairy.

Feldman[4] also cites passages from tractates *Kallah Rabbathi* (i) and *Nedarim* (20b) to the effect that "children begotten during a state of inebriety are mentally deficient."

The relevant passage from *Kallah Rabbathi*[5] occurs in chapter 52a under the discussion of who is like a bastard but is not legally such. Among those so considered are "the children of a drunken woman." The text then goes on to state that "the children of a drunken woman will have children who will [be thought of] as though they were drunk, as it is written, How long wilt thou be drunken? which is rendered in the *Targum* 'demented.'" The passage in *Nedarim* 20b[5] does not seem relevant at all since it mentions only children conceived during intoxication as being among those who are guilty of transgression.

Whereas *Kallah Rabbathi* does appear to contain some notion of alcohol-related teratogenicity, this is such an isolated passage that it received little attention and had little impact on those reading it. In the same section, for instance, the text talks about weaklings and ugly children being born to those who have been excommunicated and to men who have intercourse with their wives during menstruation. In the discussion of having intercourse while both the man and the woman are drinking, there is no mention of adverse effects on offspring.

The Jews of the postbiblical era would have had little experience with alcohol-related birth defects since they were very abstemious. Even the sending of a cup of wine to a woman was prohibited (*Kallah Rabbathi*, 51b).[5] Giving wine to women was in fact scrupulously avoided because of a fear that they would lose control of themselves sexually. According to the tractate *Kethuboth* (65a), "One glass of wine is becoming to a woman, two are somewhat degrading, and if she has three glasses she solicits coitus, but if she has four, she solicits even an ass in the street and forgets all decency." Men who were forced to leave their wives for some time were required to provide them with all the necessities, but not wine (*Kethuboth* 65a).

The Bible's and the Talmud's silence on alcohol-related birth defects is not the result of any disinterest or lack of experience with alcohol. Both contain hundreds of references to alcohol and its effects. Both also contain many references to alcohol's effects on sexual behavior.[6–8] The only conclusion that seems warranted is that fetal alcohol effects were not known to the Hebrews of the biblical or postbiblical era.

Greece and Rome

The people of the Greek and Roman empires used wine liberally. Wine was drunk at home and in public meeting places. It was a common item at almost every table and was consumed morning, noon, and night. It was used as a medicine and as a flavoring in cooking. Large amounts were consumed at banquets and religious festivals. The writers of the ancient world, especially the Greek writers, vividly portrayed the drinking habits of their contemporaries, and the artists painted drinking-related themes. They drew and spoke of the pleasant side of drinking and of its destructive side when too much was consumed.

In Greece there were few constraints against drinking by women by the 5th century B.C., and drunkenness was not confined to men. The plays of Aristophanes and Euripides are filled with scenes of women drinking wine. In Aristophanes' *Thesmophoriazusae* (*Festival Women*),[9] for example, one of the male characters berates the women around him for their drinking: "O ever thirsty, ever tippling women, O ever ready with fresh schemes for drink, To vintners what a blessing; but to us and all our goods and chattles what a curse!" (*Festival Women* 735–740). Euripides' *Bacchae*[10] portrays the same picture of women and drinking.

The early Romans were very circumspect in their drinking during the times of the kings of Rome, and women were not permitted to have wine at all. Pliny[11] (*Natural History* 14.90) says that some women were even put to death by their husbands if caught drinking. A number of other writers also refer to this law.[12] However, by the 2nd century B.C. it no longer was enforced, according to Athenaeus[13] (*Dipnosophistae* x.440).

The reason for this law was the belief that wine was a powerful aphrodisiac for women, not because of any perceived effects on offspring. In this regard, Polybius is quoted as saying that "it is almost impossible for them [women] to drink wine without being found out. For the woman does not have charge of the wine; moreover, she is bound to kiss all of her male relatives and those of her husband down to her second cousins every day on seeing them for the first time; and as she cannot tell which of them she will meet she has to be on her guard. For if she has but tasted wine there is no occasion for any formal accusation" (Athenaeus,[13] x.440).

By the 1st century B.C. drunkenness was not uncommon in Rome, and many of the great generals were among those who drank to excess (e.g., Pliny,[11] *Natural History* 14.148). Restrictions against women drinking appear to have been totally removed. Seneca[14] (*Epistles* 45.12) mentions women who drink as much as men, and the wives and mothers of the Roman emperors often drank to excess (e.g., Suetonius,[15] *Augustus* 65.1; Tacitus,[16] *Annals* 11.31).

The writings of the Church fathers also contain notices of drinking among women. Beginning with Paul, who urged older women not to become so enamored with wine so that they could set a better example for younger women (*Titus* 2:3–5), the Church was constantly after its female members to exercise more restraint in their drinking. Since the early Church was largely made up of people of Hellenistic background, it is not surprising that they engaged in many of the behaviors typical of their Greek forebears, including drinking to excess.

The ancient Greeks and Romans thus had ample opportunity to observe any instances of "fetal alcohol effects," and some writers have credited them with an awareness of alcohol's teratogenic potential. But in many instances more has been read into what was said than what seems to have been originally intended. In other instances, there is no evidence that the people cited as saying something about alcohol ever said anything of the sort.

An interesting example of what appears to be an invention of modern scholarship is the embellishment of the Vulcan cycle of myths to the effect that this Roman god was lame because his father conceived him while he was drunk. This anecdote was repeated most recently by Green[17] and by Haggard and Jellinek,[18] and can also be found in works by Ballantyne,[19] Crother,[20] and Matthews Duncan.[21] None of these authors, except for Ballantyne, gives a source for this information, and he cites Matthews Duncan.

I have not been able to trace citation of this anecdote back beyond Matthews Duncan, but he cites it as if it were already well known. In ancient mythology, the Roman god Vulcan was the counterpart of the Greek god Hephaestus. He was the god of fire and metalworking and was portrayed as a lame and ugly deformed deity. His lameness was attributed in one account to being thrown out of heaven by his father, Zeus (Jupiter in Rome), for having rescued his mother from a punishment imposed upon her by Zeus. Another story says that his mother threw him out of heaven and he became lame. Because of this insult, Hephaestus/ Vulcan anonymously sent her a throne that kept her locked into it by invisible bonds. Only by getting him drunk were the gods able to get him to release his mother (Plato, *Republic* 378[d]; Pausanius, *Description of Greece* 1, xx, 3).

This latter story was elaborated in Greek art.[22] Hephaestus was portrayed as riding back to heaven on an ass (which was a phallic symbol) surrounded by satyrs, either holding a drinking horn in his hand or with a wine pitcher on the ass's phallus. Whether this story and its associated portrayal in art formed the basis for the story of the god's eventual lameness due to being conceived while his father was drunk I do not know. Suffice is it to say that there is no mention of Vulcan's lameness being due to parental drinking in any of the standard works on Greek and Roman mythology. While such a myth indicates a recognition of alcohol-related teratogenicity, such recognition belongs to the modern, not the ancient world. Furthermore, the story emphasizes paternal, not maternal drinking. This paternal contribution is, in fact, the predominant theme in all the ancient writings containing any possible reference to fetal alcohol effects.

The second dubious anecdote of interest is one suggesting that the Carthaginians forbade a bridal couple to drink wine. This interdiction is interpreted as suggestive of an awareness of possible harm coming from exposure of a fertilized ovum to alcohol. This anecdote was cited by Jones and Smith[2] in their paper coining the term *fetal alcohol syndrome* and has been widely repeated, although rarely is any source given for the quotation by those following Jones and Smith or by Jones and Smith themselves.

The source for the Jones and Smith reference may have been Haggard and Jellinek's classic book, *Alcohol Explored* (1944),[18] but those authors also do not cite any source for their reference to this law. Hoppe in 1910 likewise cites this law without giving any reference. Matthews Duncan[21] cites the same law but adds that the Romans also had such a law and the reason for it was "lest the foetus should get harm." Matthews Duncan's reference for this law is a 1784 German translation of a Swedish text on alcohol.[23]

The historical basis of this anecdote may be a passage from Plato's *Laws*[24] in which he discusses a Carthaginian law prohibiting soldiers on the march from having wine. After stating this law, Plato then suggests some other people who should not drink, among them any "man or woman—when proposing to procreate children," and he terminates his list with the comment that "many other occasions, also, might be mentioned when wine should not be drunk by men who are swayed by right reason and law" (*Laws* 2.674ᵇ).

From this passage it is uncertain whether Plato was referring to an actual Carthaginian law forbidding men and women to drink if they were going to have children, or was suggesting that such a law should exist. A subsequent passage in the same book, however, suggests the latter interpretation. Thus, in speaking of drinking to excess, Plato says that it is especially unsafe "for those who take marriage seriously; for at such a time above all it behooves both bride and bridegroom to be sober, seeing that the change in their life is a great one, and in order to ensure, so far as possible, in every case that the child that is begotten may be sprung from the loins of sober parents: for what shall be, with God's help, the night or day of its begetting is quite uncertain" (*Laws* 6.775ᶜ). The reason for abstinence is then explained:

> Moreover, it is not right that procreation should be the work of bodies dissolved by excess of wine, but rather that the embryo should be compacted firmly, steadily and

> quietly in the womb. But the man that is steeped in wine moves and is moved himself in every way, writhing both in body and soul; consequently, when drunk, a man is clumsy and bad at sowing seed, and is thus likely to beget unstable and untrusty offspring, crooked in form and character (*Laws* 6.775^{c-d}).

Although Plato appears from this passage to have had a suspicion that alcohol could have an adverse effect on pregnancy, his emphasis is on the father rather than the mother, although both are mentioned. Furthermore, his statements are based on deduction, not observation. He says that alcohol makes a man "clumsy" and gives him "bad seed" and contends that as a result, any children that he sires will be defective.

Robert Burton[25] attributes to several other Greek and Roman writers statements about the adverse effects of drinking during pregnancy. Examination of the original sources for these quotations indicates that Burton was interpreting these ancient writings to fit his own moralistic views about drinking.

For example, Burton quotes Aristotle (*Problemata* 4.2) as stating that "foolish, drunken, or hairbrain women [for] the most part bring forth children like unto themselves, morosos et languidos [morose and feeble]. . . " (p. 213). However, nowhere in the *Problemata*[26] does Aristotle make such a statement literally or figuratively. Instead, Aristotle's comments about wine and reproduction are confined to his views on how alcohol affects sexual intercourse and male fertility. In this regard, he poses two questions. The first is: "Why is it that those who are drunk are incapable of having sexual intercourse?" (*Problemata* 872^b, 875^b). The answer, he says, is that alcohol causes a loss of heat from the lower body and therefore sperm become sluggish.

Although he could have used the same argument to answer his second question: "Why is the semen of drunkards generally infertile?"(*Problemata* 871^a), Aristotle instead says that their infertility is caused by the excessive dilution of semen by wine.

Another ancient writer quoted by Burton is Aulus Gellius. To him Burton attributes the statement in *Attic Nights* (12.1) that "if a drunken man get a child, it will never likely have a good brain" (p. 213). Gellius, however, makes no such statement in the place cited or anywhere else. Instead, his remarks deal with the Roman custom of forbidding women to drink, not because of any adverse effects on pregnancy, but because of the belief that alcohol would make them unable to control themselves sexually (see below).

The one author that Burton has not tampered very much with is Plutarch, to whom Burton attributes the saying, in *Symposiacs* (1.5), that "one drunkard begets another" (p. 213). However, it is not in the *Symposiacs* that Plutarch makes a comment of this nature, but in *Education of Children* (3):

> In this connection [having children] we should speak of a matter which has not been overlooked by our predecessors [Plato?]. What is this? It is that husbands who approach their wives for the sake of issue should do so only when they have either not

taken any wine at all, or at any rate, a very moderate portion. For children whose
fathers have chanced to beget them in drunkenness are wont to be fond of wine, and to
be given to excessive drinking.

While Plutarch suggests that paternal drinking may adversely affect children, he is proposing a Lamarkian mode of transmission. To Plutarch, and to
Plato, whom he may have had in mind when mentioning "our predecessors,"
the state of mind and body of the parents, especially the father, were of utmost
importance since these momentary traits were capable of being transmitted to any
children conceived at this time. This idea is also behind Plutarch's quotation of
Diogenes, who, "observing a crack-brained youth, said, 'Young man, your
father must have been drunk when he begot you!' "(*Education of Children* 3).

Plutarch, along with many of the other ancient writers, seemed to be clearly
aware, however, of alcohol's effects on libido and on fertility. In *Symposiacs* (5.2) Plutarch states that "the great drinkers are very dull, inactive fellows,
no women's men at all; they eject nothing strong, vigorous, and fit for generation, but are weak and unperforming by reason of the bad digestion and coldness
of their seed." In this context, Plutarch also mentions that because of his exes-
sive drinking, Alexander the Great was "cold in love . . ." (*Symposiacs* 6.1).

Here, then, is the basis of Plutarch's remarks about alcohol's effects on the
unborn. It was probably the basis for any statements by the other writers of this
period. These writers were all men. Their interests concerned men. They were in
a position to observe how alcohol affected their own sexual activities and their
own reproductive capabilities, and they would get additional information from
their male companions.

The last of the ancient writers worth quoting in this context is Macrobius. In
his *Saturnalia* (7.8) (which Burton also incorrectly cites and interprets), Macrobius says that "all hot substances provoke to venery, stir the seed, and favor
procreation, but after copious draughts of unmixed wine men become less active
lovers and the seed which they sow is unfitted for generation, since the excess of
wine, as a cold substance, makes it thin or weak." Here Macrobius follows
Aristotle and Plutarch in attributing alcohol's effects on male infertility to a
hypothermic effect in the lower part of the body.

The only writer of the ancient world who even considered women in the
procreation process, and the impact of alcohol in it, is Soranus, often considered
to be the "father" of gynecology. In his book, *Gynecology* (1), Soranus states
that the optimal state for intercourse is sobriety. The reason for this opinion is
given in Lamarkian terms: "In order that the offspring may not be rendered
misshapen, women must be sober during coitus because in drunkenness the soul
becomes the victim of strange phantasies; this furthermore, because the offspring
bears some resemblance to the mother as well not only in body but in soul. . . ."

To Soranus, as to most of his contemporaries, a conceptus was imprinted with its parents' spiritual as well as physical attributes. The disfigurement he refers to, however, does not seem to be that of the body but rather that of the "soul," suggesting that he in fact was not aware of any physical or cognitive damage resulting from prenatal alcohol exposure. However, it is noteworthy that Soranus was one of the few of the ancient writers even to consider the possibility that alcohol could affect the conceptus by way of the mother.

Before leaving this survey of what the Greek and Roman writers had to say about alcohol's effects on libido, fertility, and offspring, there is one more related topic worth mentioning, and this is alcohol's effects on spontaneous abortion.

Some of the ancient authors believed, or had heard, that alcohol could cause abortions. However, their writings on the subject are mixed with so many imaginative and incredible reports that it is likely that these ideas were not generally held by many people but were merely part of the encyclopedia of nonsense that was current even in the ancient world. In any case, among the relevant statements are those by Pliny,[11] who refers to a wine made from cucumbers that "is called by a Greek name denoting miscarriage, because it produces abortion" (*Natural History* 14.14.108–112). Elsewhere, Pliny also mentions a wine from Egypt "called in Greek 'delivery wine' which causes abortion" (*Natural History* 14.21,22).

The other statement is by Athenaeus,[13] who quotes Theophrastus as saying that "there is a kind of vine [in Achaea] the wine from which causes pregnant women to miscarry, and if they but eat of the grapes, he declares, they miscarry. Troezenia wine, he says, makes drinkers of it childless"(*Dipnosophistae* I.31). The original comment by Theophrastus[27] (*History of Plants* 9.18.10), however, refers to dogs, not to humans.

The Middle Ages

During the Middle Ages alcoholic beverages continued to be consumed in great quantities, and many of the best known and most popular drinks were made in the many monasteries of Europe. Ale became a very popular drink among the common people, and various parishes became known for their ales. In fact, "ale" became synonymous with parish festival.

The term *bride-ales,* which was later shortened to *bridals,* was applied to parish wedding feasts in which the bride and the drinking of ale were both central features.[6] Wine, of course, was still an integral part of the marriage ceremony, as stated in *The Complete Vintner,* written about 1720:

> What priest can join two lovers' hands
> But wine must seal the marriage bands?

The poem (quoted by Wasson,[6] p. 163) then goes on and intimates that it was not just a cupful of wine that sealed the marriage:

> As if celestial wine was thought
> Essential to the sacred knot,
> And that each bridegroom and his bride
> Believed they were not firmly tied
> Till Bacchus, with the bleeding tun,
> Had finished what the priest begun.

If the Church or anyone else had any intimation of possible aftereffects on a pregnancy from such drinking, there was no notice of it. Chaucer, in his *Canterbury Tales*,[28] is not aware of alcohol-related effects on pregnancy but is well aware of the ages-old belief that alcohol has the potential to arouse promiscuity in women, as the wife of Bath confesses in the story of the same name:

> After wine, I think mostly of Venus
> For just as it's true that cold engenders hail
> A liquorous mouth must have a liquorous tail.
> Women have no defense against wine
> As lechers know from experience.

The French writer and physician François Rabelais[29] likewise commented on alcohol and sex, but seems only to have been aware of alcohol's potential to cause a loss of male libido and decrease in sperm production:

from intemperance, proceeding from excessive drinking of strong liquor, there is brought upon the body . . . a chillness in the blood, a slackening in the sinews, a dissipation of the generative seed, a numbness and dulling of the senses, with a pervasive wryness and convulsion of the muscles, all of which are great lets and impediments to the act of generation. Wine, nevertheless, taken moderately, worketh quite contrary effects. . . .

The only writers of note in the Middle Ages who seemed concerned or aware of the possibility of alcohol-related problems during pregnancy are Robert Burton[25] and Francis Bacon.[30]

Burton's writings on the subject have already been discussed (see above), and while he may have deliberately misinterpreted the writings of Aristotle and others to conform with his own ideas, the fact that he had such ideas at all is noteworthy.

A far more influential and important writer and observer was Francis Bacon, generally considered to be the father of the modern scientific method. Bacon did not have much to say about alcohol and reproduction, but he was more accurate than Burton in quoting his sources. For instance, in *Sylva Sylvarum*, posthumously published in 1627,[30] when referring to Aristotle, he cites the Greek writer's observations about how alcohol adversely affects sperm production and adds that in his own time "we have a merry saying, that they that go drunk to bed get daughters" (p. 571). Later, he mentions the possible ill effects of drinking during pregnancy in the context of maternal dietary habits in general: "if the mother eat [much] onions or beans, or such vaporous food; or drink wine or strong drink immoderately; or fast much; or be given to much musing; (all of which send or draw vapours to the head;) it endangereth the child to become lunatic, or of imperfect memory: and I make the same judgment of tobacco often taken by the mother" (p. 665).

During the 18th century, England was the scene of the so-called gin epidemic, and for the first time there were numerous warnings and statements regarding alcohol's potential to affect the outcome of pregnancy. This episode has been admirably documented by Warner and Rosett,[31] and much of the information discussed here can also be found in this previous survey of the period.

The "gin epidemic" came about as a result of the availability of gin at a very cheap price. During the early 18th century, prices for cereals were very low and England faced the prospect of an unfavorable balance of trade. Distilling was regarded as a way of providing revenues from producers and a way of providing farmers with a market for their crop. It was also a way of reducing imports of distilled spirits from other countries.

Some idea of the amount of gin that was consumed during the gin mania that followed the lowering of prices is the change in consumption figures. In 1714 about 2 million gallons were drunk annually. By 1735 the figure increased to about 5½ million gallons, and by 1750 it was up to 11 million gallons.[32] In 1736 there were about 7000 gin houses in London alone—about 1 for every 6 houses in the entire city![33]

As early as 1725 there were dire warnings about how this increased drinking was damaging the citizenry, including the unborn. In 1726 the College of Physicians petitioned Parliament to increase the taxes on gin so that fewer people could afford it. Gin, it said, was causing "weak, feeble and distempered children."[34]

In 1736 a report from Middlesex was submitted to Parliament concerning the widespread drunkenness in the area that was now even encompassing women, with attendant effects on their children:[34]

> With regard to the female sex, we find the contagion has spread even among them, and that to a degree hardly possible to be conceived. Unhappy mothers habituate themselves to these distilled liquors, whose children are born weak and sickly, and often look shrivel'd and old as though they had numbered many years.

In 1751 Henry Fielding added his voice to the many that had already decried the menace of cheap gin.[35] Although concerned primarily about the relation of drinking to crime, Fielding also commented on the children of women who drank. "What must become of an infant," he asked, "who is conceived in gin, with the poisonous distillations of which it is nourished, both in the womb and at the breast?" (p. 19).

In the same year another author, Corbyn Morris,[36] commented on "the diminution of births set out from the time that the consumption of these liquors by the common people became enormous. [Moreover] as this consumption hath been continually increasing since that time, the amount of the birth hath been continually diminishing. . . . Can it be necessary to add to this shocking loss . . . the sickly state of such infants as are born, who with difficulty pass through the first stages of life and live very few of them to years of manhood?" (p. 115).

The year 1751 also saw the printing of William Hogarth's well-known caricature of the era, *Gin Lane*, which was drawn out of the artist's dismay and disgust at the excesses of gin drinking during the era. The print, shown in Figure 1, depicts a baby falling from a drunken mother's arms, starved children fighting, and other maladies of the era.

These books and paintings and the many petitions sent to Parliament asking for something to be done to make gin less available eventually led to the Act of 1751, which increased the taxes on distilled spirits so that they would become more expensive, and curtailed retail outlets for their sale. The new law apparently had the desired impact. By 1757 one writer noted that "the lower people of late years have not drank spirituous liquors so freely as they did before the good regulations and qualifications for selling them. . . . We do not see the hundredth part of poor wretches drunk in the streets since the said qualifications as before."[34]

Whereas the increase in gin drinking certainly contributed to the death rate and the increase in unhealthy children, the impact of such drinking may have been only one of many factors responsible for these calamities. M. Dorothy George[34] reports that the period of the gin mania coincided with periods of fever, epidemic disease, and poor harvests. The winter of 1740–1741 was especially cold and the summer was especially hot. Fever broke out in London and corn prices rose. Unemployment rose. "Gin drinking," says George, "was essentially a disease of poverty. Gin was so cheap, so warming and brought such forgetfulness of cold and misery . . . the typical gin-drinkers were the poorest and most wretched of the community, their poverty a cause as well as a result of their craving for gin, and when gin became dearer the reduction in consumption was immediate" (p. 40).

One of the reasons for the high infant mortality rate was infanticide. Newborn children were left unattended in the streets to die or were given to nurses who left them to starve. Others were given to unscrupulous foster parents, who blinded or maimed these children so that they would arouse pity when they begged.[34]

GIN LANE.

The numerous cases of "convulsions" among children born to alcoholic women were the result not of prenatal but of postnatal alcohol consumption. The incidence of infantile convulsions was very high between 1728 and 1757 and occurred because nurses to whom these children were given poured gin or other alcoholic waters down their throats, causing them to convulse and strangle. When the authorities came to inspect the bodies and asked what the cause of death was, they were told, "convulsions."[34]

The period after the reinstatement of taxes on gin also coincided with the establishment of a Foundling Hospital in London where children would be cared for at government expense. During the first 3 years of its opening, the Foundling Hospital took in almost 15,000 children. About 50% of these infants died, compared to about 80 to 90% of those not brought in.[34]

Thus, while many of the newborn deaths and sickly children born to alcoholic women during the gin epidemic were no doubt the results of prenatal alcohol exposure, the actual impact of such abuse is difficult to determine apart from the appalling conditions that existed during those times. This was especially the point made by Charles Dickens in 1836, when he poked fun at the idea of "fetal alcohol effects" in *Pickwick Papers*.[37] In his description of the meeting of "The Brick Lane Branch of the United Grand Junction Temperance Association," Dickens tells of one of the new members, a "Betsy Martin, widow, one child and one eye. Goes out charring and washing by day; never had more than one eye, but knows her mother drank bottled stout, and shouldn't wonder if that caused it" (p. 394).

It is also important to place statements concerning alcohol and pregnancy outcome made during the gin epidemic in perspective. While the comments cited in conjunction with this problem might give the impression that child welfare was of utmost concern to those writing about this era, this is far from the case. The comments about sickly children were just an afterthought. Fielding, for example, was most concerned with how drinking affected crime.[35] He believed that the poor became thieves because they needed money for gin, and once they got it, it made them unfit for working, so they had to rob more. As far as the children born of alcoholics are concerned, Fielding was concerned that they would not be good army or navy fodder.[35] For his part, Hogarth's main interest was the way gin drinking made people idle and out of control. *Gin Lane* was not solely a depiction of how drunkenness rendered women unfit for nursing their young or led to child abandonment, but, as he wrote in the *London Evening Post*, "the subjects of these prints are calculated to reform some reigning vices peculiar to the lower class of people. . ." (quoted by Paulson,[38] p. 269).

Judging by the absence of any mention of the gin epidemic's impact on pregnancy in the writings of later physicians or social commentators, any effects on newborns appear to have created or left little impact on the minds of those who witnessed them. In 1813 Thomas Trotter, a well-known Scottish physician of his era, published a book[39] in which he faithfully quotes Robert Burton's inaccurate citations of Aristotle, Plutarch, and Gellius on the effects of prenatal alcohol exposure, but makes no mention of the more contemporary evidence of the gin epidemic. Trotter does offer some of this own insights on the subject of alcohol, sex, and reproduction, however. "Impotence," he writes, "may be occasioned here by paralysis of those muscles which are employed in the sexual intercourse; but the appetite itself is certainly destroyed in time; the sot loses all feelings of love'' (p. 132).

On the subject of alcohol-related fetal effects, Trotter cites the analogy of alcohol-induced effects on the adult brain to suggest a possible adverse impact on the developing conceptus: ''We have seen that the mental functions become deranged, when the brain is injured in its structure. And if this happens, can it be too gross to suppose, that the organs of generation must equally suffer in both sexes, from frequent intoxication; and if offspring should unfortunately be derived from such a parentage, can we doubt, that it must be diseased and puny in its corporeal parts; and beneath the standard of a rational being in its intellectual faculties?'' (p. 133).

Apparently Trotter had little firsthand evidence of fetal alcohol damage to call upon. His comments, though they foreshadowed what has come to be known as ''fetal alcohol effects,'' were based on intuition rather than observation. As such, they were merely one more interesting but unsubstantiated consideration for the medical profession to entertain—and judging from the lack of attention afforded to it, it was not accorded much attention and was rarely cited.

During the 19th century, the Lamarkian doctrine of inheritance of acquired characteristics dominated the thinking of many writers on the subject of alcohol and offspring. ''Children born of intemperate parents bear in their birth the germs of disease, die prematurely, or drag along a languishing existence, useless to society, depraved and possessed with evil instincts,'' wrote Barry.[40] Figg[41] likewise wrote, ''The brain of the drinker's child is as often the miniature of that of his father, as is the impress of his features. Education may do much for him, conscience and self-respect more; yet the germs of those vices which precipitated the parent's ruin will, in too many instances, defy eradication.'' Similarly, J. P. Stevens[42] stated matter-of-factly: ''When the brain and nervous system have been the subject of such torturing persecution; at one time lashed into fury, and at another, sunk to the lowest depths of depression, is it wonderful that the offspring of such parents should inherit a weak and perverted nervous system—overthrown by the least unusual exciting cause, subject to spasms, convulsions, and falling readily into attacks of epilepsy or idiocy. Not only is this peculiarly delicate and irritable temperament transmissible from parent to child, but descends even to the third generation'' (p. 461).

By the middle of the 1800s, more and more attention was being focused on the possible damage drinking might have on the fetus, but in many cases, no distinction was made as to the parental source of such damage. Roesch,[43] for example, noted that ''the children of men and women who are given to drink have always a weak constitution, are either delicate and nervous to excess, or heavy and stupid. In the former case they often fall victims to convulsions and die suddenly, or become prey to water on the brain, and later pulmonary phthisis.

In the latter case they are seized by atrophy, and sink into imbecility. In both cases they are exposed to all the varied forms of scrofula, rash, and on reaching maturity, gout.''

Morel, in his *Degeneration of the Human Race,*[44] added: "There is no other disease in which hereditary influences are so fatally characteristic. Imbecility and idiocy are the extreme terms of the degradation in the descendants of drinkers, but a great number of intermediary stages develop themselves . . . beyond the positive data afforded by observation of hereditary influences, it is impossible for us to form a just idea of certain monstrosities, physical and moral. . . . It is a law for the preservation of the race, which strikes alcoholics with early impotence, and their descendants are not only intellectually feeble, but this degradation is joined with congenital impotence.''

The most important contribution to the literature of the mid-1800s on alcohol's effects on the offspring, however, was that of Samuel Howe.[45] In a report to the legislature, Howe noted that parental alcoholism was a characteristic of almost one-half of the 300 institutionalized "idiots" whose family histories he was able to uncover. In one case, Howe found that seven "idiot" children came from a single family, in which both the mother and the father were alcoholic.

This study was the first epidemiological attempt to evaluate the impact of parental drinking on offspring, and it was widely quoted in the United States and Europe as definite proof that parental alcoholism could damage offspring. It was not until the latter part of the 19th century, however, that other epidemiological studies were undertaken to examine the influence of parental drinking on offspring. However, when these studies were finally instituted, the focus began to narrow and prenatal alcohol exposure itself became the issue.

Early Epidemiological Studies

Among the more interesting approaches taken in this regard were the various epidemiological studies correlating the birth of "imbeciles" with the various drinking seasons that recurred at specific times of the year throughout Europe. During these times, especially large amounts of alcohol were consumed compared to the rest of the year. If *in utero* alcohol exposure were related to drinking, epidemiologists of the period reasoned that a preponderance of children would be born with subnormal intelligence and other problems in due course.

A classic example of one such study was conducted in Switzerland by Bezzola.[46] In that country, the periods of greatest drinking before the turn of the century occurred around the New Year and between April and June, coinciding with Easter and weddings, whereas from July to September, the "months of unusual labor,'' there was much less drinking.

Bezzola was able to determine that during 1880–1890, 8196 "imbeciles and idiots'' were born out of the approximately 1 million births. Bezzola then calculated the average number of births per month for normal children and these imbeciles for the 10-year period. Bezzola assigned the value of 100 to the average number of births per month and used this figure to compare the monthly averages for normals and imbeciles. The data are shown in Figure 2.

If the monthly average for normals or imbeciles is greater than the general average, it exceeds 100; if less, it will be below. As indicated by Figure 2, the number of conceptions was highest during the festival seasons and the number of conceptions for ''imbeciles'' was also highest at this time. However, the rate for birth of ''imbeciles'' exceeded the expected increase for this time of year, as predicted. Figure 2 also shows a dramatic drop in the number of imbeciles born during the ''months of increased labor,'' when drinking was minimal, although the birth rate itself was relatively unchanged at this time.

Another classic study of this era was published in 1899 by William Sullivan.[47] Sullivan compared children born to 120 alcoholic women, most of whom were inmates of Liverpool prison, with those born to 28 nonalcoholic female relatives. Women with tuberculosis, syphilis, and other problems were

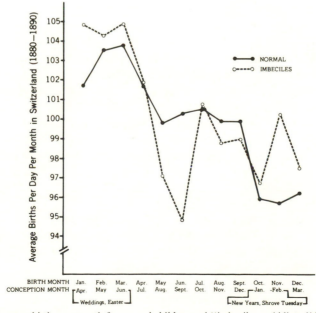

Figure 2. Average births per month for normal children and ''imbeciles and idiots.'' Data from early study by Bezzola[46] (see text for explanation).

omitted. Infant mortality and stillborn rates were about 2½ times higher among the children of alcoholics. Sullivan also was able to compare children born to women prior to imprisonment, when there were no restrictions on their drinking, with those born to the same women after imprisonment, when they were unable to drink. Although there were not many such cases, he invariably found that those born after the forced abstention were healthier than those born beforehand.

An epidemiological study by Laitenen[48] is also of interest. Laitenen reported his analysis of 5848 families and how their drinking affected their 19,515 children. Abortions among abstainers averaged 1.07%; among the moderate drinkers (one glass of beer or less per day), the average was 5.26%; and among the "immoderate" drinkers, the percentage was 7.11. The death rate among children of abstainers was also lower—13.45%, versus 23.17% for moderate drinkers and 32.02% for "immoderate" drinkers. The children of abstainers also developed faster, as measured by the age at which their teeth erupted.

Elderton–Pearson Controversy

In 1910, however, a very influential report on the relation between drinking and the outcome of pregnancy was published by Elderton and Pearson.[49] Elderton and Pearson suggested that one of the main factors that had not been fully considered in assessing the link between parental alcoholism and offspring was the parents themselves, apart from their use of alcohol. In their approach to the problem, which was novel for its time, Elderton and Pearson suggested that children of alcoholics might be defective not because their parents were alcoholic but "because it [alcoholism] is the product like the parent of a defective germ plasm." Another possibility was the effects on these children were due to an environmental influence. In one case, this influence could take the form of a poor home environment. Another source of environmental harm to offspring that was the accepted tenet of the times was "an enfeeblement of the physique, or possibly of the germ plasm of the parents owing to a toxic property of alcohol."

After outlining the various sociological factors that also had to be considered in addition to the "enfeebling hypothesis," Elderton and Pearson then argued that the medical profession was not in the best position to assess the problem of drinking and offspring as far as the population as a whole was concerned. Physicians, they said, had no opportunity of dealing with random samples. Individual physicians saw many individual and extreme cases, but it was the social worker who had a better appreciation of the overall situation. In addition, physicians were not trained in the kinds of statistical procedures needed to analyze the relationships between parental drinking, parental socioeconomic status, and similar factors, and the health and behavior of offspring.

The authors then described the analyses they had conducted of this problem in the Edinburgh area. Parents, they said, were divided into three classes, consisting of cases in which both parents drank, only one parent drank, or neither parent drank. The income of these families was then determined on the presumption that income and use of alcohol were related.

Anticipating the modern approach to categorization, Elderton and Pearson did not confine their drinkers only to the "chronic alcoholism" of medical literature, but instead they included what today would be considered "problem drinkers." This was defined according to "the opinion of trained social workers—assisted by the judgment of police and employers—as drinking more than is good for them or their homes." Nondrinkers were not abstainers only, but they also included "cases in which the use of alcohol is so moderate, if it exists, that it does not appear to interfere with the health of the individual or the welfare of the home."

After studying the various relations between parents and children, Elderton and Pearson concluded that "no marked relation had been found between the intelligence, physique or disease of the offspring and parental alcoholism in any of the categories investigated. On the whole the balance turns as often in favour of the alcoholic as of the non-alcoholic parentage. It is needless to say that we do not attribute this to the alcohol but to certain physical and possibly mental characters which appear to be associated with the tendency to alcohol. Other categories when investigated may give a different result, but we confess that our experience as to the influence of environment has now been so considerable, that we hardly believe large correlations are likely to occur" (p. 32).

Elderton and Pearson then related their findings to the temperance movement and waved the proverbial red flag at their efforts: "If, as we think, the danger of alcoholic parentage lies chiefly in the direct and cross-hereditary factors of which it is the outward or somatic mark, the problem of those who are fighting alcoholism is one with the fundamental problem of eugenics. We fear it will be long before the temperance reformer takes this to heart. He is fighting a great and in many respects a good fight, and in war all is held fair, even to a show of unjustifiable statistics. Yet the time is approaching when real knowledge must take the place of energetic but untrained philanthropy in dictating the lines of feasible social reform" (p. 32).

Representatives of the temperance movement were not slow to respond. Within months of the appearance of the Elderton and Pearson report, physician C. W. Saleeby,[50] at the invitation of the editor of the *British Journal of Inebriety,* wrote a rejoinder criticizing their work. Saleeby was sarcastic. He cited Sullivan's work,[47] which he said "is familiar to every student of alcoholism (except, of course, our new recruit) . . ." and states that their report "totally ignores as non-existent all the work done on this subject throughout the civilized world for decades past. These characters are part of the Pearsonian, if not necessarily the biometic (i.e. statistical) method" (p. 58).

Saleeby claimed that Elderton and Pearson did not speak for the eugenics movement, although the report came from the Eugenics Laboratory, claiming that the authors were "welcome to what opinions they please regarding biometrics, but they must not confound eugenics with biometrics." He also offered some valid criticisms of Elderton and Pearson's methods, but in general, the depth and breadth of the Elderton and Pearson report was very impressive, and in Saleeby's words, it was "gravely injurious to the great cause of temperance."

Saleeby was correct in this assessment of the report. Pearson was a well-respected statistician and member of the eugenics movement, and Saleeby says that his "conclusions have been gleefully quoted, not only in trade journals, but in that large and influential section of the Press which is involved with the alcoholic interest." Apparently these alcoholic interests were extremely wide, for the *Times* even mentioned the Elderton and Pearson report in an article on lawn tennis: "But if the examination be conducted without bias, its critics will obtain about as much satisfaction as was derived by the teetotallers from the investigation that was to establish the degeneracy of the children of drunkards. These children were to serve as an awful warning—the only service that, with such a parentage, they could render their country—and did they immolate themselves on the altar of patriotism? They did not; they proved their unfitness to be citizens by being quite normal."[50] Saleeby also says that he had heard that even "a large German brewery is widely using Professor Pearson's conclusions for the purposes of advertisement."

There were other denunciations of the Elderton and Pearson report, but the main points made by these authors convinced many readers and shifted the idea from parental alcoholism being the cause of damage to offspring, to one that saw alcoholism, feeblemindedness, and various health problems in offspring as all stemming from some basic hereditary defect. This idea soon entered medical texts such as Rosenau's *Preventative Medicine and Hygiene,*[51]: "It is necessary to recognize that what may be inherited is not the result of alcoholism, but rather the predisposition which led the parent to become alcoholic" (p. 311).

Early "Animal Model" Studies

At the same time that these epidemiological studies were being initiated, experiments were also being done for the first time with animals to examine how alcohol affected pregnancy under more controlled conditions. While these studies were often naive in their experimental design, they were supportive of the clinical and epidemiological evidence being reported, and in many ways, the data from these studies have been corroborated even when more stringent procedures were incorporated.

One of the earliest of these experimental studies was Combemale's[52] examination of the effects of absinthe on dogs. Combemale mated a male dog to which he had given absinthe for 8 months with a normal female. Twelve pups were born, and all died by 70 days of age. Two pups were stillborn. While this study involved only one pair of animals, the results did not go unnoticed, and considerable interest was generated.

A few years later, a series of studies by Feré[53,54] generated even more interest in using animals to study the prenatal effects of alcohol, and his method became one of the standard practices in animal experimentation. Feré's procedure involved exposing chicken eggs to alcohol vapor. Eggs were left exposed to alcohol fumes for various times and were then transferred to an incubator. Exposing the eggs to the vapor often resulted in the birth of abnormal chicks. If exposed for an extended period, the eggs did not hatch.

One of the more interesting observations from these studies was the wide variability in susceptibility to the effects of the alcohol fumes. While many chicks were deformed, there were also many that appeared perfectly normal, despite exposure to exactly the same conditions.

Stockard[55,56] subsequently repeated these studies in chicken and minnow eggs to verify the results and to compare exposure to alcohol with exposure to other agents. On the basis of these studies he concluded that the type of defect, e.g., absence of eyes, was nonspecific.

Stockard also conducted many studies of the effects of alcohol on the offspring of guinea pigs.[e.g.,57,58] Again the method of alcohol inhalation was used. Animals were first mated without treatment to make sure they were fertile. Males and females were then treated separately or together. Males previously fertile became infertile after exposure to alcohol vapor, and those that remained fertile often sired defective offspring.

Although newborn weights did not seem to be affected by parental alcohol exposure, neonatal mortality was considerably higher among treated offspring. Spontaneous abortion rates were also considerably increased among treated females. As a result of this prenatal effect, Stockard suggested that the survivors would be heavier and possibly stronger than control offspring because of the reduction in litter size and the weeding out of weaker offspring.

This selective effect was later used to interpret data from other studies, using chick eggs and mice, which found that animals prenatally exposed to alcohol vapor were heavier at birth than control animals.

In summarizing his own exhaustive studies, which involved matings of over 5000 guinea pigs, and those of other workers at the time, Stockard[59] derived the following conclusions: First, the type of abnormality produced by any teratogen was due not to the specific nature of the teratogen itself but rather to the time of exposure during development.

Next, Stockard introduced the "developmental delay" hypothesis. Alcohol (or any other agent), he said, had no specific action on the embryo. Instead, it acted to slow the rate of development.

Finally, he related his observations and hypothesis to humans: "All of the extensive and carefully conducted experimental studies on the influences of alcohol on the germ cells and developing embryos of mammals would seem to indicate that the surviving stock is not decidedly injured by the treatments. There are indications that the less resistant germ cells are affected by the treatments but the hardy, more resistant cells seem to escape. It might be thought that if alcohol does affect some cells it might in large enough doses injure the most resistant cells. This is of course probable but it is not certain that the mammalian blood stream can tolerate the presence of enough alcohol to injure the most resistant members of the germ-cell population" (p. 119).

Stockard concluded his overview with a remark that seemed to allay existing concerns about possible embryo/fetal damage from prenatal alcohol exposure: "With full appreciation of all the difficulties in transferring the results obtained from the study of one animal kind to another, we may assume from the experiments on the effects of alcohol in development and inheritance that it is highly improbable that the quality of human stock has been at all injured or adversely modified by the long use of alcohol" (p. 119).

The debate about alcohol's effects on offspring would undoubtedly have generated considerably more attention in the United States in the 1920s and in later years had Prohibition not been introduced. Prohibition, however, effectively reduced interest in the problem. In England, where Prohibition was not passed into law, there was also a noticeable decline in interest as Elderton and Pearson's emphasis of hereditary and environmental influences gained more acceptance. In addition, there was also the impact of the eugenicists, who offered the interesting argument that by being a selective toxin, alcohol actually improved mankind. This argument was entertained by the social Darwinists like Reid[60] and was supported by experimental data in animals such as that reported by Stockard, and especially by Pearl.[e.g.,61–63] On the basis of years of research, for instance, Pearl[63] summarized his own work and that of other researchers as follows: "The racial effect of alcohol is preponderantly either beneficial, or at the worst, not harmful. This is true for characters depending upon general vigor in guinea pigs (after early generations are passed), fowls, rats, mice, rabbits, insects, and probably frogs.

"This beneficial racial effect appears to be the result primarily of the fact that alcohol acts as a definite, but not too drastic selective agent, both upon germ cells and developing embryos, eliminating the weak and leaving the strong" (p. 224).

Pearl then concluded by expressing a sense of satisfaction about what these data had done to clarify the issue of alcohol's effects on development: "regardless of any immediate application to man, it is an extremely satisfactory thing to have such a large body of critical experimental results, so consistently agreeing in regard to their main, broad conclusions. That much more work needs to be done in this field goes without saying, but the experimenter who begins now has a definite and consistent body of solidly grounded knowledge to start from, instead of the indefinite conjectures of fifteen years ago'' (p. 225).

During the 1940s there was virtually no interest or work on the subject of alcohol and pregnancy. In 1940, in the newly formed *Quarterly Journal of Studies on Alcohol,* Jellinek and Jolliffe wrote what was to become the definitive statement on the issue for the next 30 years: "In spite of the practically unanimous opinion that the idea of germ poisoning by alcohol in humans may be safely dismissed, the spook of Forel's blastophthoria is still haunting German journals" (p. 162). Two years later, in their influential book, *Alcohol Explored,*[18] Haggard and Jellinek again minimized alcohol's teratogenic potential. In tacit recognition of Stockard's and Pearl's work, they wrote: "Germ cells do not have nerves; they do not become intoxicated, and they are injured by alcohol only when it is present in concentrations far higher than those causing death from failure of respiration—concentrations which are strong enough to be 'germicidal.' Thus, in a sense, the body protects the germ cells; it is sacrificed before they can be injured.''

Next, they leveled their sights at the belief that procreation during intoxication could be damaging, stating that "in this same category [of uncontrolled observations] fall the efforts of those investigators who have tried to gather evidence of the birth of idiots and other types of defective children conceived while the parents were said to have been in a state of acute intoxication. Such spectacular studies do not yield valid evidence; they belong more in the realm of rumormongering than in that of scientific study'' (p. 207).

As for the argument that alcohol damaged the reproductive organs, Haggard and Jellinek countered with the argument that such damage does not necessarily mean that the germ cells are also damaged. Similar kinds of changes in reproductive organs, they said, also occurred in conjunction with diseases such as those affecting the liver. Furthermore, they noted that the changes in reproductive organs noted in connection with alcoholism in humans generally occurred after age 45. However, men over 45 accounted for only 6% of all the births in the United States.

Next, Haggard and Jellinek revived Edlerton and Pearson's[49] arguments about the need to separate the impact of alcohol on the germ from its impact on the home environment and noted that this had important implications: "The child of the inebriate may suffer great handicaps, but these handicaps are inherent not in the germ but in the unfavorable environment which the inebriety of the parent creates . . . when the belief is held that the ill effects are due to germ damage, the prevention seems hopeless. . . . When, however, it is realized that the effect is not due to fundamental weakness of the child, but instead to home and social conditions, its remedy is no longer impossible'' (p. 208).

In response to the many studies purporting to prove that children born to alcoholics had a higher incidence of mental retardation and epilepsy then normal, Haggard and Jellinek said that "the explanation is to be found in the fact that while alcohol does not make bad stock, many alcoholics come from bad stock. The offspring inherit the defects of the parents" (pp. 213–214).

The arguments that Haggard and Jellinek marshaled in support of their position that alcohol was not a threat to the developing conceptus were very impressive and convincing. For the next three decades they went virtually unchallenged. Inquiries about possible damage to the fetus from maternal drinking were given reassuring answers in the *Journal of the American Medical Association*,[64] and the *Practitioner*.[65] The *British Medical Journal*[66] cautioned that alcohol could affect fertility but was noncommittal on fetal effects.

By 1955 Keller said in a pamphlet distributed by the Rutgers Center of Alcohol Studies that "the old notions about children of drunken parents being born defective can be cast aside, together with the idea that alcohol can directly irritate and injure the sex glands" (quoted by Warner and Rosett[31]).

Ten years later, Ashley Montague[67] felt no hesitation in writing that "it can now be stated categorically, after hundreds of studies covering many years, that no matter how great the amounts of alcohol taken by the mother—or by the father, for that matter—neither the germ cells nor the development of the child will be affected. . .'' (p. 114).

It was not long before this categorical statement and those like it had to be reconsidered, however. In 1968 a French team headed by Lemoine[68] published a study of 127 children born to alcoholic parents. These children, they said, exhibited a distinctive pattern of anomalies consisting of prenatal growth retardation, peculiar facial features, a high frequency of malformations, and psychomotor disturbances. Lemoine further stated that these children so resembled one another that a diagnosis of maternal alcholism could be made almost entirely from their physical appearance.

This report of physical and behavioral anomalies in the children of alcoholics predated by 5 years Jones and Smith's[1,2] description of the "fetal alcohol syndrome," but it had no impact since it was published in French and was received with skepticism by those who read it. It was only after Jones and Smith published their own report that they were informed of Lemoine's previous contributions.

Although it can be debated to whom the modern rediscovery of the fetal alcohol syndrome should be credited, Jones and Smith must undoubtedly be given credit for bringing the syndrome to international attention and for the term *fetal alcohol syndrome* itself. It was their systematic clinical efforts and those of

Table 1. Articles on Fetal Alcohol Effects

Year	Animal studies	Human studies
1973	8	11
1974	6	21
1975	27	40
1976	29	68
1977	56	127
1978	52	137
1979	96	147
1980	161	211
1981	112	129
Totals	547	891
Grand total		1438

their colleague, Streissguth,[e.g.,69] that clearly identified prenatal alcohol exposure as a serious health risk to the developing fetus.

Since 1973 over 1000 articles have been published concerning the effects of alcohol on reproduction,[70] most of them dealing with fetal alcohol effects (see Table 1).

References

1. Jones, K. L., Smith, D. W., Ulleland, C. N., and Streissguth, A. P. Pattern of malformation in offspring of chronic alcoholic mothers. *Lancet*, 1973, *1*, 1267–1271.
2. Jones, K. L., and Smith, D. W. Recognition of the fetal alcohol syndrome in early infancy. *Lancet*, 1973, *2*, 999–1001.
3. *The interpreter's bible*. New York: Abingdon Press, 1953.
4. Feldman, W. M. *The Jewish child*. New York: Bloch, 1918.
5. Cohen, A. (Ed.). *The minor tractates of the Talmud*. London: Soncino Press, 1965.
6. Wasson, E. A. *Religion and drink*. New York: Burr Printing House, 1914.
7. Preuss, J. *Biblical and talmudic medicine*. New York: Sanhedrin Press, 1971.
8. O'Brien, J. M., and Seller, S. C. Attributes of alcohol in the Old Testament. *Drinking and Drug Practices Surveyor*, 1982, *18*, 18–23.
9. Aristophanes. *Thesmophoriazusae*. In B. B. Rogers (Ed.), *Aristophanes*. New York: Putnam, 1924.
10. Euripides. *Bacchae*. In H. H. Milman (Ed.), *The Bacchanals and other plays*. London: Routledge, 1888.
11. Pliny. *Natural history*. In H. Rackman (Ed.), *Pliny's natural history*. Cambridge, Mass.: Harvard University Press, 1958.
12. McKinlay, A. P. The Roman attitude toward women's drinking. *Classical bulletin*, 1945, *22*, 222–223.

13. Athenaeus. *Dipnosophistae.* In C. B. Gulick (Ed.), *Athenaeus, The deipnosophists.* New York: Putnam's, 1928.
14. Seneca. *Epistles.* In R. H. Gummere (Ed.), *Seneca, epistles.* Cambridge, Mass.: Harvard University Press, 1953.
15. Suetonius. *Augustus.* In J. C. Rolfe (Ed.), *Suetonius, lives of the caesars.* Cambridge, Mass: Harvard University Press, 1960.
16. Tacitus. *Annals.* In C. H. Moore (Ed.), *Tacitus. The annals.* New York: Putnam's, 1925.
17. Green, H. G. Infants of alcoholic mothers. *American Journal of Obstetrics and Gynecology,* 1974, *118,* 713–716.
18. Haggard, H. W., and Jellinek, E. M. *Alcohol explored.* Garden City: Doubleday, 1942.
19. Ballantyne, J. W. Alcohol and antenatal child welfare. *British Journal of Inebriety,* 1917, *14,* 93–108.
20. Crother, T. D. *Inebriety.* Cincinnati: Harvey, 1911.
21. Matthews Duncan, J. On alcoholism and gynaecology and obstetrics. *Transactions of the Edinburgh Obstetrical Society,* 1888, *12,* 105–120.
22. Goodenough, E. R. *Jewish symbols in the Greco-Roman period* (Vol. 6). New York: Pantheon, 1956.
23. Frank, J. P. *System einer vollständingen medicinischen Polizei.* Mannheim, Germany, 1784.
24. Plato. *Laws.* In R. G. Bury (Ed.), *Plato.* Cambridge, Mass.: Harvard University Press, 1952.
25. Burton, R. *The anatomy of melancholy.* New York: Vintage Books, 1977. (Originally published, 1621.)
26. Aristotle. *Problemata.* In W. D. Ross, (Ed.), *The works of Aristotle* (Vol. 7). Oxford: Clarendon Press, 1927.
27. Theophrastus. *History of plants.* In A. Hort (Ed.), *Theophrastus.* New York: Putnam, 1916.
28. Chaucer, G. *Canterbury tales.* In A. C. Cawley (Ed.), *The Canterbury tales.* New York: Dutton, 1958.
29. Rabelais, F. Quoted by Benedik, T. G. Food and drink as aphrodisiacs. *Sexual Behavior,* 1972, *2,* 5–10.
30. Bacon, F. *Sylva Sylvarum: or A natural history* (1627). In J. Spedding, R. L. Ellis, and D. D. Heath (Eds.), *The works of Francis Bacon.* London: Longmans, 1887.
31. Warner, R. H., and Rosett, H. L. The effects of drinking on offspring: An historical survey of the American and British literature. *Journal of Studies on Alcohol,* 1975, *36,* 1395–1420.
32. Coffey, T. G. Beer street: Gin Lane. Some views of 18th-century drinking. *Quarterly Journal of Studies on Alcohol,* 1966, *27,* 669–692.
33. Rodin, A. E. Infants and gin mania in 18th-century London. *Journal of the American Medical Association,* 1981, *245,* 1237–1239.
34. George, M. D. *London life in the eighteenth century.* New York: Harper & Row, 1964.
35. Fielding, H. *An enquiry into the causes of the late increase of robbers, etc. with some proposals for remedying this growing evil.* London: A. Millar, 1751. (Quoted by Zirker, M. R. *Fielding's social pamphlets.* Berkeley: University of California Press, 1966.)
36. Morris, C. *A collection of the yearly bills of mortality from 1657 to 1758 inclusive. To which are subjoined . . . III. Observations on the past growth and present state of the city of London,* 1751. (Quoted by George.[34])
37. Dickens, C. *The Pickwick papers.* New York: Dodd, Mead, 1944.
38. Paulson, R. *Hogarth: His life, art, and times.* New Haven: Yale University Press, 1974.
39. Trotter, T. *An essay, medical, philosophical, and chemical, on drunkenness.* Philadelphia: Anthony Finley, 1813.
40. Barry, E. B. *Essay on wedlock.* Reading: 1806.
41. Figg, E. G. *The physiological operation of alcohol.* London: Temperance Spectator, 1862.

42. Stevens, J. P. Some of the effects of alcohol upon the physical constitution of man. *Southern Medical and Surgical Journal*, 1857, *13*, 451–462.

43. Roesch, C. H. *Der Missbrauch geistiger Getränke in pathologischer, therapeutischer, medicinisch-polizeilicher und gerichtlicher Hinsicht*. Tübingen: 1839.

44. Morel, B. A. *Traité des dégénérescences physiques, intellectuelles et Morales de l'espèce Humaine*. Paris: 1857.

45. Howe, S. G. *Report made to the legislature of Massachusetts upon idiocy*. Boston: Coolidge and Wiley, 1848.

46. Bezzola, D. A statistical investigation into the role of alcohol in the origin of innate imbecility. *Quarterly Journal of Inebriety*, 1901, *23*, 346–354.

47. Sullivan, W. C. A note on the influence of maternal inebriety on the offspring. *Journal of Mental Science*, 1899, *45*, 489–503.

48. Laitinen, T. A contribution to the study of the influence of alcohol on the degeneration of human offspring. *Proceedings of the Twelfth International Congress on Alcoholism*, London, 1909, *12*, 263–270.

49. Elderton, E. M., and Pearson, K. A first study of the influence of parental alcoholism on the physique and ability of the offspring. *Eugenics Laboratory Memoir*, 1910, *10*, 1–46.

50. Saleeby, C. W. Professor Karl Pearson on alcoholism and offspring. *British Journal of Inebriety*, 1910, *8*, 53–66.

51. Rosenau, M. J. *Preventive medicine and hygiene*. New York: Appleton, Century, 1916.

52. Combemale, F. *La descendance des alcooliques*. Doctoral dissertation, Montpelier, 1888.

53. Feré, C. H. Note sur l'influence de l'exposition préalable aux vapeurs d'alcool sur l'incubation de l'oeuf de la poule. *Comptes Rendus des Séances de la Société de Biologie et de Ses Filiales*, 1893, 773–775.

54. Feré, C. H. Études expérimentales sur l'influence tératogène ou dégénérative des alcools et des essences. *Journal de l'Anatomie et de la Physiologie*, 1895, *31*, 161–186.

55. Stockard, C. R. The influence of alcohol and other anaesthetics on embryonic development. *American Journal of Anatomy*, 1910, *10*, 369–392.

56. Stockard, C. R. The artifical production of eye abnormalities in the chick embryo. *Anatomical Record*, 1914, *8*, 33–41.

57. Stockard, C. R. An experimental study of racial degeneration in mammals treated with alcohol. *Archives of Internal Medicine*, 1912, *10*, 369–398.

58. Stockard, C. R. The effect on the offspring of intoxicating the male parent and the transmission of the defects to the subsequent generations. *American Naturalist*, 1913, *47*, 641–682.

59. Stockard, C. R. The effects of alcohol in development and heredity. In H. Emerson (Ed.), *Alcohol and man*. New York: Macmillan, 1932. Pp. 103–119.

60. Reid, G. A. Human evolution; with especial reference to alcohol. *British Medical Journal*, 1903, *2*, 818–820.

61. Pearl, R. On the effect of continued administration of certain poisons to the domestic fowl, with special reference to the progeny. *Proceedings of the American Philosophical Society*, 1916, *4*, 243–258.

62. Pearl, R. The experimental modification of germ cells. III. The effect of parental alcoholism, and certain other drug intoxications, upon the progeny. *Journal of Experimental Zoology*, 1917, *22*, 241–310.

63. Pearl, R. *Alcohol and longevity*. New York: Knopf, 1926.

64. Anonymous. Effect of single large alcohol intake on fetus. *Journal of the American Medical Association*, 1942, *120*, 88.

65. Bourne, A. W. Alcohol and pregnancy. *Practitioner*, 1948, *160*, 73.

66. Editorial. Effect of alcohol and tobacco on fertility. *British Medical Journal*, 1949, *2*, 768.

67. Montague, A. *Life before birth*. New York: Signet, 1965.
68. Lemoine, P., Harousseau, H., Borteryu, J. P., and Menuet, J. C. Les enfants de parents alcooliques: Anomalies observées à propos de 127 cas. *Ouest Médical,* 1968, *21,* 476–482.
69. Streissguth, A. P., Herman, C. S., and Smith, D. W. Intelligence, behavior and dysmorphogenesis in the fetal alcohol syndrome: A report on 20 clinical cases. *Journal of Pediatrics,* 1978, *92,* 363–367.
70. Abel, E. L. *Alcohol and reproduction. A bibliography*. Westport, Conn: Greenwood Press, 1982.

CHAPTER 2

Pharmacology of Alcohol Relating to Pregnancy and Lactation

The main intoxicant in alcoholic beverages is ethyl alcohol (alcohol, ethanol), a relatively simple organic chemical, made up of carbon, oxygen, and hydrogen, that is soluble in both water and fat. The various other ingredients in alcoholic beverages are called congeners. Different alcoholic beverages contain different types and different amounts of congeners and other substances, e.g., minerals, coloring agents. About 400 different ingredients have now been identified.[1] Some of the more common of the congeners are acetaldehyde, iso-amyl alcohol, iso-butanol, n-propanol, ethyl acetate, and methanol. Although some congeners may produce toxic or pharmacological effects on the fetus, thus far little attention has been focused on this possibility. Relevant studies of this issue are discussed in Chapter 9.

Absorption and Route of Administration

Alcohol is commonly consumed by humans in the form of beer, wine, or distilled spirits. In animal studies it is primarily administered as ethyl alcohol either by intragastric intubation, by placing it in the drinking water, or by incorporating it into a liquid diet. Only by intubation, however, is it possible to control dosage and time of exposure. This is because of the wide variability in amount of drinking and pattern of drinking when animals voluntarily ingest alcohol. Intubation is also the preferred method when relatively high blood alcohol levels are required. These and other related issues are discussed more fully in Chapter 10.

Other methods of administration for animals include injection by parenteral routes (e.g., intraperitoneal), vapor inhalation, and schedule-induced polydipsia.

Currently, administration is primarily by the oral route in reproductive studies. Although intraperitoneal injection results in more uniform, higher, and more rapid peak blood alcohol levels than oral administration, this method is generally avoided in pregnant animals for several reasons. Most obvious is the possibility of puncture of fetuses or misinjections elsewhere. In one study cited by Wallgren and Barry[2] 19.6% of 127 injections directed at the intraperitoneal cavity were delivered instead to the gastrointestinal tract or urinary bladder, or were injected subcutaneously or retroperitoneally. Since animals often struggle when about to be injected (or intubated), misinjections are likely. Although comparable studies evaluating the percentage of injections delivered to the fetus, uterus, or amniotic fluid have not been conducted, such a possibility cannot be dismissed. In addition, frequent intraperitoneal injection may result in peritonitis and local irritation. Concentrations of alcohol above 20% are to be especially avoided because they may cause marked local inflammation.[2]

Following oral intake, alcohol is absorbed by diffusion into the blood from all areas of the gastrointestinal system, but most rapid absorption occurs from the intestine and much less so from the stomach.

Rate of absorption is primarily determined by dosage and concentration. However, factors that delay the passage of alcohol from the stomach to the intestine will delay the rate of absorption into the blood and hence will reduce peak blood alcohol levels and rate of increase of blood alcohol levels. Among the factors that produce such delays and result in lower peak blood alcohol levels are presence of food in the stomach, which obstructs movement; ingestion of other drugs that affect gastrointestinal motility or blood flow; concentration; and type of beverage (e.g., alcohol in beer is absorbed more slowly than alcohol in distilled beverages).[2,3]

Not only does food in general delay absorption and result in lower blood alcohol levels, it is also possible that certain kinds of food may affect blood alcohol levels. Wiener and her co-workers,[4] for example, found that despite equivalent alcohol intakes on the basis of body weight in two groups of pregnant rats, animals ingesting an alcohol diet with a higher protein content had lower blood alcohol levels than those ingesting alcohol in a lower protein diet. One implication of this finding is that type of diet (and hence nutritional status) may be a factor in the occurrence of fetal alcohol effects since the lower the blood alcohol level, the lower the probability of fetal alcohol effects.

Concentrations of alcohol between 15 and 30% v/v are most rapidly absorbed. Below 15% v/v, the concentration gradient is relatively low, resulting in slower absorption. Above 20% it is relatively high enough to facilitate absorption, but as the concentration increases, gastric motility is reduced. At about 30% v/v, strong local irritation of the stomach lining may occur along with hemorrhaging.[2,3] Gottfried and his co-workers[5] reported that a single oral administration of as little as 1 g/kg may cause intestinal hemorrhaging. The severity of such hemorrhaging tends to increase with the concentration of alcohol used.[6]

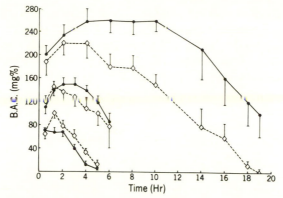

Figure 3. Blood alcohol levels in pregnant (●——●) and nonpregnant (◇——◇) female rats following oral administration of alcohol (30% w/v). Lower curves: 2 g/kg; intermediate curves: 4 g/kg; upper curves: 6 g/kg. A minimum of seven animals represented by each curve.

Pregnancy does not appear to affect the rate of absorption but does affect peak alcohol levels depending on dosage[7] (see Figure 3).

Distribution

Because of its solubility in water and fat, alcohol readily diffuses across all cell membranes and is distributed approximately equally throughout all body tissues in proportion to their tissue water content. This is an especially important consideration in comparing male and female consumption patterns. Since women generally weigh less than men and have less body water (44–55%) than men (55–65%), the volume of distribution of alcohol will be lower in women. Therefore, blood alcohol levels will be higher in women than men after consumption of identical amounts of alcohol because there is less fluid in the female body for alcohol to dissolve in.

Some studies also suggest that blood alcohol levels vary considerably during the menstrual cycle and are highest around the time of ovulation and immediately prior to menstruation.[8] This means that women are more likely than men to become "intoxicated" after consumption of the same amount of alcohol. It also means that women may be more likely to experience alcohol-related health problems at lower levels of consumption than men. Hence, comparisons of the extent of "heavy" drinking between men and women may be misleading in some cases (see Chapter 3) since at any given level of consumption, blood alcohol levels will be higher for women than for men. In other words, although actual consumption levels may be identical, women may still be "heavier" drinkers than men.

With respect to reproductive status, it is also important to note that blood alcohol levels may be considerably higher in pregnant women than in their nonpregnant counterparts. This conclusion is suggested by studies in animals in which the same amount of alcohol was administered to pregnant and nonpregnant rats. As indicated by Figure 3, blood alcohol levels were considerably higher in pregnant animals after administration of the higher dose of alcohol compared to nonpregnant animals.[7] Thus, while many studies have shown that pregnant women tend to decrease their level of consumption below their prepregnant levels (see below), these decreases may be compensated for by higher blood alcohol levels.

Another important variable affecting blood alcohol levels is age.[9] Owing to the decreasing proportion of body water associated with aging, blood alcohol levels will be higher in older compared to younger women after consumption of equivalent amounts of alcohol. The differences in blood alcohol levels in rats of different ages is shown in Figure 4. As indicated by the figure, older animals attain considerably higher peak blood alcohol levels than younger animals after administration of the same amount of alcohol. This raises the possibility that older women may be more at risk than their younger counterparts for fetal alcohol effects because they attain higher blood alcohol levels even though they may drink the same amount of alcohol.

Yet another important variable to consider is nutritional status. While this is closely related to diet, a condition of chronic undernutrition will of itself result in higher blood alcohol levels by reducing volume of distribution. Since mothers of fetal alcohol syndrome children often weigh considerably less than other women

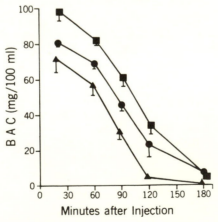

Figure 4. Blood alcohol disappearance in 2–3-month-(▲——▲), 12–14-month- (●——●), and 18–20-month-old (■——■) rats after injection (i.p.) of 1.0 g/kg alcohol.

in general (see Chapter 11), they may be at risk for such a pregnancy outcome because of their lower volumes of distribution in addition to any other nutrition-related factors.

Distribution to the Fetus

Distribution of alcohol from the mother to the fetus is of special importance as far as potential effects of alcohol are concerned.

Distribution of alcohol to the human fetus was demonstrated as early as 1899.[10] Subsequent studies, summarized in Table 2, corroborate this early finding and present quantitative estimations of newborn blood alcohol levels relative to maternal levels.

Blood alcohol levels in some of these reports were obtained following administration of alcohol to prevent premature labor, and levels were obtained at, or some time after delivery. Fetal blood alcohol levels were therefore somewhat higher.

The relatively high blood alcohol levels observed by Jung,[16] Cook,[17] and Fitzsimons[18] are noteworthy because of the levels *per se* and because the levels in the newborns were higher than in the mothers.

In the Jung[16] report, the mother was advised to consume vodka, 30 ml three times a day, to retard the early onset of labor. When contractions continued, she

Table 2. Blood Alcohol Levels in Neonates and Mothers (mg%) Clinical Studies

Source	Neonate	Mother
Belinkoff and Hall[11]	Less than 20%[a] of maternal BAL	
Chapman and Williams[12]	43	65
Fuchs *et al.*[13]	180[b]	150
	170[b]	150
Seppala *et al.*[14]	67[b]	58
	53[b]	58
Waltman *et al.*[15]	25	30
	17	26
Jung *et al.*[16]	477	277 (14 hr after birth)
	381	54 (22 hr after birth)
Cook *et al.*[17]	150	98
Fitzsimons *et al.*[18]	200	(8 hr after birth)
Puschel and Seifert[19]	94	— (13 hr after birth)
Idanpaan-Heikkila *et al.*[20]	36	58

[a]Cord blood.
[b]Twins.

Table 3. Blood Alcohol Levels (BAL) in Neonates and Mothers (mg%) Studies in Animals

Species	Day of gestation	Dose	Time after administration	Areas of distribution	Reference
Mouse	16	1.2–1.6 g/kg; i.v.	1 min	Lower concentrations in fetuses relative to maternal BAL	Akesson[21]
			10 min	Levels in fetuses equal to maternal BAL	
			.10–60 min	Slightly higher levels in fetal liver relative to maternal BAL	
			4–24 hr	Levels in fetal blood, brain, skeletal muscle, and heart higher than in corresponding tissues in mother	
Rat	16–17	6 g/kg, p.o.	1 hr	Slightly higher concentrations in fetuses relative to maternal BAL	Abel and Greizerstein[22]
			4 hr	Higher concentrations (121%) in fetuses relative to maternal BAL	
	20–21		1 hr	Identical levels in fetus and maternal BAL	
			4 hr	Slightly higher (106%) concentrations in fetuses relative to maternal BAL	
Hamster	6	1.5 g/kg, i.v.	30 min	Maternal BAL (81mg%), fetal BAL (37mg%)	Ho et al.[23]
	15		30 min	Maternal BAL (68mg%), fetal BAL (66mg%), placenta (35mg%), amniotic fluid (64mg%)	
	6		90 min	Maternal BAL (69mg%), fetal BAL (43mg%)	
	15		90 min	Maternal BAL (61mg%), fetal BAL (30mg%), placenta (28mg%), amniotic fluid (41mg%)	
	6		4 hr	Maternal BAL (48mg%), fetal BAL (19mg%)	
	15		4 hr	Maternal BAL (46mg%), fetal BAL (23mg%), placenta (27mg%), amniotic fluid (26mg%)	
Guinea pig	57–65		30–40 min	Maternal BAL (279mg%), fetal BAL (168mg%)	Bergstrom et al.[24]
			70–75 min	Maternal BAL (536mg%), fetal BAL (279mg%)	

Animal		Dose	Days	Time		Reference
Cat	60	Not stated		50 min	Maternal BAL (47mg%), fetal BAL (32mg%), amniotic fluid (22mg%)	Himwich et al.[25]
				1 hr	Maternal BAL (39mg%), fetal BAL (43mg%), amniotic fluid (32mg%)	
				2½ hr	Maternal BAL (40mg%), fetal BAL (49mg%)	
				3 hr	Maternal BAL (30mg%), fetal BAL (41mg%), amniotic fluid (48mg%)	
Dog	56	2 or 2.5 g/kg (25% w/v, p.o.)		3 hr	Maternal BAL (291 %), fetal BAL (289 %)	Ellis and Pick[26]
				4 hr	Maternal BAL (225 %), fetal BAL (224 %)	
Sheep	90	1.2 g/kg/120 min, i.v. infusion		5 hr	Maternal BAL (251 %), fetal BAL (253 %)	Dilts[27]
				30 min	Maternal BAL (64mg%), umbilical vein (54mg%)	
				60 min	Maternal BAL (127mg%), umbilical vein (81mg%)	
				90 min	Maternal BAL (175mg%), umbilical vein (115mg%)	
				120 min	Maternal BAL (188mg%), umbilical vein (137mg%)	
	Last 25 days			60 min	Maternal BAL (230mg%), fetal BAL (222mg%)	Mann et al.[28]
	109–135	1.1 g/kg/120 min, i.v. fusion		30 min	Maternal BAL (52mg%), fetal BAL (44mg%)	Ayromlooi et al.[29]
				60 min	Maternal BAL (74mg%), fetal BAL (66mg%)	
				2 hr	Maternal BAL (122mg%), fetal BAL (121mg%)	
				3 hr	Maternal BAL (98mg%), fetal BAL (97mg%)	
				4 hr	Maternal BAL (85mg%), fetal BAL (78mg%)	

(continued)

Table 3. (*Continued*)

Species	Day of gestation	Dose	Time after administration	Areas of distribution	Reference
Monkey (rhesus)	120–160	2–4 g/kg, i.v.		Lower concentrations in fetuses up to 90 min after administration, peak maternal BAL (237mg%), peak fetal BAL (165mg%)	Horiguchi et al.[30]
	Last 30 days	.5 g/kg, i.v.	15 min	Maternal levels: BAL (85%), liver (14%), brain (83%), placenta (51%), amniotic fluid (34%) Fetal levels: BAL (68%), liver (41%), brain (83%)	Ho et al.[23]
			90 min	Maternal levels: BAL (41%), liver (4%), placenta (43%), amniotic fluid (24%) Fetal levels: BAL (55%), liver (50%)	

was told to drink 30 ml per hour. Twelve hours later she was hospitalized and was placed on continuous i.v. drip of 10% alcohol. A total of 160 g of alcohol was administered during a 4-hour period. Five hours after birth, the newborn's blood alcohol level was 715 mg%! At 22 hours of life, his blood alcohol level was 381 mg%, and at 52 hours, it was 97 mg%. The infant subsequently died.

Studies in animals demonstrating passage of alcohol across the placenta are noted in Table 3.

Again, fetal levels are usually comparable to maternal levels, although in some cases exceptions have been observed. Two studies, one in the rat,[22] the other in sheep,[31] indicate that alcohol may concentrate in amniotic fluid. Data illustrating this "reservoir" effect are shown in Figure 5.

A similar reservoir effect in the amniotic fluid of pregnant women was recently reported by Loomis and his co-workers.[32] In this study, six women who were receiving prostaglandin-induced abortions consumed .3 g/kg of alcohol in a 5-minute period. Peak blood alcohol levels of 23–75 mg% occurred in the 1st hour after ingestion, but by 3.5 hours after ingestion no alcohol could be detected. By contrast, peak levels of alcohol in amniotic fluid did not occur until 2 hours after ingestion. Although these peak levels were lower (9–31 mg%) than those in blood, they could still be detected at 3.5 hours in amniotic fluid.

In the fetus itself, alcohol is distributed to all tissues. Liver, pancreas, kidney, lung, thymus, heart, and brain appear to achieve the highest levels.[21,23] In the brain, alcohol tends to concentrate more in gray matter, which has greater water content than white matter. In the telencephalon, the areas of highest concentration are the visual cortex, hippocampus, caudate nucleus, and puta-

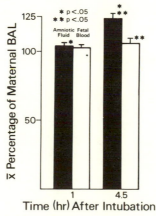

Figure 5. Ratio of alcohol in fetal blood and amniotic fluid relative to maternal blood at 1 and 4.5 hours after intubation. (Abel and Greizerstein[22])

men. The cerebellum, dentate, fastigal nucleus, and lateral geniculate also attain relatively high concentrations.

Distribution to the Neonate

Although alcohol is very rarely given to newborns, there are some instances in which alcohol may be inadvertently ingested by the newborn. One such instance is during nursing. Since the nervous system is still developing in the neonate, such exposure could conceivably affect its maturation, as suggested by studies in animals (see Chapter 12).

The fact that drugs are secreted into milk by humans and animals has long been reconized and has been the subject of several reviews.[e.g.,33,34] The mechanism whereby such secretion occurs has also been studied, the conclusion being that most drugs pass from the blood to the mammary gland by diffusion of their non-protein-bound and nonionized fractions.[34]

Like most drugs, alcohol diffuses into human milk and reaches concentrations similar to those that occur in maternal blood. Kesaniemi[35] calculated that if a nursing woman (weighing about 120 lb) drank about two drinks, her 11-lb infant would receive about .006 oz. of alcohol after drinking about 200 ml of her milk. Although this is a relatively low level of alcohol absorption, it is still possible that even this low level may be harmful. There are some reports, in fact, of adverse effects resulting from alcohol ingestion in infants via breast milk,[e.g.,36–38] although, in most cases, maternal alcohol consumption was considerable. However, such cases are rare because of alcohol's inhibitory effect on milk ejection.

In the lactating mammal, milk ejection occurs as a result of the contraction of the myoepithelial cells surrounding the alveoli of the mammary gland. This ejection process is normally triggered by the release of oxytocin from the neurohypophysis as a reflex response to stimulation of the nipples by the nursing infant. Activity of this neuroendocrine reflex is known to be inhibited by anesthetic drugs, including alcohol, as a consequence of their blocking the release of oxytocin in response to sucking.[39,40]

Inhibition of milk ejection would thus act to reduce the amount of alcohol that might otherwise be ingested by the nursing infant. However, inhibition of the milk-ejection reflex occurs only at relatively high doses. In some women, for instance, inhibition does not occur at blood alcohol levels as high as 250 mg%.[41]

Metabolism

Metabolism of alcohol occurs primarily via the hepatic enzyme alcohol dehydrogenase (ADH). Other enzyme systems such as the microsomal ethanol-oxidizing system (MEOS) or the catalase system are also capable of metabolizing alcohol,[42,43] but they do not appear to contribute much to alcohol metabolism in the body.[44]

The first metabolite of alcohol is acetaldehyde. Acetaldehyde is then in turn metabolized to acetate. The final breakdown produces carbon dioxide and water.

In the adult human, the rate of metabolism is about 15 mg% per hour. In terms of body weight, this is about 100 mg/kg/hr. In the rat and mouse, two species widely used as "animal models" for alcohol-related studies, this rate is about 3 and 5½ times faster, respectively.[2]

Pregnancy does not affect the rate of blood alcohol disappearance[7] or ADH activity.[45] During lactation, however, there is a considerable increase in blood alcohol disappearance rate.[46-49]

The rate of metabolism in the newborn infant is about 50% that of the adult. Jung and his co-workers[16] monitored blood alcohol levels for 52 hours in a woman and her newborn. At 5 hours the infant's blood alcohol level was 715 mg%, and at 52 hours it was 97 mg%. The maternal blood alcohol level was 473 mg% at 6 hours and 54 mg% at 22 hours. Jung calculated blood alcohol disappearance rates of 15 and 27 mg% per hour for the newborn and the mother, respectively. Estimates of blood alcohol disappearance from other studies are summarized in Table 4.

The data in Table 4 suggest that the disappearance rate in newborns is about 8 mg%/hr. Interestingly, the disappearance rates given for mothers are considerably below those noted by Wallgren and Barry[2] for the adult human.

The lower rate of elimination in the newborn is due to decreased ADH activity associated with the relative immaturity of the newborn's liver. In their

Table 4. Rate of Blood Alcohol Disappearance in Mothers and Newborns

Reference	Newborn	Mother
Wagner et al.[50]	7.4 mg%/hr (premature)	—[a]
	11 mg%/hr	—[a]
Gartner and Ryden[51]	8 mg%/hr	—[a]
	9 mg%/hr	—[a]
	12 mg%/hr	—[a]
	20 mg%/hr	—[a]
Seppala et al.[14]	8 mg%/hr (twin)	14 mg%/hr
	7 mg%/hr (twin)	14 mg%/hr
Idanpaan-Heikkila et al.[20]	8 mg%/hr	14 mg%/hr
Jung et al.[16]	15 mg%/hr	27 mg%/hr
Puschel and Seifert[19]	8 mg%/hr	—[a]
Cook et al.[17]	8.5 mg%/hr	—[a]

[a]Data not reported.

study of ADH activity in human fetal, early postnatal, infant, and adult liver, Pikkarainen and Raiha[52] found that while ADH activity was detectable in human fetal liver as early as the 2nd month after gestation, it was extremely low (about 3–4% of adult activity), and adult activity is not reached until 5 years of age. At term it was about 20% of the adult rate.

Taking the elimination rate of the newborn at about 8 mg%/hr, it would require about 13 hours for a newborn infant to clear its blood of alcohol if born to a mother whose blood alcohol level were 100 mg%, the legal level of intoxication in most states in the United States.

In the rat, ADH activity is first detectable in the fetus at about 18 days of gestation (about 3–4 days prior to birth).[53,54] At birth, ADH activity is about 25% that of the adult.[53] Adult activity was not reached until 18 days of age in one report,[53] 25 days in another,[54] and 47 days in a third.[55]

ADH activity may be increased in adult animals following chronic alcohol exposure.[56] Although alcohol exposure during pregnancy has not been found to increase alcohol disappearance rates in the rat or mouse dam, some studies have examined the possibility that ADH induction may occur in offspring prenatally exposed to alcohol. The data from these studies are inconclusive, however, since both increases[57,58] and decreases[59] have been reported in such offspring using the same period and method of exposure. The third alternative, that of no differences in ADH activity in rat fetuses or neonates, has also been noted.[53,54,60] Thus, there is little unequivocal evidence that chronic exposure to alcohol *in utero* affects the fetus's or the neonate's ability to eliminate alcohol from its body. The main method of elimination of alcohol from the body of the fetus is by way of passive diffusion back into the maternal body, where it is then eliminated.

Acetaldehyde dehydrogenase, the enzyme that metabolizes acetaldehyde, develops in the human fetus much earlier than alcohol dehydrogenase and is able to metabolize acetaldehyde as early as 10–16 weeks' gestation.[61] This suggests that the fetus is somewhat protected from small amounts of acetaldehyde entering its blood from maternal blood.

There are also several other methods by which the fetus is protected from acetaldehyde exposure. In contrast to ADH activity, for example, hepatic acetaldehyde dehydrogenase activity was increased about twofold in the mouse during pregnancy.[45] This was accompanied by a decrease in blood acetaldehyde levels in the body following administration of 2.0 or 3.0 g/kg, but not after administration of 1.2 g/kg. Kesaniemi,[62] on the other hand, reported slightly higher blood acetaldehyde levels in pregnant rats following administration of 1.2 g/kg of alcohol. The reason for this discrepancy, other than that due to species differences, is not apparent. As pointed out by Petersen and his co-workers,[45] however, differences in blood acetaldehyde levels between pregnant and non-pregnant animals (or humans) are not likely to be detectable after low levels of alcohol exposure such as 1.2 g/kg, and Kesaniemi's results may therefore be artifactual. The fact that differences do occur after higher levels of alcohol exposure, however, suggests the likelihood of a mechanism protecting the fetus against acetaldehyde exposure.

Another protective mechanism may occur via the placenta. Kesaniemi and Sippel[63] reported that rat placenta tissue is able to metabolize acetaldehyde, and in another study they found that only 25% of the acetaldehyde present in maternal blood was present in placental tissue and no acetaldehyde was detectable in fetal tissue[61] (cf., however, reference 64).

The issue of acetaldehyde entry into the fetus is one of major interest as far as the fetal alcohol syndrome is concerned since acetaldehyde is very toxic, and it has been suggested that acetaldehyde is a major contributor to the syndrome (see, e.g., references 65 and 66).

Although the rat placenta may be able to metabolize some of the acetaldehyde flowing to it from the maternal circulation, human placenta is about four times less capable of doing so.[67] Consequently, the role of acetaldehyde as a teratogen cannot be entirely dismissed.

Elimination

About 90% of the alcohol taken into the adult body is excreted in the form of carbon dioxide and water. The remainder is eliminated unchanged in urine, breath, and sweat.[2,3] Because of the low levels of ADH and acetaldehyde dehydrogenase activity in the fetal liver, virtually all of the alcohol and acetaldehyde entering the fetal body is eliminated unchanged back into the maternal circulation.

Toxic Blood Alcohol Levels

Blood alcohol levels are obviously related to amount of alcohol consumption. However, peak levels will be affected by factors that influence absorption into the blood (see above)—rate of drinking, time of day, metabolic rate, and various other factors.

In most cases, blood alcohol levels about 300 mg% are unusual because of the onset of stupor or coma. Blood alcohol levels of about 500 mg% can result in death in humans as a result of depression of respiratory centers.[2] However, there are clinical reports of alcoholics surviving blood alcohol levels over 500 mg% and up to 780 mg%.[68–70] Wallgren and Barry[2] present data indicating that the lethal blood level in the rat and mouse are 900 mg% and 800 mg%, respectively. The oral LD_{50} for rats and mice is about 9.5 g/kg and 8 g/kg, respectively.[2] (The wide ranges are due to differences in concentration.)

The effects of age on the LD_{50} has not received very much attention. Chesler and his co-workers[71] reported an LD_{50} of 5–6 g/kg in adult rats compared to 8 g/kg in newborn rats. This observation suggests a lower sensitivity to alcohol in the fetus and newborn than in the adult.

Withdrawal

Prenatal exposure to alcohol may result in withdrawal symptoms at birth. Reports of such withdrawal, however, are sporadic (see, e.g., references 72–74). Withdrawal signs in the newborn are similar to those occurring in the adult and include hyperactivity, sweating, and prolonged twitching for several days after birth. The relative scarcity of such reports in conjunction with fetal alcohol syndrome is surprising and may be due to failure to detect the milder symptoms of alcohol, compared to narcotics withdrawal in infants (see, e.g., reference 75). Other reasons for the absence of such reports may be related to administration of medication during labor resulting in suppression of withdrawal, or to the occurrence of withdrawal in the womb prior to delivery if maternal drinking stops sometime prior to birth. Jitteriness, on the other hand, is frequently noted in conjunction with fetal alcohol syndrome, and this may be indicative of withdrawal.

References

1. Kricka, L. J., and Clark, P. M. S. *Biochemistry of alcohol and alcoholism.* Chichester, England: Ellis Horwood, 1979.
2. Wallgren, H., and Barry, H. *Actions of alcohol.* Amsterdam: Elsevier, 1970.
3. Kalant, H. Absorption, diffusion, distribution, and elimination of ethanol: Effects on biological membranes. In B. Kissin, and H. Begleiter (Eds.), *The biology of alcoholism.* New York: Plenum Press, 1971. Pp. 1–62.
4. Wiener, S. G., Shoemaker, W. J., Koda, L. Y., and Bloom, F. E. Interaction of ethanol and nutrition during gestation: Influence on maternal and offspring development in the rat. *Journal of Pharmacology and Experimental Therapeutics, 1981, 216,* 572–579.
5. Gottfried, E. B., Korsten, M. A., and Lieber, C. S. Gastritis and duodenitis induced by alcohol: An endoscopic and histologic assessment. *Gastroenterology, 1976, 70,* 890.
6. Barone, E., Pirola, R. C., and Lieber, C. S. Small intestinal damage and changes in cell population produced by ethanol ingestion in the rat. *Gastroenterology, 1974, 66,* 226–234.
7. Abel, E. L. Prenatal effects of alcohol on adult learning in rats. *Pharmacology, Biochemistry and Behavior, 1979, 10,* 239–243.
8. Jones, B. M., and Jones, M. K. Alcohol effects in women during the menstrual cycle. *Annals of the New York Academy of Sciences, 1976, 273,* 576–587.
9. Abel, E. L., and York, J. L. Age-related differences in response to ethanol in the rat. *Physiological Psychology, 1979, 7,* 391–395.

10. Nicloux, M. Sur le passage de l'alcool ingéré de la mère au foetus, en particulier chez la femme. *Comptes Rendus des Séances de la Société de Biologie et de Ses Filiales,* 1899, *51,* 980–982.
11. Belinkoff, S., and Hall, O. W. Intravenous alcohol during labor. *American Journal of Obstetrics and Gynecology,* 1950, *59,* 429–432.
12. Chapman, E. R., and Williams, P. T. Intravenous alcohol as an obstetrical analgesia. *American Journal of Obstetrics and Gynecology,* 1951, *61,* 676–679.
13. Fuchs, F., Fuchs, A. R., Poblete, V. F., and Risk, A. Effect of alcohol on threatened premature labor. *American Journal of Obstetrics and Gynecology,* 1967, *99,* 627–637.
14. Seppala, M., Raiha, N. C., and Tamminen, V. Ethanol elimination in a mother and her premature twins. *Lancet,* 1971, *1,* 1188–1189.
15. Waltman, R., Iniquez, F., and Iniquez, E. S. Placental transfer of ethanol and its elimination at term. *American Journal of Obstetrics and Gynecology,* 1972, *40,* 180–185.
16. Jung, A. L., Roan, Y., and Temple, A. R. Neonatal death associated with acute transplacental ethanol intoxication. *American Journal of Diseases of Children,* 1980, *134,* 419–420.
17. Cook, L. N., Shott, R. J., and Andres, B. F. Acute transplacental ethanol intoxication. *American Journal of Diseases of Children,* 1975, *129,* 1075–1076.
18. Fitzsimons, R. B., Mahony, M. J., and Cussen, G. H. Ethanol intoxication of the newborn: A case report and review of the literature. *Irish Medical Journal,* 1981, *74,* 230–231.
19. Puschel, K., and Seifert, H. Bedeutung des Alkohols in der Embryofetalperiode und beim Neugeborenen. *Zeitschrift für Rechtsmedizin,* 1979, *83,* 69–76.
20. Idanpaan-Heikkila, J. E., Jouppila, P., Akerblom, H. K., Isoaho, R., Kouppila, E., and Koivisto, M. Elimination and metabolic effects of ethanol in mother, fetus, and newborn infant. *American Journal of Obstetrics and Gynecology,* 1972, *112,* 387–393.
21. Akesson, C. Autoradiographic studies on the distribution of ^{14}C-2-ethanol and its non-volatile metabolites in the pregnant mouse. *Archives Internationales de Pharmacodynamie et de Thérapie,* 1974, *209,* 296–304.
22. Abel, E. L., and Greizerstein, H. B. Relation of alcohol content in amniotic fluid, fetal and maternal blood. *Alcoholism: Clinical and Experimental Research,* 1980, *4,* 209.
23. Ho, B. T., Fritchie, G. E., Idänpään-Heikkilä, J. E., and McIsaac, W. M. Placental transfer and tissue distribution of ethanol-1-[14]C: A radioautographic study in monkeys and hamsters. *Quarterly Journal of Studies on Alcohol,* 1972, *33,* 485–493.
24. Bergstrom, R. M., Sainio, K., and Taalas, J. The effect of ethanol on the EEG of the guinea pig foetus. *Medicina et Pharmacologia Experimentalis,* 1967, *16,* 448–452.
25. Himwich, W. A., Hall, J. S., and MacArthur, W. F. Maternal alcohol and neonatal health. *Biological Psychiatry,* 1977, *12,* 495–505.
26. Ellis, F. W., and Pick, J. R. An animal model of the fetal alcohol syndrome in beagles. *Alcoholism: Clinical and Experimental Research,* 1980, *4,* 123–134.
27. Dilts, P. V., Jr. Effect of ethanol on external and fetal umbilical hemodynamics and oxygen transfer. *American Journal of Obstetrics and Gynecology,* 1970, *106,* 221–228.
28. Mann, L. I., Bhakthavathsalan, A., Liu, M., and Marowski, P. Placental transport of alcohol and its effect on maternal and fetal acid-base balance. *American Journal of Obstetrics and Gynecology,* 1975, *122,* 837–844.
29. Ayromlooi, J., Tobias, M., Berg, P. D., and Desiderio, D. Effects of ethanol on the circulation and acid-base balance of pregnant sheep. *Obstetrics and Gynecology,* 1979, *54,* 624–630.
30. Horiguchi, T., Suzuki, K., Comas-Urrutia, A. C., Mueller-Heubach, E., Boyer-Milic, A. M., Baratz, R. A., Morishima, H. O., James, L. S., and Adamsons, K. Effect of ethanol upon uterine activity and fetal acid-base state in the rhesus monkey. *American Journal of Obstetrics and Gynecology,* 1971, *109,* 910–917.
31. Ng, P. K., Cottle, M. K., Baker, J. M., Johnson, B., Van Muyden, P., and Van Petten, G. R.

Ethanol kinetics during pregnancy. Study in ewes and their fetuses. *Progress in Neuro-Psycho-pharmacology and Biological Psychiatry,* 1982, *6,* 37–42.

32. Loomis, C. W., Tranmer, J., and Brien, J. F. Disposition of ethanol in human maternal blood and amniotic fluid during pregnancy. *Pharmacologist,* 1982, *24,* 204.
33. Catz, C. S., and Giacoia, G. P. Drugs and breast milk. *Pediatric Clinics of North America,* 1972, *19,* 151–167.
34. Rasmussen, F. Excretion of drugs by milk. In O. Eichler (Ed.), *Handbook of pharmacology.* New York: Springer-Verlag, 1971. Pp. 390–402.
35. Kesaniemi, Y. A. Ethanol and acetaldehyde in the milk and peripheral blood of lactating women after ethanol administration. *Journal of Obstetrics and Gynecology of the British Empire,* 1974, *81,* 84–86.
36. Bessey, W. E. On the act of alcoholic stimulants by nursing mothers. *Canadian Medical Record,* 1872, *1,* 195–200.
37. Bisdom, C. J. W. Alkohol- en nicotinevergiftiging bij zuigelingen. *Mundschrift Kindergenese,* 1936, *6,* 332–341.
38. Binkiewicz, A., Robinson, M. J., and Senior, B. Pseudo-Cushing syndrome caused by alcohol in breast milk. *Journal of Pediatrics,* 1978, *93,* 965–967.
39. Cowie, A. T., and Tindal, J. S. *The physiology of lactation.* Baltimore: Williams and Wilkins, 1971.
40. Fuchs, A.-R. Ethanol and the inhibition of oxytocin release in lactating rats. *Acta Endo-crinologica,* 1969, *62,* 546–554.
41. Cobo, E., and Quintero, C. A. Milk-ejecting and antidiuretic activities under neurohypophyseal inhibition with alcohol and water overload. *American Journal of Obstetrics and Gynecology,* 1969, *105,* 877–887.
42. Lieber, G. S., and DeCarli, L. M. The role of the hepatic microsomal ethanol oxidizing system (MEOS) for ethanol metabolism *in vivo. Journal of Pharmacology and Experimental Therapeutics,* 1970, *170,* 78–80.
43. Thurman, R. C., Levy, H. G., and Scholz, R. Hepatic microsomal ethanol oxidation: Hydrogen peroxide formation and the role of catylase. *European Journal of Biochemistry,* 1972, *25,* 420–426.
44. Khanna, J. M., Kalant, H., and Linc, C. Significance in vivo of the increase in microsomal ethanol-oxidizing system after chronic administration of ethanol, pentobarbital, and chlorcyclizine. *Biochemical Pharmacology,* 1972, *21,* 2215–2226.
45. Petersen, D. R., Panter, S. S., and Collins, A. C. Ethanol and acetaldehyde metabolism in the pregnant mouse. *Drug and Alcohol Dependence,* 1977, *2,* 409–420.
46. Abel, E. L., Greizerstein, H. B., and Siemens, A. J. Influence of lactation on rate of disappearance of ethanol in the rat. *Neurobehavioral Toxicology,* 1979, *1,* 185–186.
47. Thiessen, D. D., Whitworth, N. S., and Rodgers, D. A. Reproductive variables and alcohol consumption of the C57BL/Crgl female mouse. *Quarterly Journal of Studies on Alcohol,* 1966, *27,* 591–595.
48. Abel, E. L. Effects of lactation on rate of blood ethanol disappearance, ethanol consumption and serum electrolytes in the rat. *Bulletin of the Psychonomic Society,* 1979, *14,* 365–367.
49. Greizerstein, H. B., and Abel, E. L. Time parameters for increased blood ethanol disappearance rates in lactating rats. *Alcoholism: Clinical and Experimental Research,* 1980, *4,* 216.
50. Wagner, L., Wagner, G., and Guerrero, J. Effect of alcohol on premature newborn infants. *American Journal of Obstetrics and Gynecology,* 1970, *108,* 308–315.
51. Gartner, U., and Ryden, G. The elimination of alcohol in the premature infant. *Acta Paediatrica Scandinavica,* 1972, *61,* 720–721.
52. Pikkarainen, P. H., and Raiha, N. C. R. Development of alcohol dehydrogenase in the human liver. *Pediatric Research,* 1967, *7,* 165–168.

53. Raiha, N. C. R., Koskinen, M., and Pikkarainen, P. Developmental changes in alcohol dehydrogenase activity in rat and guinea-pig liver. *Biochemical Journal*, 1967, *103*, 623–626.
54. Yavorsky, V. M., and Menshchishen, I. F. Effect of chronic alcoholic poisoning on the activity of liver alcohol dehydrogenase in the progeny. *Farmakologiya i Toksikologiya*, 1980, *43*, 622–625.
55. Sjoblom, M., Pilstrom, L., and Morlund, J. Activity of alcohol dehydrogenase in the liver and placenta during the development of the rat. *Enzyme*, 1978, *23*, 108–115.
56. Hawkins, D., Kalant, H., and Khanna, I. M. Effects of chronic intake of ethanol on rate of ethanol metabolism. *Canadian Journal of Physiology and Pharmacology*, 1966, *44*, 241.
57. Sze, P. Y., Yanai, J., and Ginsburg, P. W. Effects of early ethanol input on the activities of ethanol-metabolizing enzymes in mice. *Biochemical Pharmacology*, 1976, *25*, 215–217.
58. Niimi, Y. Studies on effects of alcohol on fetus. *Sanfujinka No Shimpo*, 1973, *25*, 55–78.
59. Duncan, R. J. S., and Woodhouse, B. The lack of effect on liver alcohol dehydrogenase in mice of early exposure to alcohol. *Biochemical Pharmacology*, 1978, *27*, 2755–2756.
60. Sjoblom, M., Oisund, J. F., and Morlund, J. Development of alcohol dehydrogenase and aldehyde dehydrogenase in the offspring of female rats chronically treated with ethanol. *Acta Pharmacologica et Toxicologica*, 1979, *44*, 128–131.
61. Sippel, H. W., and Kesaniemi, Y. A. Placental and foetal metabolism of acetaldehyde in the rat. II. Studies on metabolism of acetaldehyde in the isolated placenta and foetus. *Acta Pharmacologia et Toxicologica*, 1975, *37*, 49–55.
62. Kesaniemi, Y. A. Metabolism of ethanol and acetaldehyde in intact rats during pregnancy. *Biochemical Pharmacology*, 1974, *23*, 1157–1162.
63. Kesaniemi, Y. A., and Sippel, H. W. Placental and foetal metabolism of acetaldehyde in rat. *Acta Pharmacologica et Toxicologica*, 1975, *37*, 43–48.
64. Randall, C. L., Taylor, W. J., Tabakoff, B., and Walker, D. W. Ethanol as a teratogen. In R. G. Thurman (Ed.), *Alcohol and aldehyde metabolizing systems*. New York: Academic Press, 1977. Pp. 659–670.
65. Veghelyi, P. V., Osztovics, M., Kardos, G., Leisztner, L., Szaszovsky, E., Igali, S., and Imrei, J. The fetal alcohol syndrome: Symptoms and pathogenesis. *Acta Paediatrica Academiae Scientiarum Hungaricae*, 1978, *19*, 171–189.
66. Majewski, F. Alcohol embryopathy: Some facts and speculations about pathogenesis. *Neurobehavioral Toxicology and Teratology*, 1981, *3*, 129–144.
67. Kouri, M., Koivula, T., and Koivusalo, M. Aldehyde dehydrogenase activity in human placenta. *Acta Pharmacologica et Toxicologica*, 1977, *40*, 460–463.
68. Lindblad, B., and Olsson, R. Unusually high levels of blood alcohol? *Journal of the American Medical Association*, 1976, *236*, 1600–1602.
69. Hammond, K. B., Rumack, B. H., and Rodgerson, D. O. Blood ethanol: A report of unusually high levels in a living patient. *Journal of the American Medical Association*, 1973, *226*, 63–64.
70. Poklis, A., and Pearson, M. An unusually high blood ethanol level in a living patient. *Clinical Toxicology*, 1977, *10*, 429–431.
71. Chesler, A., La Belle, G. C., and Himwich, H. E. The relative effects of toxic doses of alcohol on fetal, newborn and adult rats. *Quarterly Journal of Studies on Alcohol*, 1942, *3*, 1–4.
72. Schaefer, O. Alcohol withdrawal syndrome in a newborn infant of a Yukon Indian mother. *Canadian Medical Association Journal*, 1962, *87*, 1333–1334.
73. Nichols, M. M. Acute alcohol withdrawal syndrome in a newborn. *American Journal of Diseases of Children*, 1967, *113*, 714–715.
74. Pierog, S., Chandavasu, O., and Wexler, I. Withdrawal symptoms in infants with the fetal alcohol syndrome. *Journal of Pediatrics*, 1977, *90*, 630–633.
75. Zelson, C. Acute management of neonatal addiction. *Addictive Diseases*, 1975, *2*, 159–168.

CHAPTER 3

Consumption Patterns for Alcohol during Pregnancy

This chapter examines current information about alcohol usage in the United States, although some comparisons will be made with drinking practices in other countries. The main intent of this chapter is to provide a context for evaluating the impact of alcohol on reproduction rather than an analysis of the factors that contribute to drinking. Much of the data and definitions used are based on the *Fourth Special Report to the U.S. Congress on Alcohol and Health.*[1] More complete information concerning the data upon which this report was based can be found in the excellent surveys* by Clark and Midanik[2] and Malin *et al.*[3]

Total per capita Consumption

Countries that have the highest rates of per capita alcohol consumption also tend to have the highest rates of alcohol-related problems. For example, cirrhosis rates are considerably higher in France and Portugal than in Norway or Finland.[4] Similarly, one could also assume that countries with high alcohol consumption would also have a high prevalence of alcohol-related birth anomalies. Determination of such a relationship is not possible at present due to a lack of available data. However, it is interesting that fetal alcohol syndrome was first "rediscovered" in France, where 127 cases were identified in 1967,[5,6] and France continues to be a country reporting a relatively high incidence of this syndrome,[7]

---

*A number of errors were made in transcribing information from the Clark and Midanik and Malin *et al.* reports to the *Alcohol and Health* report. Where such discrepancies exist, the data from the original reports have been used.

along with West Germany.[8] Both countries are among the five leading alcohol consumers in the world.[9]

Compared with other countries for which data are available, the United States ranks about 15th in overall annual alcohol consumption per adult.[9] Per capita consumption is highest in Portugal (1613 drinks/year) followed by France (1510 drinks/year), Italy (1203 drinks/year), Switzerland (998 drinks/year), and West Germany (973 drinks/year). The estimate for the United States is 691 drinks per year (i.e., about 2 drinks/day) for each adult. These estimates are based on gallons of absolute alcohol consumed and assumption of ½ oz. of absolute alcohol in a can of beer (12 oz.), a glass of wine (4 oz.), or a "shot" of distilled spirits (1 oz.).

These figures are based on total adult populations and include drinkers and nondrinkers. As such they are misleading because they greatly underestimate the amount of alcohol consumed by those who drink. In the United States, for instance, only about two-thirds of the population 14 years and older drink (see Table 5). If only those who actually drink are considered, the average number of drinks per day is about 3 rather than 2. However, this figure is also misleading since most people who drink do not consume this much. In fact, only about 11% (about 16 million) of the adult population consumes about 65% of the alcohol sold. It is this 11% that consumes at least 2 or more drinks per day. Of these 16 million adults, about 9 million (6% of the adult population) consumes about 8+ drinks a day.[2] It is this minority that is especially at risk for alcohol-related problems.

Although these data do not differentiate between men and women, there is a need to do so since self-reported consumption rates among men are considerably higher than for women.[2] Also evident is the need to conduct separate pharmacological studies of drinking in women since blood alcohol levels may be higher in women than in men even though the same amount of alcohol is consumed.[10] This is because women have a smaller volume of distribution. Therefore, they do not have to drink as much as men to obtain a comparable blood alcohol level.[10]

Table 5. Estimated Percentages of the Adult American Population that Drinks[a]

Category	Percentage	Number of adults
Abstainers/1–2 drinks per year	35%	51 million
2 drinks per day	54%	78.5 million
2–4 drinks per day	5%	7 million
8+ drinks per day	6%	9 million

[a]Data derived from Malin et al.[2]

Even though most alcohol consumers do not experience health-related or personal problems from drinking, many do. Unfortunately, there is no agreement as to definition of such problems or criteria. This has led to a number of different descriptors that may be useful for some purposes but of limited value for others. In the fourth *Alcohol and Health* report[1] alcohol-related drinking problems were divided into three main divisions, consisting of alcohol dependence, adverse effects, and heavier alcohol consumption.

Alcohol dependence was defined in terms of the presence of physical dependence and loss of control. Adverse effects were defined in terms of "negative consequences of consumption other than physical dependence and include physical diseases and psychological and social impairment." Heavier alcohol consumption was defined in terms of amount of drinking. Drinking problems can be defined in terms of any of these dimensions or in terms of any combination of these three.

Using these definitions and criteria, Table 6 indicates the estimated percentages of drinking problems among drinkers in the United States.

Table 7 translates these percentages into absolute numbers based on total population data for men and women, 18 years and older, using estimated abstinence percentages of 15% and 40%, respectively.

Several points are worth noting in regard to these data. The first is that survey data generally underestimate the number of heavy drinkers.[8] These estimates are therefore likely to be conservative.

The second is that these estimates differ somewhat from those of Malin *et al.*[3] The latter estimated the number of people drinking 2 or more drinks a day at 16 million, whereas the *Alcohol and Health*[1] report put this estimate considerably higher at 20.5 million. The reason for this discrepancy is in part due to the criteria used for adults; Malin *et al.*[3] classified anyone 14 years or older as an adult, whereas the *Alcohol and Health*[1] report, which relied on Clark and Midanik's[2] calculations, used 18 years as its criterion. Inclusion of the lower age

Table 6. Incidence (%) of Drinking Problems among Drinkers in the United States[a]

	Alcohol dependence[b]			Heavy consumption[b]	
	2 or more symptoms	3 or more symptoms	Adverse social consequences	2 drinks/day (60+/mon)	4 drinks/day (120+/mon)
Men	12	6	9	29	16
Women	5	2	5	9	3

[a]Data from Clark and Midanik (Table 13).[2]
[b]See text for definitions.

Table 7. Number of Adult Americans with Drinking Problems according to Different Criteria

| | Total population (18 years +) | N drinkers (%) Total | Alcohol-dependent | | Adverse social consequences | Heavy consumption | |
			2 or more symptoms	3 or more symptoms		60+ drinks/month	120+ drinks/month
Men	74,155,000	(75%) 55,616,250	6,673,950	3,336,975	5,005,462	16,128,712	8,898,600
Women	85,142,000	(60%) 51,085,200	2,554,260	1,021,704	2,554,268	4,597,673	1,532,556

[a]Data from Clark and Midanik,[2] and Bureau of Census.[7]

group will have the effect of lowering the overall percentage in the heavy drinking groups if one assumes that fewer teenagers drink as much as older adults.
There were also differences in the assumptions each study made about how much
alcohol is contained in a particular drink. These and other differences underscore
the difficulties in arriving at a concensus about drinking habits. Labels such as
"heavy" or "moderate" drinking may be identical from study to study, but this
does not necessarily mean that the same amount of drinking has been included in
the category.

A third point is that while level of consumption may be positively related to
both alcohol dependence and adverse effects, frequency of consumption must
also be considered. Perhaps the important question is not how many drinks are
consumed in an average day, but how many drinks are consumed in a drinking
day.[11] If "heavy" drinkers do not drink every day, but every other day, for
instance, then instead of their consuming 4 drinks per day, the data would be
better considered in terms of 8 drinks per drinking day.

Using the estimates from Table 7 and the criteria specifying three or more
alcohol-dependent symptoms or consumption of 4 drinks/day, or adverse social
consequences associated with drinking, the total number of women with serious
drinking problems in the United States ranges from 1.0 to 2.6 millions.

Consumption during Pregnancy

In addition to examining consumption patterns among all women, a number
of studies have also examined consumption patterns during pregnancy. A summary of these studies is presented in Table 8.

As indicated by this table, "heavy" drinking varies from a low of .1% to a
high of 9% during pregnancy in studies that have attempted to assess such
behavior.

One reason for the considerable variability among the various estimates of
"heavy" drinking during pregnancy is that "heavy" drinking is defined differ-
ently according to the index used. The three main indices used in these studies
are the Cahalan et al.[12] Quantity-Frequency-Variability (QFV) index, the Jessor
et al.[13] absolute alcohol (AA) index, and the Cahalan et al.[12] volume variability
(VV) index. The criteria for heavy drinking in these three indices are (1) QFV:
drinking 3 or more times per day regardless of amount or 3–5 times per month
with at least 5 drinks more than half the time; (2) AA: 2 or more drinks per day;
(3) VV: 1.5 drinks per day or 5 or more drinks per occasion.

Russell and Bigler[14] evaluated drinking behavior among obstetric patients
using each of these three scales and found relatively good agreement with about a
2% discrepancy. Relatively good agreement among these three scales, ranging
from 1.7% to 2.9%, was also observed by Streissguth and her co-workers.[15]

Table 8. Incidence of "Heavy" Drinking during Pregnancy in the United States and Other Countries

Study site	Socioeconomic status	Sample size	N heavy drinkers	% heavy drinkers	Scale	Reference
Boston	Low SES (inner city, mainly black)	633	58	9	VV	Ouellette et al.[16]
Boston	Same	1,690	36	2	VV	Alpert et al.[17]
Buffalo	Cross-sectional	88	7	8	QFV	Russell and Bigler[14]
			5	6	AA	
			5	6	VV	
Cleveland	Lower SES (inner city)	12,127	204	1.7	Medical diagnosis	Sokol et al.[18]
California	Middle SES (mainly white)	12,406	478	3.9	AA (2 drinks/day)	Kuzma and Kissinger[19]
			187	1.5	AA (4 drinks/day)	
California	Middle SES	32,019		.4	(3½ drinks/day)	Harlap and Shiono[20]
				.1	(6 drinks/day)	
Colorado	Middle-low SES	278	5	2	AA (1½ drinks/day)	Tennes and Blackard[21]
New York	Cross-sectional	657		1.2	AA	Kline et al.[22]
Seattle	Middle and upper SES	801	73	9	AA	Little[23]
Seattle	Same	1,529		2.9	QFV	Streissguth et al.[15]
				2.4	AA	
				1.7	VV	
Seattle	Same	156	3	2	AA	Little et al.[24]
England	Not stated	200		6		Murray et al.[25]
France	Cross section	9,236		5.5		Kaminski et al.[26]
Germany	Middle SES	5,200		.1	(drank "frequently")	Mau and Netter[27]
Brazil	Very low SES	179		14.5		da Silva et al.[28]

There are also differences in the subject populations in these studies worth noting. The data from the Kuzma and Kissinger[19] report was based on a high percentage of Mormons and Seventh Day Adventists, two religious groups that strongly discourage drinking among their members. The low percentage of "heavy" drinkers in this study is thus probably due to the region in which it was conducted.

The lower percentage in the Alpert *et al.*[17] study compared to the Ouellette *et al.*[16] study is surprising, however, since the former includes data from the latter. One reason for the discrepancy and lower reported percentages from the Alpert study may have been that its data were collected postpartum (whereas Ouellette's data were collected prior to birth), and it is possible that many of these women may have felt guilty if they said they drank heavily and their children were born with defects, or they may have felt their children would be taken from them if they made such an admission.

On the other hand, the data from Cleveland also reflect a relatively low incidence of "heavy" drinking. In this study about 1.7% of the women were identified as being "alcoholic."

The median percentage of "heavy" drinking based on American studies summarized in Table 8 (using AA scores where more than one measure is given) is 2%. This is also the modal score. While this score is closer to Clark and Midanik's[2] estimate for women who drink 4 or more drinks per day (3% of adult women) than to their estimate for women drinking 2 or more drinks per day (9% of adult women; see Table 6), it is important to keep in mind that Clark and Midanik's estimates are based on all women, whereas the estimate from Table 8 is based only on pregnant women. This is an important consideration, since alcohol intake decreases considerably during pregnancy (see below).

The "Perinatal-Protective" Mechanism

The question of when women are asked about their drinking is an especially important one in light of recent studies indicating that during pregnancy, many women develop a distaste for alcohol, which results in a sharp decrease in their drinking.[18,23,24,29-31] For example, in a study of 156 predominantly white middle-socioeconomic-class women at a health maintenance clinic in Seattle, two-thirds said they drank less during early pregnancy than before, and alcohol consumption decreased to about half prepregnancy levels.[24] The decrease in consumption after pregnancy was directly proportional to prepregnancy levels— the heaviest drinkers prior to pregnancy continued to be the heaviest drinkers during pregnancy.[24] Similar results were obtained when a group of alcoholic women were studied.[29] However, while regular drinking decreased, the number of "binge" drinking episodes (drinking double the regular intake) increased considerably during pregnancy.

The main reasons given for the decrease in drinking during pregnancy were an unpleasant physiological reaction (e.g., nausea, stomach irritation, headache) and lack of appeal (e.g., unpleasant taste and smell), rather than concern for the welfare of unborn children. An excellent summary of these studies is contained in the review by Little.[31]

Studies in monkeys,[32] mice,[33–35] rats,[36] and hamsters[37] have likewise noted a decrease in alcohol consumption during pregnancy. Such studies eliminate the possibility that the decrease in drinking during pregnancy is in fact solely due to social pressures or other nonphysiological factors. One interpretation of these data is that a "perinatal-protective" mechanism operates during pregnancy (and lactation) to reduce the risks of fetal/neonatal exposure to potentially damaging agents such as alcohol. The nature of this mechanism is as yet unknown, although some relevant studies have already been conducted.

In some instances, for example, the decreased preference for alcohol during pregnancy or lactation arose because of an increase in water intake combined with a constant level of alcohol consumption.[36,38] In other words, alcohol consumption itself remained relatively unaltered by pregnancy or lactation but water intake increased considerably. As a result, preference ratios, determined by calculating alcohol intake relative to total fluid consumption, fell during pregnancy and lactation. Interestingly, Randall and her co-workers[33] observed an increase in total fluid intake in mice only during lactation but not during pregnancy, although preference ratios for alcohol were lower during both periods.

Several attempts have been made to determine if changes in hormonal status underlie the decrease in alcohol intake during pregnancy. During pregnancy and lactation, for instance, estrogen levels are decreased, whereas progesterone levels are increased. This relationship also occurs as a result of ovariectomy in animals. Under conditions of ovariectomy, animals also decrease their preference for alcohol over concentrations ranging from 2 to 9% v/v.[36] Maximum preference for alcohol versus water occurs at a concentration of 3% v/v for ovariectomized rats versus a 6% v/v concentration for intact animals.[36] These results suggest that as in ovariectomy and during pregnancy and lactation, sensitivity to the taste or negative internal effects of alcohol are enhanced, resulting in decreased consumption of alcohol. The fact that increased estrogen levels did not affect alcohol consumption in women[39] is in keeping with the possibility that the hypothesized perinatal-protective mechanism is associated with a decrease in estrogens or is not associated with estrogens at all but rather with progesterone, or the ratio of the two.

Regardless of the nature of the perinatal-protective mechanism, the fact that alcohol intake decreases during pregnancy, often by half prepregnancy rates, means that there is fairly good agreement between Clark and Midanik's estimated 3% of women who drink 4 or more drinks per day prior to pregnancy and the median and modal estimate of 2% for women who drink 2 or more drinks per day during pregnancy.

At-Risk Levels of Consumption

Determination of at-risk levels of alcohol consumption for fetal alcohol effects may not be possible. This is because in addition to actual consumption, factors such as time of embryo/fetal exposure, genetic susceptibility, pattern of exposure, and type of beverage all interact in affecting pregnancy outcome. Thus far, the lowest level of drinking at which the conceptus has been shown to be affected is 2 drinks per day. However, the effect was a decrease of 160 grams.[23] While this was a statistically significant effect, its biological relevance is unclear since it is well within the normal expected range in birth weight for all children. (This topic is discussed in much greater detail in Chapter 7.)

There are, in fact, no unequivocal data from human studies establishing a risk-level of maternal drinking for fetal alcohol effects. In a retrospective study of the available data presented in the clinical literature dealing with fetal alcohol syndrome (summarized in Abel[40]), information about drinking during pregnancy was presented for 72 women from around the world. An attempt was made to convert this information into common units, which in some cases was admittedly guesswork. Nevertheless, based on this arbitrary transformation, average daily consumption for these women was about 14 drinks per day (standard error = ±1). For a 120-lb (55-kg) woman, this would produce a peak blood alcohol level of about 350 mg% if this number of drinks were consumed over a 4-hour period.

Yet even with such high blood alcohol levels, many women do not give birth to children with identifiable fetal alcohol syndrome (see Chapter 11). If even at these high levels the probability of predicting the occurrence of fetal alcohol syndrome is relatively low, it is unlikely that unequivocal predictions can be made about levels of considerably lower intake such as 2 drinks per day.

References

1. Secretary of Health and Human Services. *Fourth Special Report to the U.S. Congress on Alcohol and Health* (DHHS Publication No. (ADM) 81-1080). Washington, D.C.: U.S. Department of Health and Human Services, 1981.

2. Clark, W. B., and Midanik, L. Alcohol use and alcohol problems among U.S. adults: Results of the 1979 national survey. In National Institute on Alcohol Abuse and Alcoholism, *Alcohol consumption and related problems,* Alcohol and Health Monograph No. 1 (DHHS Publication No. (ADM) 82-1190). Rockville, Md.: National Institute on Alcohol Abuse and Alcoholism, 1982. Pp. 3–52.

3. Malin, H., Coakley, J., Kaelber, C., Munch, N., and Holland, W. An epidemiologic perspective on alcohol use and abuse in the United States. In National Institute on Alcohol Abuse and Alcoholism, *Alcohol consumption and related problems,* Alcohol and Health Monograph No. 1 (DHHS Publication No. (ADM) 82-1190). Rockville, Md.: National Institute on Alcohol Abuse and Alcoholism, 1982. Pp. 99–153.

4. Schmidt, W., and Popham, R. E. Heavy alcohol consumption and physical health problems: A review of the eipdemiological evidence. *Drug and Alcohol Dependence,* 1975, *1,* 27–50.

5. Lemoine, P., Harousseau, H., Borteryu, J. P., and Menuet, J. C. Les enfants de parents alcooliques; anomalies observées, à propos de 127 cas. *Archives Francaises de Pédiatrie*, 1967, *25*, 830–832.
6. Lemoine, P., Harousseau, H., Borteryu, J. P., and Menuet, J. C. Les enfants de parents alcooliques: Anomalies observées à propos de 127 cas. *Ouest Médical*, 1968, *21*, 476–482.
7. Dehaene, P. H., Crepin, G., Delahousse, G., Querleu, D., Walbaum, R., Titran, N., and Samaille-Villette, C. Aspects épidémiologiques du syndrome d'alcoolisme foetal: 45 observations en 3 ans. *Nouvelle Presse Médicale*, 1981, *10*, 2639–2643.
8. Majewski, F., Bierich, J. R., Loser, H., Michaelis, R., Leiber, B., and Bettecken, F. Zur Klinik und Pathogenese der Alkohol-Embryopathie; Bericht über 68 Falle. *Münchener Medizinische Wochenschrift*, 1976, *118*, 1635–1642.
9. Secretary of Health, Education, and Welfare. *Third Special Report to the U.S. Congress on Alcohol and Health. Technical Support Document* (DHEW Publication No. (ADM) 79-832). Rockville, Md.: National Institute on Alcohol Abuse and Alcoholism, 1979.
10. Braiker, H. B., Meshokoff, J. E., and Armor, D. J. A thirty-month follow-up of treated female alcoholics (in press).
11. Sokol, R. J., Miller, S. I., and Reed, G. Alcohol abuse during pregnancy: An epidemiologic study. *Alcoholism: Clinical and Experimental Research*, 1980, *4*, 135–145.
12. Cahalan, D., Cisin, I., and Crossley, H. *American drinking practices: A national study of drinking behavior and attitudes*. New Brunswick, N.J.: Rutgers Center of Alcohol Studies, 1969.
13. Jessor, R., Graves, R. D., Hanson, R. C., and Jessor, S. L. *Society, personality and deviant behavior: A study of a tri-ethnic community*. New York: Holt, Rinehart & Winston, 1968.
14. Russell, M., and Bigler, L. Screening for alcohol related problems in an out-patient obstetric-gynecologic clinic. *American Journal of Obstetrics and Gynecology*, 1979, *34*, 4–12.
15. Streissguth, A. P., Martin, D. C., and Buffington, V. E. Identifying heavy drinkers: A comparison of eight alcohol scores obtained on the sample sample. In F. A. Sexias, (Ed.)., *Currents in alcoholism*. New York: Grune and Stratton, 1977. Pp. 395–420.
16. Ouellette, E. M., Rosett, H. L., Rosman, N. P., and Weiner, L. Adverse effects on offspring of maternal alcohol abuse during pregnancy. *New England Journal of Medicine*, 1977, *297*, 528–530.
17. Alpert, J. J., Day, N., Dooling, E., Hingson, R., Oppenheimer, E., Rosett, H. L., Weiner, L., and Zuckerman, B. Maternal alcohol consumption and newborn assessment: Methodology of the Boston City Hospital prospective study. *Neurobehavioral Toxicology and Teratology*, 1981, *3*, 195–202.
18. Sokol, R. J., Miller, S. I., and Reed, G. Alcohol abuse during pregnancy: An epidemiological study. *Alcoholism: Clinical and Experimental Research*, 1980, *4*, 134–145.
19. Kuzma, J. W., and Kissinger, D. G. Patterns of alcohol and cigarette use in pregnancy. *Neurobehavioral Toxicology and Teratology*, 1981, *3*, 211–221.
20. Harlap, S., and Shiono, P. H. Alcohol, smoking, and incidence of spontaneous abortions in the first trimester. *Lancet*, 1980, *2*, 173–176.
21. Tennes, K., and Blackard, C. Maternal alcohol consumption, birth weight, and minor physical anomalies. *American Journal of Obstetrics and Gynecology*, 1980, *138*, 774–780.
22. Kline, J., Shrout, P., Stein, Z., Susser, M., and Warburton, D. Drinking during pregnancy and spontaneous abortion. *Lancet*, 1980, *1*, 176–180.
23. Little, R. E. Moderate alcohol use during pregnancy and decreased infant birth weight. *American Journal of Public Health*, 1977, *38*, 544–562.
24. Little, T. E., Schultz, F. A., and Mandell, W. A. Drinking during pregnancy. *Journal of Studies on Alcohol*, 1976, *37*, 375–379.
25. Murray-Lyon, I. M., Barrison, I. G., Wright, J. T., Morris, N., and Gordon, M. Alcohol abuse in pregnancy: A problem in London. *Lancet*, 1980, *1*, 27.

26. Kaminski, M., Rumeau-Rouquette, C., and Schwartz, D. Consommation d'alcool chez les femmes enceintes et issue de la grossesse. *Revue d'Épidémiologie, Médecine Sociale et Santé Publique,* 1976, *24,* 27–40.
27. Mau, G., and Netter, P. Kaffee- und Alkoholkonsum—Risikofactoren in der Schwangerschaft? *Geburtshilfe und Frauenheilkunde,* 1974, *34,* 1018–1022.
28. da Silva, V. A., Masur, J., Laranjeira, R. R., Dolnikoff, M., and Grinfeld, H. *Alcohol consumption during pregnancy by mothers of a low socioeconomical condition and their newborn.* Paper presented at the Fetal Alcohol Syndrome Workshop, Seattle, May 2–4, 1980.
29. Little, R. E., and Streissguth, A. P. Drinking during pregnancy in alcoholic women. *Alcoholism: Clinical and Experimental Research,* 1978, *2,* 179–183.
30. Hook, E. B. Dietary cravings and aversions during pregnancy. *American Journal of Clinical Nutrition,* 1978, *31,* 1355–1362.
31. Little, R. E. Maternal alcohol use during pregnancy: A review. In E. L. Abel, (Ed.), *Fetal alcohol syndrome* (Vol. 2). *Human studies.* Boca Raton, Fla.: CRC Press, 1982. Pp. 47–64.
32. Elton, R. H., and Wilson, M. E. Changes in ethanol consumption by pregnant pig-tailed macaques. *Journal of Studies on Alcohol,* 1977, *38,* 2181–2183.
33. Randall, C. L., Lochry, E. A., Hughes, S. S., and Boggan, W. O. Decreased ethanol consumption as a function of pregnancy and lactation in C57B1 mice. *Pharmacology, Biochemistry and Behavior,* 1980, *13* (Suppl. 1), 149–153.
34. Komura, S., Niimi, Y., and Yoshitake, Y. Alcohol preference during reproductive cycle in female C57BL mice. *Japanese Journal of Studies on Alcohol,* 1970, *5,* 91–96.
35. Thiessen, D. D., Whitworth, N. S., and Rodgers, D. A. Reproductive functions and metabolic capacity as determinants of alcohol preference in c57Bl/crgL female mouse. *Quarterly Journal of Studies on Alcohol,* 1966, *27,* 591–595.
36. Forger, N. G., and Morin, L. P. Reproductive state modulates ethanol intake in rats: Effects of ovariectomy, ethanol concentration, estrous cycle and pregnancy. *Pharmacology, Biochemistry and Behavior,* 1982, *17,* 323–331.
37. Carver, W. Nash, J. B., Emerson, G. A., and Moore, W. T. Effects of pregnancy and lactation on voluntary alcohol intake of hamsters. *Federation Proceedings,* 1953, *13,* 309.
38. Abel, E. L. Effects of lactation on rate of blood ethanol disappearance, ethanol consumption, and serum electrolytes in the rat. *Bulletin of the Psychonomic Society,* 1979, *14,* 365–367.
39. Little, R. E., Moore, D. E., Guzinski, G. M., and Perez, A. Absence of effect of exogenous estradiol on alcohol consumption in women. *Substance and Alcohol Actions/Misuse,* 1980, *1,* 551–556.
40. Abel, E. L. *Marihuana, tobacco, alcohol, and reproduction.* Boca Raton, Fla.: CRC Press, 1983.

CHAPTER 4

Acute Effects of Alcohol on the Fetus

As a result of studying the acute effects of alcohol on the fetus and the newborn, researchers and clinicians have gained considerable insight into the adverse consequences of chronic *in utero* exposure to alcohol comparable to what might occur in connection with chronic maternal alcoholism. While many of these studies were directed primarily at postponing premature labor by inhibiting uterine contractions, much of the data from such studies is directly relevant to the issue of alcohol's effects on the fetus and the newborn.

During the 1950s, several tests of alcohol's potential as an anesthetic during labor were conducted. Although the clinicians felt that such treatment greatly reduced maternal discomfort, a patient in one instance delivered a stillborn child after 8 hours of infusion of alcohol. No cause of death was apparent at autopsy.[1] In a second study, respiration was depressed in 5% of the newborns born to women who had received alcohol infusion resulting in maternal blood alcohol levels of 12.5 to 125 mg%.[2] In a third study, occasional "sluggishness" was noted in newborns, although no alcohol could be detected in cord blood for 50% of the infants.[3]

Despite the enthusiasm of the clinicians regarding alcohol's anesthetic actions in these studies, alcohol was not endorsed as an anesthetic for childbirth. However, the Chapman and Williams[2] observation that alcohol inhibited uterine contractions during labor was subsequently tested by Fuchs and co-workers,[4] following preliminary studies indicating alcohol-induced delay of parturition in animals.[5]

Although a number of clinical studies have reported successful postponement of labor following alcohol infusion, the efficacy of the procedure has been frequently questioned (see review by Abel[6]), especially in light of possible adverse effects resulting from it.

For example, blood alcohol levels generally reach a concentration of 150 mg% during the course of treatment.[7] As a result, maternal inebriety, nausea, and vomiting are often encountered. Since blood alcohol levels in the fetus tend to correspond to maternal blood alcohol levels (see Chapter 2), there is also the potential for CNS depression in the fetus.

Other studies have in fact reported effects suggestive of fetal CNS depression. For example, Fox and co-workers[8] observed fetal apnea lasting for over 50 minutes after pregnant women drank 1 ounce of vodka. In each case, fetal breathing stopped shortly after consumption of alcohol. Comparable cessation of fetal breathing was not observed in control patients. Fox attributed these results to the direct pharmacological effects of alcohol on the fetal brain.

Comparable observations were reported by Lewis and Boylan.[9] In this study, pregnant women drank vodka in orange juice or drank orange juice alone. Prior to consumption of any fluids, fetal breathing movements occupied 46% of the pretest period. After consumption of orange juice, breathing movements still occupied 46% of the test period. However, after consumption of the orange juice containing vodka, breathing movements occupied only 14% of the test period.

Cook and his co-workers[10] reported a case study in which a woman consumed bourbon 30 minutes prior to delivery. One hour after birth, the infant's blood alcohol level was 150 mg% and he appeared "lethargic, responded poorly to stimulation, and had diminished muscle tone and incomplete Moro, rooting, and grasp reflexes [and] respirations were very shallow" (p. 1075). Since the blood alcohol levels encountered in this case study were not markedly different from those frequently encountered in connection with ethanol infusion to postpone labor, one might also expect comparable effects in infants born to women who receive such treatment.

In a retrospective study of infants born to mothers who received ethanol infusion to delay labor, infants born within 12 hours of such infusion had a higher incidence of low Apgar scores and a higher incidence of respiratory distress compared to infants born to mothers that did not receive such treatment. These effects were especially observable in children weighing less than 2000 g at birth. There was also an increased incidence of neonatal mortality among ethanol-exposed infants weighing 1001–1500 g at birth.[11]

Kim and Hodgkinson[12] reported a case in which a woman accidentally received an infusion of 5% alcohol instead of lactated Ringer's solution during labor. The infant's Apgar score was 3 at 1 minute. In later tests for tone, rooting, alertness, and various other neurobehavioral measures, the infant scored the lowest of the 35 infants that were tested. Since testing occurred prior to the discovery of the accidental infusion of alcohol, evaluation of the infant's performance was essentially conducted "blind." At 7 days of age, the infant was still rated hypotonic.

Bone marrow anomalies lasting more than a month have also been reported in children that were exposed to alcohol prior to birth.[13]

Jung and his co-workers[14] attributed an infant's death shortly after birth to *in utero* alcohol exposure. The mother had been advised to drink vodka to retard labor, and when she was in labor she received alcohol infusion. Her newborn's Apgar scores were 2 at 1 minute and 3 at 5 minutes. Death occurred at 56 hours after birth. Blood analysis revealed severe metabolic acidosis.

Similar effects have been reported in animal studies. Infusion of alcohol to pregnant monkeys, for example, causes acidosis, decreased arterial blood pressure, and an increase in heart rate in the fetus, all of which are suggestive of fetal asphyxia.[15]

Acidosis, decreased blood oxygen content, and decreased blood pressure have also been reported in fetal sheep 30 minutes after mothers were infused with alcohol.[16,17] Comparable changes in blood gases or pH were not observed when observations were made during the actual period of infusion.[18,19]

Changes in EEG also occur in fetal sheep following exposure to alcohol. During the first 90 minutes of an alcohol infusion that produced a blood alcohol level of about 170 mg%, EEG decreased in amplitude and frequency. At a blood alcohol level of about 220 mg%, EEG frequency and amplitude were further decreased. During the postinfusion period, EEG activity could not be detected at all in some fetuses.[20]

Similar effects on EEG activity have been observed in fetal guinea pigs following *in utero* alcohol exposure. At blood alcohol levels of 100–150 mg%, EEG amplitude and frequency were reduced. At levels of 200–250 mg%, delta activity was observable. At blood alcohol levels above 250 mg%, EEG activity disappeared in some fetuses.[21]

In summary, *in utero* alcohol exposure has the potential of producing fetal CNS depression and various symptoms of fetal asphyxia such as acidosis, decreased blood oxygen content and breathing activity, and flattening of EEG activity, as well as other adverse effects such as bone cell anomalies and, in some instances, death.

These observations suggest the occurrence of comparable effects in the fetus as a response to brief but intense exposures to alcohol such as might be associated with binge drinking especially, and with chronic alcohol exposure in general.

References

1. Belinkoff, S., and Hall, W. O. Intravenous alcohol during labor. *American Journal of Obstetrics and Gynecology*, 1950, *59*, 429–432.
2. Chapman, E. R., and Williams, P. T. Intravenous alcohol as an obstetrical analgesia. *American Journal of Obstetrics and Gynecology*, 1951, *61*, 676–679.
3. Fetchko, A. M., Wever, J. E., Carroll, J. H., and Thomas, G. J. Intravenous alcohol used for preinduction analgesia in obstetrics. *American Journal of Obstetrics and Gynecology*, 1951, *62*, 662–664.

4. Fuchs, F., Fuchs, A. R., Problete, V. F., and Risk, A. Effect of alcohol on threatened premature labor. *American Journal of Obstetrics and Gynecology,* 1967, *99,* 627–637.
5. Fuchs, A. R. The inhibitory effect of ethanol on the release of oxytocin during parturition in the rabbit. *Journal of Endocrinology,* 1966, *35,* 125–134.
6. Abel, E. L. A critical evaluation of the obstetric use of alcohol in preterm labor. *Drug and Alcohol Dependence,* 1981, *7,* 367–378.
7. Caritis, S. N., Edelstone, D. I., and Mueller-Heubach, E. Pharmacologic inhibition of preterm labor. *American Journal of Obstetrics and Gynecology,* 1979, *133,* 557–578.
8. Fox, H. E., Steinbrecher, M., Pessel, D., Inglis, J., Medvid, L., and Angel, E. Maternal ethanol ingestion and the occurrence of human fetal breathing movements. *American Journal of Obstetrics and Gynecology,* 1978, *132,* 354–358.
9. Lewis, P. J., and Boylan, P. Alcohol and fetal breathing. *Lancet,* 1979, *1,* 388.
10. Cook, L. N., Schott, R. J., and Andrews, B. F. Acute transplanental ethanol intoxication. *American Journal of Diseases in Children,* 1975, *129,* 1075–1076.
11. Zervoudakis, I. A., Kruass, A., and Fuchs, F. Infants of mothers treated with ethanol for premature labor. *American Journal of Obstetrics and Gynecology,* 1980, *137,* 713–718.
12. Kim, S. S., and Hodgkinson, R. Acute ethanol intoxication and its prolonged effect on a full-term neonate. *Anesthesia and Analgesia Current Research,* 1976, *55,* 602–603.
13. Lopez, R., and Montoya, M. F. Abnormal bone marrow morphology in the premature infant associated with maternal alcohol infusion. *Journal of Pediatrics,* 1971, *79,* 1008–1010.
14. Jung, A. L., Roan, Y., and Temple, A. R. Neonatal death associated with acute transplacental ethanol intoxication. *American Journal of Diseases of Children,* 1980, *134,* 419–420.
15. Horiguchi, T., Suzuki, K., Comas-Urrutia, A. C., Mueller-Heubach, E., Boyer-Milic, A. M., Baratz, R. A., Morishima, H. O., James, L. S., and Adamsons, K. Effect of ethanol upon uterine activity and fetal acid-base state in the rhesis monkey. *American Journal of Obstetrics and Gynecology,* 1971, *109,* 910–917.
16. Mann, L. I., Bhakthavathsalan, A., Liu, M., and Makowski, P. Placental transport of alcohol and its effect on maternal and fetal acid-base balance. *American Journal of Obstetrics and Gynecology,* 1975, *122,* 837–844.
17. Ayromlooi, J., Tobias, M., Berg, P. D., and Desiderio, D. Effects of ethanol on the circulation and acid-base balance of pregnant sheep. *Obstetrics and Gynecology,* 1979, *54,* 624–630.
18. Dilts, P. V. Effect of ethanol on maternal and fetal acid-base balance. *American Journal of Obstetrics and Gynecology,* 1970, *107,* 1018–1021.
19. Kirkpatrick, S. E., Pitlick, P. T., Hirschklau, M., and Friedman, W. F. Acute effects of maternal ethanol infusion on fetal cardiac performance. *American Journal of Obstetrics and Gynecology,* 1976, *126,* 1034–1037.
20. Mann, L. I., Bhakthavathsalan, A., Liu, M., and Makowski, P. The effect of alcohol on fetal cerebral function and metabolism. *American Journal of Obstetrics and Gynecology,* 1975, *122,* 845–851.
21. Bergstrom, R. M., Sainion, K., and Taalas, J. The effect of ethanol on the EEG of the guinea-pig foetus. *Medicina et Pharmacologia Experimentalis,* 1967, *16,* 418–452.

CHAPTER 5

Adverse Consequences of Drinking during Pregnancy

Although not included in estimates of the incidence of fetal alcohol syndrome or fetal alcohol effects (see Chapter 6), increases in spontaneous abortion, stillbirth, and perinatal death have been linked to *in utero* alcohol exposure. The nature of this link, however, can be debated. While *in utero* alcohol exposure may be directly responsible for these effects, it is also conceivable that it is the "alcoholic" rather than the alcohol that is accountable. In other words, it is possible that those physiological factors that predispose a woman to become an alcoholic, and that precede her doing so, may also render her more prone to adverse pregnancy outcomes.

Spontaneous Abortion

The possible link between alcohol and spontaneous abortion was noted more than a thousand years ago. The Roman historian-naturalist Pliny, for example, commented about several different wines that prevented childbearing. "Egypt," he wrote, "also possesses a wine called in Greek, 'delivery wine' which causes abortion" (*Natural History* 14.22).

Just before the turn of the 20th century, Haddon[1] commented on the frequency of abortions during the early months of pregnancy among female alcoholics. McDaniel[2] likewise commented that "a succession of alcoholic debauches might, I think, be very likely to cause the death of the foetus in utero. . . ."

More recently, several epidemiological studies and experimental studies in animals concerning alcohol and spontaneous abortion have now been conducted supporting these earlier clinical impressions.

63

Alcoholic Women

In their large prospective study of over 12,000 women, Sokol and his co-workers[3] found that alcoholic women were almost twice (1.7 times) as likely as nonalcoholics to have had a spontaneous abortion in a previous pregnancy and were 2.3 times as likely to have had three or more consecutive spontaneous abortions.

Vitez and Czeizel[4] likewise reported an almost twofold increase in spontaneous abortion rate (18.8% vs. 9.6%) among 323 alcoholic women compared to an equal number of nonalcoholics.

In their study of mothers of fetal alcohol syndrome children, Seidenberg and Majewski[5] reported that a higher percentage of mothers of FAS children had histories of spontaneous abortions, hemorrhage, or threatened premature delivery, compared to women who bore healthy children. A high percentage of spontaneous abortions among alcoholic mothers was also reported by Dehaene and his colleagues.[6]

The one exception to this general pattern was reported by Bark,[7] who found that a group of Irish alcoholic women did not experience greater reproductive dysfunction than a control group of women suffering from endogenous depression. This result does not necessarily contradict other results, however, as Bark's "control" group may have been inappropriate. Since many female alcoholics also suffer from depression (see, e.g., references 8–10), Bark's control group may have been more similar to than different from his alcoholic group.

Nonalcoholic Women

In a case control study, Kline and her co-workers[11] retrospectively compared 616 women who aborted spontaneously with 632 who delivered after 28 weeks' gestation. Women were matched for age, maternal status, ethnic background, education, and religion.

Women who aborted were twice as likely to drink more than twice per week. The minimum threshold for increasing the likelihood of spontaneous abortion was calculated to be about 2 drinks twice weekly. Wine conferred the highest increased risk (odds ratio of 3:15) followed by distilled spirits (2:26) followed by beer (1:58). Overall, the authors calculated that drinking during pregnancy increases the risk of spontaneous abortion 2.62-fold.

While this study suggests that a very high risk of spontaneous abortion is associated with a minimal amount of drinking (2 drinks twice weekly), there are a number of factors that acted to inflate the reported relationship and that warrant attention. The first is that women who aborted were interviewed earlier than controls and after admission to hospital, whereas controls were interviewed during attendance in a prenatal clinic. Both factors may have affected recall.

**Table 9. Relative Risk of Miscarriage Associated with
Alcohol Consumption during Pregnancy (N = 32,019)[a]**

N drinks per day	% of sample	First trimester risk factor	Second trimester risk factor
1	44.6	1.12	1.03
1–2	2.4	1.15	1.98
3+	.4	1.16	3.53

[a]Data from Harlap and Shiono.[12]

A larger prospective study involving over 32,000 women,[12] on the other hand, is much less open to criticism. In this study, women responded to a questionnaire on alcohol use at the time of their first prenatal visit. The relationship between alcohol use and spontaneous abortion is shown in Table 9.

As indicated by the table, there was a dose-related increase in the number of spontaneous abortions. As alcohol consumption increased, so did the risk of spontaneous abortion. This was especially so during the second trimester, when consumption of more than 2 drinks per day increased the rate 3.5-fold. This increased risk could not be accounted for by age, parity, race, marital status, smoking, or prior history of abortion. However, in the preliminary publication of these findings,[13] the authors did find that drinking slightly increased the risk of abortion during the second trimester for "slender" women. This relation was not pointed out in the more complete publication of these findings, however, nor was it mentioned, for some unknown reason. Conceivably the relation may have disappeared after further analysis of the data.

Berkowitz[14] has also reported a slight, but significantly higher incidence of spontaneous abortion among women who consumed 2.4 drinks per week compared to those consuming 1.9 drinks per week, after factors such as smoking, marital status, and socioeconomic status were taken into account.

These studies thus support the likelihood that drinking during pregnancy increases the risk of spontaneous abortion. This risk is dose-related and varies from a 1.2-fold to a 3.5-fold increase in relative risk.

Alcohol versus the Alcoholic

Although there is good evidence that women who drink during pregnancy have an increased risk of spontaneous abortion, it is conceivable that these women would also be at risk even if they did not drink.

Alcoholic women tend to have an increased incidence of gynecological problems to begin with, and it is conceivable that these problems preceded their drinking and may even have precipitated it. Menstrual disorders such as dys-menorrhea and menorrhagia, for example, are not uncommon among alcoholic women.[15,16] In his survey of 321 chronic alcoholic women attending an obstet-rical/gynecological clinic in Yugoslavia, Moscovic[15] found that about two-thirds had ovarian dysfunction. Beckman[17] reported that 51% of a group of alcoholic women experienced "menstrual or other female problems" compared to 36% for controls. There are also several reports of increased drinking during pre-menstruum due to an attempt to relieve menstrual distress.[18-21]

Wilsnack[22] reported that alcoholic women had a higher incidence of diffi-culty conceiving and being able to carry pregnancies to term than did controls matched for age, socioeconomic status, and ethnicity. Only women who indi-cated that their reproductive problems preceded their drinking were sampled, suggesting that their infertility (and reproductive problems) may have precipi-tated drinking rather than the reverse. However, uncertainty about recall of events cannot be dismissed in this study. Moreover, it is also possible that "moderate" or "heavy" drinking precipitated reproductive dysfunction, which in turn led to "alcoholism" and further reproductive problems.

Studies in animals, however, leave no doubt that alcohol can affect ovarian function and can precipitate spontaneous abortion.

While consumption of relatively low amounts of alcohol resulting in blood alcohol levels below 100 mg% do not affect fertility,[23,24] when larger blood alcohol levels are achieved, ovulation has been blocked in rabbits,[25] rats,[26] and mice.[27]

Van Thiel and co-workers[28] reported that rats consuming a liquid alcohol diet for 7 weeks had ovaries that weighed 40% less than those of control rats. The uterus and fallopian tubes of these animals weighed about 25% that of controls. When the ovaries were examined, evidence of atrophy was also present.

These studies indicate that alcohol can precipitate ovarian dysfunction. Although such studies do not rule out the possibility that "alcoholics" experi-ence such dysfunction prior to becoming alcoholics, they indicate that the ob-verse is more likely.

One additional possibility that should also be mentioned in the context of reduced fertility among alcoholic women is that their infertility is also contrib-uted to by the father. Since women who drink heavily also tend to be married to men who drink heavily,[29] and since alcohol adversely affects sperm produc-tion,[30] difficulty in conceiving may not be due solely to ovarian dysfunction but also to paternal aspermia.

With respect to spontaneous abortion, however, studies in animals leave no doubt that alcohol can precipitate pregnancy loss. Table 10 summarizes some of these studies in mice. (In rodents, fetuses are resorbed rather than aborted.)

As in the epidemiological studies, these studies in mice also demonstrate that alcohol exerts a dose-related effect on spontaneous abortion (i.e., resorption rate). There is also some indication that genetic factors affect the extent of the increase in spontaneous abortion[33,39] and that time of exposure to alcohol is also important,[39] as noted by Harlap and Shiono.[12]

Pregnancy loss following alcohol exposure has also been reported in rats,[40] dogs,[41] and monkeys.[42] In the monkey, spontaneous abortion occurred in the first trimester when blood alcohol levels were around 200 mg% but did not occur when levels were below 150 mg%.[42] Similarly, spontaneous abortion rate was increased in dogs when blood alcohol levels exceeded 205 mg%.[41]

Alcohol has also been used to induce spontaneous abortion in both humans and animals Gomel and Carpenter,[43] for example, induced midterm abortions in women by first removing amniotic fluid and then replacing it with a comparable volume of fluid containing alcohol (47.5%) Fetal heart sounds disappeared within an hour after alcohol administration. Abortions occurred between 20 and 40 hours after treatment. The final concentration of alcohol in the amniotic fluid was estimated at between 100 and 150 mg%.

Dubin and his co-workers[44] induced abortion in monkeys by applying alcohol (70% v/v) topically to the amniotic sac. Abortions have also been induced in pregnant rats by introducing alcohol into the uterus.[45]

Although these deliberate attempts to induce abortion involved very high concentrations of alcohol, the fact that abortion occurs with such methods is in keeping with data from experiments in which animals and humans ingested alcohol in much lower concentrations and quantities.

In summary, both epidemiological studies and experimental studies in animals indicate that alcohol consumption can increase the risk of spontaneous abortion, and this risk increases as the amount of drinking increases. Although alcohol consumption has frequently been associated with ovarian dysfunction and fertility problems, these data demonstrate that it is the alcohol, and not the alcoholic, that is primarily responsible for this increased rate of spontaneous abortion.

Stillbirths

The reported effects of alcohol ingestion during pregnancy on stillbirth rates have not been consistent. In their first prospective study involving over 9000 French women, Kaminski and her co-workers[46] noted a significant increase in stillbirth rate among women who drank 3 or more drinks per day compared to women who drank less. In their second study[47] there was a similar trend, but it was not statistically significant. No significant increase in stillbirth rates was noted by Sokol and his co-workers[3] in their prospective study of alcoholic women.

At present there is no clear evidence that drinking during pregnancy causes an added risk for stillbirths in humans.

A dose-related increase in stillbirth rate associated with alcohol exposure

Table 10. Effects of Alcohol on Resorption Rate in Mice

Source	Strain	Duration of exposure during pregnancy	Route of exposure	Amount administered	% resorptions
Chernoff[31]	CBA/J	Prior to and during pregnancy	p.o. (liquid diet)	0 (EDC)[a]	0
				15	57
				20	72
				25	73
				30	100
	C$_3$H/1g	Prior to and during pregnancy	p.o. (liquid diet)	0 (EDC)	0
				20	0
				25	30
				30	72
				35	100
Chernoff[32]	CBA	Prior to and during pregnancy	p.o. (liquid diet)	0 (EDC)	~4[b]
				20	~73
	C$_3$H	Prior to and during pregnancy	p.o. (liquid diet)	0 (EDC)	5
				20	7
	C$_{57}$BL/6J	Prior to and during pregnancy	p.o. (liquid diet)	0 (EDC)	7
				20	7
Giknis et al.[33]	Swiss Webster	Days 8, 10, 12, and 14 of pregnancy	i.p.	0 g/kg	~6
				4	~38
				6	~45
	CD$_1$	Days 8, 10, 12, and 14 of pregnancy	i.p.	0	~14
				4	~21
				6	~31
	C$_{57}$BL/6J	Days 8, 10, 12, and 14 of pregnancy	i.p.	0	~18
				4	~28
	DBA/6J	Days 8, 10, 12, and 14 of pregnancy	i.p.	0	~46
				4	~36
Kronick[34]	C$_{57}$BL/6J	Days 8 and 9 of pregnancy	i.p.	0 g/kg	6
				~6	37
	x DBA/6J	Days 10 and 11 of pregnancy	i.p.	0	6
				~6	~60
		Day 7	i.p.	6	7
		Day 8	i.p.	6	19
		Day 9	i.p.	6	28
		Day 10	i.p.	6	45
		Day 11	i.p.	6	38
Randall et al.[35]	C$_{57}$BL/6J	Days 5–10 of pregnancy	p.o. (liquid diet)	0 (EDC)	6
				25	16
Randall and Taylor[36]	C$_{57}$BL/6J	Days 5–10 of pregnancy	p.o. (liquid diet)	0 (EDC)	8
				17	15
				25	16
				30	23

(continued)

Table 10. (*Continued*)

Source	Strain	Duration of exposure during pregnancy	Route of exposure	Amount administered	% resorptions
Rasmussen and Christensen[37]	C_3H	Days 1–18 of pregnancy	p.o. (water)	0% v/v 10 20	7 9 21
Schwetz et al.[38]	CF_1	Days 6–15 of pregnancy	p.o. (water)	0% v/v 15	~3 6
Webster et al.[39]	$C_{57}BL/6J$	Day 7 of pregnancy	i.p.	0 g/kg 2.9 4.3 5.9	20 17 25 34
	$C_{57}BL/6J$	Day 8 of pregnancy	i.p.	2.9 g/kg 4.3 5.9	13 16 47
		Day 9 of pregnancy	i.p.	2.9 4.3 5.9	15 27 48
		Day 10 of pregnancy	i.p.	2.9 4.3 5.9	10 49 70
		Day 11 of pregnancy	i.p.	4.3 5.9	35 66
	QS	Day 7 of pregnancy	i.p.	5.9	9
		Day 8 of pregnancy	i.p.	5.9	10
		Day 9 of pregnancy	i.p.	5.9	15
		Day 10 of pregnancy	i.p.	5.9	17
		Day 11 of pregnancy	i.p.	5.9	4

[a]EDC = ethanol-derived calories.
[b]~ = approximately.

during pregnancy has been reported in some animal studies, although here too the data are inconsistent. Ellis and Pick[41] reported a dose-related increase in stillbirth rate among beagles intubated with alcohol during pregnancy. The stillbirth rate for control mothers was 7%. At blood alcohol levels of about 100 mg%, the stillbirth rate was 24%. At levels of 130 mg%, stillbirth rate increased to 45%. Levels above 130 mg% did not cause any further increases in stillbirth rate but did increase rate of spontaneous abortions (see above).

A major problem in assessing stillbirth rates in rodents is that dams may cannibalize stillborn pups before they can be identified and removed. This is especially so if births occur during the night hours, when investigators may not be monitoring animals. The inability to monitor births continuously may be one reason for the absence of any consistent data in conjunction with alcohol exposure and stillbirth rate in animals.

Neonatal Mortality

Maternal consumption of alcohol does not appear to be associated with an increase in neonatal mortality in humans. This conclusion is based on epidemiological studies involving large numbers of patients.[3,29,30] Two studies[48,49] reporting an increase in neonatal mortality associated with maternal drinking were based on relatively small sample sizes. For example, in the study reported by Jones and co-workers,[48] sample size was 4 out of 23 cases, the data were gathered retrospectively, and there was no determination of alcoholic status at the time the data were originally obtained. However, the fact that a diagnosis of alcoholism could be made in these few cases probably means that consumption was very high in these women. Consequently, the reported association between heavy drinking and neonatal mortality may indeed be valid.

The other study reporting an increase in neonatal mortality among alcoholic women was reported by Olegård and his colleagues.[49] Again sample size was relatively small (3 cases out of 52), but again these women may have been heavier drinkers than those studied in the larger epidemiological evaluations.

Studies in animals, on the other hand, have frequently noted an increase in neonatal mortality resulting from prenatal alcohol exposure (see, e.g., references 40, 41, and 50). This effect is dose-related and is not attributable to residual effects on maternal nurturing or lactation.[40]

The reason effects on neonatal mortality are more readily apparent in animal studies than in human studies is no doubt related in large part to the intensive care newborn human infants receive. In the animal world there is no equivalent of the "intensive care unit," so that weak and puny offspring are either cannibalized or are ignored and die.

References

1. Haddon, J. On intemperance in women, with special reference to its effects on the reproductive system. *British Medical Journal*, 1876, *1*, 748–750.
2. McDaniel, W. H. The effect of alcohol upon the foetus through the blood of the mother. *Maryland State Medical Journal*, 1883, *10*, 39–40.
3. Sokol, R. J., Miller, S. I., and Reed, G. Alcohol abuse during pregnancy: An epidemiological study. *Alcoholism: Clinical and Experimental Research*, 1980, *4*, 135–145.

4. Vitez, M., and Czeizel, E. Az iszakos—alkoholista nok termekenysege. *Alkohologia*, 1982, *13*, 79–83.
5. Seidenberg, J., and Majewski, F. Zur Haufigkeit der Alkoholembryopathie in den verschiedenen Phasen der mutterlichen Alkoholkrankheit. *Suchtgefahren*, 1978, *24*, 63–75.
6. Dehaene, P. H., Samaille-Villette, C. H., Samaille, P. P., Crepin, G., Walbaum, R., Deroubaix, P., and Blanc-Garin, A. P. Le syndrome d'alcoolisme foetal dans le nord de la France. *Revue de l'Alcoolisme*, 1977, *23*, 145–158.
7. Bark, N. Fertility and offspring of alcoholic women: An unsuccessful search for the fetal alcohol syndrome. *British Journal of Addiction*, 1979, *74*, 43–49.
8. Winokur, G., and Clayton, P. Family history studies. IV. Comparison of male and female alcoholics. *Quarterly Journal of Studies on Alcohol*, 1968, *29*, 885–891.
9. Rimmer, J., Reich, T., and Winokur, G. Alcoholism. V. Diagnosis and clinical variation among alcoholics. *Quarterly Journal of Studies on Alcohol*, 1972, *33*, 658–666.
10. Schuckit, M., Pitts, F. N., Reich, T., King, L. J., and Winokur, G. Alcoholism. I. Two types of alcoholism in women. *Archives of General Psychiatry*, 1969, *20*, 301–306.
11. Kline, J., Shrout, P., Stein, Z., Susser, M., and Warburton, D. Drinking during pregnancy and spontaneous abortion. *Lancet*, 1980, *2*, 176–180.
12. Harlap, S., and Shiono, P. H. Alcohol, smoking, and incidence of spontaneous abortions in the first and second trimester. *Lancet*, 1980, *2*, 173–176.
13. Harlap, S., Shiono, P. H., and Ramcharan, S. Alcohol and spontaneous abortions. *American Journal of Epidemiology*, 1980, *110*, 372.
14. Berkowitz, G. S. An epidemiologic study of preterm delivery. *American Journal of Epidemiology*, 1981, *113*, 81–92.
15. Moskovic, S. Effect of chronic alcohol intoxication on ovarian dysfunction. *Srpski Arhiv za Celokupno Lekarstvo*, 1975, *103*, 751–758.
16. Wall, J. H. A study of alcoholism in women. *American Journal of Psychiatry*, 1937, *93*, 943.
17. Beckman, L. J. Reported effects of alcohol on the sexual feelings and behavior of women alcoholics and nonalcoholics. *Journal of Studies on Alcohol*, 1979, *40*, 272–282.
18. Belfer, M. L., Shader, R. I., Carroll, M., and Harmatz, J. S. Alcoholism in women. *Archives of General Psychiatry*, 1971, *25*, 540–544.
19. James, J. E. Symptoms of alcoholism in women: A preliminary survey of AA members. *Journal of Studies on Alcohol*, 1975, *36*, 1564–1569.
20. Lolli, G. Alcoholism in women. *Connecticut Review on Alcoholism*, 1953, *5*, 9–11.
21. Podolsky, E. The woman alcoholic and premenstrual tension. *Journal of the American Medical Women's Association*, 1963, *18*, 816–818.
22. Wilsnack, S. C. Sex role identity in female alcoholism. *Journal of Abnormal Psychology*, 1973, *82*, 253–259.
23. Oisund, J. F., Fjorden, A. E., and Morlund, J. Is moderate ethanol teratogenic in the rat? *Acta Pharmacologica et Toxicologia*, 1978, *43*, 145–155.
24. Tze, W. J., and Lee, M. Adverse effects of maternal alcohol consumption on pregnancy and foetal growth in rats. *Nature*, 1975, *257*, 479–480.
25. Saul, G. Blockade of ovulation in the rabbit by intoxicating doses of ethyl alcohol. *Anatomical Record*, 1959, *133*, 332.
26. Kieffer, J. D., and Ketchel, M. M. Blockade of ovulation in the rat by ethanol. *Acta Endocrinologica*, 1970, *65*, 117–124.
27. Cranston, E. M. Effect of tranquilizers and other agents on sexual cycle in mice. *Proceedings of the Society of Experimental Biology and Medicine*, 1958, *98*, 320–322.
28. Van Thiel, D. H., Gavaler, J. S., and Lester, R. Alcohol-induced ovarian failure in the rat. *Journal of Clinical Investigation*, 1978, *61*, 624–632.
29. Gomberg, E. S. *Alcoholism and women: State of knowledge today.* Paper presented at the National Alcoholism Forum, Milwaukee, 1975.

30. Lester, R., and Van Thiel, D. H. Gonadal function in chronic alcoholism. *Advances in Experimental Medicine and Biology*, 1977, *85A*, 399–414.
31. Chernoff, G. F. The fetal alcohol syndrome in mice: An animal model. *Teratology*, 1977, *15*, 223–229.
32. Chernoff, G. F. The fetal alcohol syndrome in mice: Maternal variables. *Teratology*, 1980, *22*, 71–75.
33. Giknis, M. L., Damjanov, I., and Rubin, E. The differential transplacental effects of ethanol in four mouse strains. *Neurobehavioral Toxicology*, 1980, *2*, 235–237.
34. Kronick, J. B. Teratogenic effects of ethyl alcohol administered to pregnant mice. *American Journal of Obstetrics and Gynecology*, 1976, *124*, 676–680.
35. Randall, C. L., Taylor, W. J., and Walker, D. W. Ethanol-induced malformations in mice. *Alcoholism: Clinical and Experimental Research*, 1977, *1*, 219–223.
36. Randall, C. L., and Taylor, W. J. Prenatal ethanol exposure in mice: Teratogenic effects. *Teratology*, 1979, *19*, 305–312.
37. Rasmussen, B. B., and Christensen, N. Teratogenic effect of maternal alcohol consumption of the mouse fetus: A histopathological study. *Acta Pathologica et Microbiologica Scandinavica, Section A, Pathology*, 1980, *88*, 285–289.
38. Schwetz, B. A., Smith, F. A., and Staples, R. E. Teratogenic potential of ethanol in mice, rats, and rabbits. *Teratology*, 1978, *18*, 385–392.
39. Webster, W. S., Walsh, D. A., Lipson, A. H., and McEwen, S. E. Teratogenesis after acute alcohol exposure in inbred and outbred mice. *Neurobehavioral Toxicology*, 1980, *2*, 227–234.
40. Abel, E. L., and Dintcheff, B. A. Effects of prenatal alcohol exposure on growth and development in rats. *Journal of Pharmacology and Experimental Therapeutics*, 1978, *207*, 916–921.
41. Ellis, F. W., and Pick, J. R. An animal model of the fetal alcohol syndrome in beagles. *Alcoholism: Clinical and Experimental Research*, 1980, *4*, 123–134.
42. Altschuler, H. L., and Shippenberg, T. S. A subhuman primate model for fetal alcohol syndrome research. *Neurobehavioral Toxicology and Teratology*, 1981, *3*, 121–126.
43. Gomel, V., and Carpenter, C. W. Induction of midtrimester abortion with intrauterine alcohol. *Journal of Obstetrics and Gynecology*, 1973, *41*, 455–458.
44. Dubin, N. H., Blake, D. H., Parmley, T. H., Conner, E. A., Cox, R. T., and King, T. M. Intrauterine ethanol-induced termination of pregnancy in cynomolgus monkeys (*Macaca fascicularis*). *American Journal of Obstetrics and Gynecology*, 1978, *132*, 789–790.
45. Conner, E. A., Blake, D. A., Parmley, T. H., Burnett, L. S., and King, T. M. Efficacy of various locally applied chemicals as contragestational agents in rats. *Contraception*, 1976, *13*, 571–582.
46. Kaminski, M., Rumeau-Rouquette, C., and Schwartz, D. Consommation d'alcool chez les femmes enceintes et issue de la grossesse. *Revue d'Épidémiologie, Médecine Sociale et Santé Publique*, 1976, *24*, 27–40.
47. Kaminski, M., Franc, M., Lebouvier, M., Du Mazaubrun, C., and Rumeau-Rouquette, C. Moderate alcohol use and pregnancy outcome. *Neurobehavioral Toxicology and Teratology*, 1981, *3*, 173–181.
48. Jones, K. L., Smith, D. W., Streissguth, S., and Myrianthopoulos, N. C. Outcome in offspring of chronic alcoholic women. *Lancet*, 1974, *1*, 1076–1078.
49. Olegård, R., Sabel, K. G., Aronsson, M., Sandin, B., Johansson, P. R., Carlsson, C., Kyllerman, M., Iverson, K., and Hrbek, A. Effects on the child of alcohol abuse during pregnancy. *Acta Paediatrica Scandinavica (Supplement)*, 1979, *275*, 112–121.
50. Lochry, E. A., Shapiro, N. R., and Riley, E. P. Growth deficits in rats exposed to alcohol in utero. *Journal of Studies on Alcohol*, 1980, *41*, 1031–1039.

CHAPTER 6

Incidence of Fetal Alcohol Syndrome and Fetal Alcohol Effects

As noted in Chapter 1, recognition of alcohol's teratogenic potential is far from new. Even during the 1950s there were studies attributing teratogenicity to alcohol,[1,2] but these studies were not published in English and they went largely unnoticed. A similar lack of attention was accorded Lemoine's report in 1968[3] in which the main clinical features of the fetal alcohol syndrome were described. It was not until 1973, when Jones and Smith[4,5] published their own observations of children born to alcoholic women and labeled the pattern of defects they observed as the "fetal alcohol syndrome," that general scientific attention was once again attracted to alcohol's potentially adverse effects on fetal development. Since those two publications, literally hundreds of research articles have appeared in connection with this syndrome (see Table 1). Moreover, alcohol has now been singled out as "the most common chemical teratogen presently causing problems of malformation and mental deficiency in the human."[6]

As of 1979, over 600 cases of fetal alcohol syndrome have been identified.[6] These cases have not been confined to any specific geographical area. Instances of fetal alcohol syndrome have now been observed in Australia,[7] Belgium,[8] Brazil,[9] Canada,[10] Chile,[11] Czechoslovakia,[12] France,[13] Germany,[14] Hungary,[15] Ireland,[16] Italy,[17] Reunion,[18] South Africa,[19] Spain,[20] Sweden,[21] Switzerland,[22] and the United States.[4]

For a diagnosis of fetal alcohol syndrome to be made, the Fetal Alcohol Study Group of the Research Society on Alcoholism[23] has proposed that a patient should exhibit the three basic criteria outlined in Table 11. If all three criteria cannot be met, the study group has recommended the term *possible fetal alcohol effects* for characteristics suspected of being related to prenatal alcohol exposure. Even in cases in which fetal alcohol effects seem evident, however, this diagnosis should be corroborated if at all possible, with a diagnosis of

73

**Table 11. Minimal Criteria for Diagnosis of
Fetal Alcohol Syndrome Proposed by
Research Society on Alcoholism's Fetal
Alcohol Study Group**[23]

1. Prenatal or postnatal growth retardation (below
   10th percentile for body weight, length, or head
   circumference)
2. Characteristic facial anomalies (at least 2 of 3)
   a. Microcephaly (below 3rd percentile)
   b. Microphthalmia or short palpebral fissures
   c. Underdeveloped philtrum, thin upper lip, and
      maxillary hypoplasia
3. Central nervous system dysfunction (neurological
   abnormality, mental deficiency, developmental
   delay)

maternal alcoholism because of the close resemblance between fetal alcohol
effects and fetal hydantoin effects and other syndromes such as Noonan and
Cornellia de Lange syndromes.[24]

Estimated Incidence

Despite its ubiquity, the overall incidence of fetal alcohol syndrome per
total live births is relatively low and ranges between .4 and 3.1 per 1000,
depending on the study population and the methodology used for estimation. The
average minimal incidence, as indicated by Table 12, which summarizes the
various studies making such estimates, is 1.1 cases per 1000 live-born infants.

In 1980 approximately 3,598,000 children were born in the United States.
Assuming these were all single-borns, the number of children born with fetal
alcohol syndrome was 3958 (3,598,000 × .0011), based on the number of births
and the estimated average incidence from Table 12.

Fetal alcohol syndrome, however, represents only one of the extremes of a
broad range of fetal alcohol effects, which are described more fully in Table 13.

Not surprisingly, the estimated incidence of patients with some, but not all,
of the effects associated with fetal alcohol syndrome, i.e., "possible fetal alcohol effects," is higher than for fetal alcohol syndrome. Estimates of the number
of such patients are presented in Table 14.

As indicated by Table 14, estimates from the Boston study are considerably
higher than estimates from all other sites. This is because the Boston study
included any minor irregularity such as hemangioma along with more serious

Table 12. Estimated Incidence of FAS per 1000 Live Births (Total Population)

Study site (source)	Socioeconomic status/race	Sample size	N cases	Estimated incidence
Boston				
Ouellette et al.[25]	Low SES/black (inner city)	322	1[a]	3.1 per 1000
Cleveland				
Sokol et al.[26]	Low SES (inner city)	12,127	5	.4 per 1000
Seattle				
Hanson et al.[27]	Middle SES/white	1,529	2[b]	1.3 per 1000
France				
Dehaene et al.[28]	Low SES/white	8,284	12	1.4 per 1000
Sweden				
Olegård et al.[21]	White	7,600	12	1.6 per 1000
Average minimal incidence		29,862	32	1.1 per 1000

[a]Case diagnosed at 1 year of age.
[b]Same mother gave birth to both.

anomalies in its calculations. If the Boston study's data are included in the overall estimation, the average minimal incidence for fetal alcohol effects is about 4.4 cases per 1000 live-born infants. If it is not included, the estimated incidence 3.1 cases per 1000 live-borns.

Using the 1980 birth data statistics, there were 3,598,000 live births in the United States for that year. If the more conservative estimated incidence of 3.1 cases per 1000 live births is used, this would suggest a minimum of 11,154 children born with fetal alcohol effects per year.

Another way of estimating the incidence of fetal alcohol syndrome and fetal alcohol effects is to take into consideration the statistics for women who are "heavy" drinkers during pregnancy (see Table 8). The median estimate of such women in the United States is 2%.

Table 15 presents a summary of the estimated incidence of fetal alcohol syndrome and fetal alcohol effects among alcohol-abusing women. As indicated by the table, the average minimal incidence for each is 25 and 91 per 1,000 (omitting the Boston data because of inflated reporting for fetal alcohol effects), respectively.

Using these data, the estimated number of children born with fetal alcohol syndrome per year can be calculated by multiplying the total number of children born in 1980 (3,598,000) by the percentage of heavy drinkers (2%) by the average minimal incidence of fetal alcohol syndrome (.025) among heavy drink-

Table 13. Characteristics Associated with *in Utero* Alcohol Exposure (Fetal Alcohol Effects)

Pre- and Postnatal growth retardation
Microcephaly
Abnormal facial features
Eyes
   Short palpebral fissures (eye slits)   Strabismus, nystagmus, myopia, esotropia, Abnormal retinal
   Epicanthal folds   vasculature
   Microphthalmia (small eyes)
   Antimongoloid slant (eyes slant downward)
   Ptosis (drooping eyelid)
   Hyperteleorism (wide-set eyes)
Ears
   Low-set (below eyes)   Persistent rhinorrhea, otitis media
   Posterior rotation (toward back of head)
   Prominent (large)
   Abnormal pinna (external ear)
   Poorly formed concha (hollow of external ear)
Nose
   Shortened
   Hypoplasia of nasal bridge (underdeveloped bridge of nose)
   Anteverted nostrils (upturned nose)
Mouth
   Wide
   Thin upper vermilion border (red pigment)
   High arched palate (interior of upper mouth)
   Cleft palate
   Cleft lip
   Prominent lateral palantine ridge (top of mouth)
   Poorly formed teeth

(continued)

Other facial features
  Indistinct philtrum (groove between nose and mouth)
  Midface hypoplasia (small middle area of face)
  Hypoplastic maxilla (small upper jaw)
  Micrognathia (small lower jaw)
  Hirsutism (excess hair on face)
  Prominent occiput (bulging rear of head)
  Occipital flattening (back of head flattened)
Abnormal organ development
  Heart
    Ventricular septal defect (hole between heart chambers)
    Atrial septal defect (hole between heart chambers)
    Patent ductus arteriosus (opening in artery)
    Tetralogy of Fallot
    Heart murmur
  Urogenital
    Hydronephrosis (enlarged area of kidney)   Obstruction of urinary flow
    Small kidney
    Hypospadia (orifice of penis too low)
    Undescended testicle
    Clitoromegaly (enlarged clitoris)
    Hypoplastic labia majora (small external genitalia)
    Biseptate vagina (fold in vagina)
    Absent clitoris
    Gynecomastia (enlarged breasts)
  Respiratory
    Small trachea   Respiratory distress syndrome
    Thin epiglottis
  Liver   Abnormal liver function

Table 13 (*Continued*)

Limb and joint abnormalities
  Skeletal anomalies
    Small nails
    Polydactyly (additional fingers or toes)
    Camptodactyly (permanent flexion of finger)
    Clinodactyly (permanent bending of one or more fingers)
    Tetradactyly (absence of one or more fingers or toes)
    Phocomelia of upper limb (absence of limb)
    Amelia of lower limb (absence of limb)
    Shortened fingers
    Overlapping fingers
    Increased interdigital skin fold (extra webbing between fingers
      and toes)
    Talipes (clubfoot)
    Cervical spinal fusion
    Scoliosis (spinal curvature)
    Carpal fusion (fusion of wrist bones)
    Fusion of ribs
    Hip dislocation
    Spina bifida
    Limited joint movement
    Pectus excavatum (funnel breast)
    Pectus carinatum (pigeon breast)
    Radioulnar stenosis (narrowing of junction between bones of
      forearm)

Cutaneous anomalies
  Aberrant palmar creases
  Abnormal fingerprint patterns
  Hemangiomas (abnormal pigmented areas)
  Accessory nipple (extra nipple)
  Hypoplastic nipple (small nipple)
  Hirsutism
  Abnormal scalp-hair pattern
  Hair whorls
  Presacral dimple (dimple in sacrum area of spine)
Muscular abnormalities
  Hernias
  Anal stenosis (narrowing of anal canal)
  Hypotonia (poor muscle tone)
Central nervous system abnormalities
  Abnormal brain structures
  Hydrocephalus (excessive fluid in brain)
  Anencephaly (absence of brain)

Mental retardation
Hyperactivity
Poor eye–hand coordination
Learning disability (in absence of mental retardation)
Cerebral palsy
Seizure disorders
Electroencephalograph irregularities
Sleep problems
Neonatal irritability
Neonatal alcohol withdrawal
Low Apgar scores

Table 14. Estimated Incidence of FAE per 1000 Live Births (Total Population)[a]

Study site (source)	Sample size	N cases	Estimated incidence
Boston			
Ouellette et al.[25]	322	29	90.1 per 1000
Cleveland			
Sokol et al.[26]	12,127	21	1.7 per 1000
Seattle			
Hanson et al.[27]	1,529	9	5.9 per 1000
Sweden			
Olegård et al.[21]	7,600	24	3.2 per 1000
France			
Dehaene et al.[13]	8,284	39	4.7 per 1000
Average minimal incidence			4.4 per 1000
			3.1 per 1000[b]

[a]Combined classification of anomalies, including congenital, growth, or neurological anomalies (does not include spontaneous abortions).
[b]Estimate does not include data from Boston study (see text).

Table 15. Estimated Incidence of FAS and FAE per 1000 Live Births among Alcohol-Abusing Women

Study site (source)	Sample size	N FAS cases	N FAE cases	Estimated incidence per 1000	
				FAS	FAE
Boston					
Ouellette et al.[25] 1977	42	1	29	24	690
Cleveland					
Sokol et al.[26] 1980	204	5	16	25	78
Seattle					
Hanson et al.[27] 1978	70	2	9	29	129
Average minimal incidence	316	3	54	25	171
	274[a]		25[a]		91[a]

[a]Data from Boston omitted due to inflated estimate (see text).

ers. On the basis of these data, the estimated annual number of cases of fetal alcohol syndrome is about 1800 (3,598,000 × .02 × .025).

Similarly, the estimated annual number of children born with fetal alcohol effects is about 6550 (3,598,000 × .02 × 091).

When estimates are calculated in this way, they fall considerably under the estimates of approximately 4000 fetal alcohol syndrome cases and 11,000 fetal alcohol effects cases determined by evaluating all pregnant women.

In summary, the estimated number of children born each year with fetal alcohol syndrome and fetal alcohol effects is as follows:

Estimated Annual Cases of Fetal Alcohol Syndrome: 1800 to 4000
Estimated Annual Cases of Fetal Alcohol Effects: 6550 to 11,000

References

1. Heuyer, H., Mises, R., and Dereux, J. F. La descendance des alcooliques. *Presse Médicale,* 1957, 29, 657–658.
2. Uhlig, H. Missbildungen unerwunschter Kinder. *Arztliche Wochenschrift,* 1957, 12, 61–65.
3. Lemoine, P., Harousseau, H., Borteryu, J. P., and Menuet, J. C. Les enfants de parents alcooliques: Anomalies observées à propos de 127 cas. *Ouest Medical,* 1968, 21, 476–482.
4. Jones, K. L., and Smith, D. W. Recognition of the fetal alcohol syndrome in early infancy. *Lancet,* 1973, 2, 999–1001.
5. Jones, K. L., Smith, D. W., Ulleland, C. N., and Streissguth, A. P. Pattern of malformation in offspring of chronic alcoholic mothers. *Lancet,* 1973, 1, 1267–1271.
6. Smith, D. W. The fetal alcohol syndrome. *Hospital Practice,* 1979, 14, 12–28.
7. Collins, E., and Turner, G. Six children affected by maternal alcoholism. *Medical Journal of Australia,* 1978, 2, 606–608.
8. Van Biervliet, J. P. The fetal alcohol syndrome. *Acta Paediatrie Belge,* 1977, 30, 113–116.
9. da Silva, V. A., Laranjeira, R. R., Dolnikoff, M., Grinfeld, H., and Masur, J. Alcohol consumption during pregnancy and newborn outcome: A study in Brazil. *Neurobehavioral Toxicology and Teratology,* 1981, 3, 169–172.
10. Smith, D. F., Sander, G. G., Macleod, P. M., Tredwell, S. Wood, B., and Newman, D. E. Intrinsic defects in the fetal alcohol syndrome: Studies on 76 cases from British Columbia and the Yukon territory. *Neurobehavioral Toxicology and Teratology,* 1981, 3, 145–152.
11. Mena, M., Albornoz, C., Puente, M., and Moreno, M. Fetal alcohol syndromes. A study of 19 clinical cases. *Revue Chile Pediatrie,* 1980, 51, 414–423.
12. Ticha, R. Alkoholova embryopatie. *Ceskoslovenska Gynekologie,* 1979, 34, 615–617.
13. Dehaene, P. H., Samaille-Villette, C. H., Samaille, P. P., Crepin, G., Walbaum, R. Deroubaix, P., and Blanc-Garin, A. P. Le syndrome d'alcoolisme foetal dans le nord de la France. *Revue de l'Alcoolisme,* 1977, 23, 145–158.
14. Majewski, F. Über schadigende Einflusse des Alkohols auf die Nachkommen. *Der Nervenarzt,* 1978, 49, 410–416.
15. Pocsy, T., and Balassa, E. Alkohoos embryopathia. *Orvosi Hetilap,* 1978, 119, 209–211.
16. Barry, R. G. G., and O'Nuallain, S. Case report: Foetal alcoholism. *Irish Journal of Medical Science,* 1975, 144, 286–288.

17. Fiocchi, A., Colombini, A., and Codara, L. La embriopatìa alcoòlica; rassègna della lètteratùra e contribùto personàle. *Minerva Pediatrica,* 1978, *30,* 19–28.
18. Lesure, J. F. Syndrome d' alcoolisme foetal à l'Ile de la Réunion. *Nouvelle Presse Médicale,* 1980, *9,* 1708, 1710.
19. Beyers, N., and Moosa, A. The fetal alcohol syndrome, case reports. *South Africa Medical Journal,* 1978, *54,* 575–578.
20. Cahuana, A., Krauel, J., Molina, V., Lizarraga, I., and Alfonso, H. Fetopatiea alcoholica. *Anales Espanoles de Pediatria,* 1977, *10,* 673–676.
21. Olegård, R., Sabel, K. G., Aronsson, M., Sandin, B., Johansson, P. R., Carlsson, C., Kyllerman, M., Iverson, K., and Hrbek, A. Effects on the child of alcohol abuse during pregnancy. *Acta Paediatrica Scandinavica, Supplement,* 1979, *275,* 112–121.
22. Villermaulaz, A. Syndrome de l'alcoolisme foetal. *Révue Médicale de la Suisse Romande,* 1977, *97,* 613–619.
23. Rosett, H. L. A clinical perspective of the fetal alcohol syndrome. *Alcoholism: Clinical and Experimental Research,* 1980, *4,* 119–122.
24. Smith, D. W. Fetal drug syndromes: Effects of ethanol and hydantoins. *Pediatrics in Review,* 1979, *1,* 165–172.
25. Ouellette, E. M., Rosett, H. L., Rosman, N. P., and Leiner, L. Adverse effects on offspring of maternal alcohol abuse during pregnancy. *New England Journal of Medicine,* 1977, *297,* 528–530.
26. Sokol, R. J., Miller, S. I., and Reed, G. Alcohol abuse during pregnancy: An epidemiological study. *Alcoholism: Clinical and Experimental Research,* 1980, *4,* 135–145.
27. Hanson, J. W., Streissguth, A. P., and Smith, D. W. The effects of moderate alcohol consumption during pregnancy on fetal growth and morphogenesis. *Journal of Pediatrics,* 1978, *92,* 457–460.
28. Dehaene, P. H., Crepin, G., Delahousse, G., Querlu, D., Walbaum, R., Titran, M., and Samaille Villette, C. Aspects épidémiologiques du syndrome d'alcoolisme foetal. 45 observations dans 3 ans. *Nouvelle Presse Médicale,* 1981, *10,* 2639–2643.
29. Little, R. E. Moderate alcohol use during pregnancy and decreased infant birth weight. *American Journal of Public Health,* 1977, *67,* 1154–1156.
30. Kaminski, M., Rumeau-Rouquette, C., and Schwartz, D. Consommation d'alcool chez les femmes enceintes et issue de la grossesse. *Révue d'Épidémiologie, Médecine Sociale et Santé Publique,* 1976, *24,* 27–40.

CHAPTER 7

Intrauterine Growth Retardation

Intrauterine growth retardation is one of the most common characteristics associated with prenatal exposure to alcohol. A retrospective analysis of over 300 clinical case studies[1] indicated that the average birth weight for a term-birth infant was 2179 grams for infants born with diagnosed fetal alcohol syndrome. By contrast, the median birth weight for all children born in the United States during 1975 was 3320 grams.[2] About 66% of all term fetal alcohol syndrome infants were also characterized by "low birth weight," i.e., they weighed less than 2500 grams at birth compared to an overall incidence of 7% for the general population.[2] A reduction in birth weight of this magnitude is a serious risk factor for increased perinatal mortality,[3,4] postnatal growth retardation,[5,6] delayed reflex and motor development,[5,6] sleep disturbances,[7] mental retardation,[5,6,8] speech problems,[6] and many other effects. Thus, while the reduction in birth weight associated with *in utero* alcohol exposure may not seem as serious as some of the other morphological effects of such exposure, it is without doubt one of the more serious consequences in terms of subsequent mortality and morbidity. Furthermore, while a decrease in birth weight of this size is usually not considered a teratological effect, it should be so considered since it, like other morphological anomalies, represents a considerable departure from normal development.

Clinical and Epidemiological Studies

The decrease in birth weight associated with maternal drinking is not restricted to chronic alcoholic women or to fetal alcohol syndrome. Alcohol can also reduce birth weight in children of more moderate drinkers and need not be associated with any other fetal alcohol effects. For example, Little[9] reported that for each ounce of absolute alcohol (2 drinks) consumed per day during late

83

pregnancy, birth weight was reduced by 160 grams. The women in this study were primarily white and middle class and they were interviewed during their 5th and 8th week of pregnancy.

As noted in Chapter 3, the average alcohol consumption for mothers of children with fetal alcohol syndrome is about 14 drinks per day. Translating this amount into Little's dose–response paradigm means that the fetal alcohol syndrome child should weight about 7×200 grams less than normal or about 1400 grams below normal. Taking 3320 grams as the median birth weight for all children born in the United States,[2] the average birth weight of the fetal alcohol syndrome child should be about 1900 grams, if Little's formula is correct, and indeed, this is very close to the 2000-gram average arrived at independently.

Various large-scale epidemiological studies have also noted decreased birth weights associated with maternal drinking, but these decreases have rarely been found to be as great as those just mentioned. This is because women who are at risk for fetal alcohol syndrome rarely obtain prenatal care and therefore they are not included in most epidemiological studies. Since women who do agree to participate in such studies generally drink considerably less than these other women, it is not surprising that the decreases in birth weight among those who drink are not as great, although such decreases are present.

For example, in their prospective study of over 12,000 women in Cleveland, Sokol and his colleagues[10] found that the average weight of children born to alcohol abusers was about 190 grams below that of offspring of non-alcohol abusers.

In Boston, Ouellette and her colleagues[11] also reported a decrease in birth weight associated with drinking. In this prospective study, women were divided into three groups on the basis of consumption levels. Group I women were abstinent or rare drinkers. Group III were "heavy" drinkers (5 or more drinks per drinking occasion), and Group II women were intermediate. The incidence of "low birth weight" ($\leq$ 2500 grams) in Group III was 27% compared to 7–8% among the other two groups.

Rosett and his co-workers[12] have noted that alcoholic women who were able to abstain or considerably reduce their drinking during the last trimester of pregnancy gave birth to infants who were less growth-retarded than those born to women who continued to drink heavily during pregnancy. This observation has been corroborated in animal studies (see below) and indicates that alcohol's impact on growth occurs primarily during this stage of pregnancy.

Recently, a number of studies have examined the effects of various beverage alcohols on growth in humans and animals.[13–16] Kuzma and Sokol,[13] for example, have found that beer drinking during pregnancy represents a significant factor in intrauterine growth retardation in newborn children. This conclusion, based on a prospective study of over 5000 women, was independent of smoking, coffee consumption, and gestational age and was most apparent among those women who reported the highest amount of beer intake (3% of the sample). This finding corroborated an earlier French study involving over 9000 pregnancies during the 1960s, which also found that birth weight was significantly decreased among children born to heavy beer drinkers (1.7% of the women studied) compared to non-beer drinkers.[14]

A study in animals,[15] however, did not find any differences between beer or other forms of alcoholic beverages with respect to birth weight, although all beverages did produce a significant decrease in birth weight compared to nutritionlly matched controls. The reason for this discrepancy between the human and animal data is unclear at present. One possibility is that the ingredients present in beer acted synergistically with other substances used by the women in the epidemiological studies.

To examine the relation between beer drinking and intrauterine growth retardation in children further, Bottoms and her colleagues[16] measured maternal and cord blood thiocyanate levels associated with drinking during pregnancy, since thiothiocyanate is present in beer and has previously been linked with decreased birth weight.[17,18] Maternal beer consumption was found to be significantly correlated with cord-blood thiocyanate levels after controlling for smoking, whereas consumption of wine and liquor were not. However, beer accounted for only 3.6% of the total variance of cord blood thiocyanate compared to 68% for smoking. This finding suggests that one of the reasons beer is more strongly associated with intrauterine growth retardation is because of its thiocyanate content. However, compared to the levels of thiocyanate resulting from smoking, the thiocyanate levels obtained from drinking beer are relatively low. Conceivably, the interaction of thiocyanate and alcohol may be the important variable responsible for beer's added impact in intrauterine growth retardation, but this hypothesis has yet to be examined experimentally.

Studies in Animals

Decreased weight at birth is also the most reliable effect of prenatal alcohol exposure in animals (see Table 16). This effect is observed even after maternal consumption of food has been equalized between alcohol-consuming and non-consuming animals by the method of pair feeding (see below).

The effects of increasing doses of alcohol on birth weights in rats is shown in Figure 6. As indicated by the figure, birth weight is depressed by about 25% when mothers are given 6 g/kg of alcohol each day of pregnancy. An almost identical decrease occurs when these data are calculated on the basis of birth weight for pair-fed control animals (see Figure 6). This indicates that the decrease associated with *in utero* alcohol exposure is not due to any decrease in maternal food or water consumption. Figure 6 also indicates that birth weight is affected only to a very minor extent when mothers are given doses of alcohol of 1

Table 16. Effects of Prenatal Exposure to Alcohol on Litter Size and Birth Weight

Source	Species and strain	Duration of exposure	Amount consumed or administered (B.A.C. Levels)	Pair-fed	Litter size	Body weight (g)
Abel[19]	Long Evans rat	Pregnancy	1,2 g/kg/day, p.o. (30, 80 mg%)	Yes	→	→
Abel and Dintcheff[20]	Long Evans rat	Pregnancy	4,6 g/kg/day, p.o. (150, 260 mg%)	Yes	—	→
Abel et al.[21]	Long Evans rat	Pregnancy	6 g/kg/day, p.o.	Yes	→	→
Abel[22]	Long Evans rat	Pregnancy day 1–21	6 g/kg/day, p.o.	Yes	→	→
		1–7			→	—
		8–15			→	—
		16–21			→	→
Buttar[23]	Wistar rat	Pregnancy	3 g/kg/day	No	—	—
Chen and Smith[24]	Long Evans rat	Pregnancy day 7–birth	10% v/v in .125% saccharine	—	—	—
Detering et al.[25]	Wistar rat	Pregnancy day 14–birth	6.6% v/v liquid diet (61 mg%)	Yes	—	→
Dexter et al.[26]	Miniature swine	Prior to and during pregnancy	20% v/v in water	Yes	→	→
Druse-Manteuffel and Hofteig[27]	Sprague-Dawley rat	Prior to and during pregnancy	6.6% v/v liquid diet	Yes	—	—
Ellis and Pick[28]	Beagle	Pregnancy	1.2–2.8 g/kg twice daily, p.o. (3.7–346 mg%)	Yes	→	→

Reference	Species	Period	Dose	Pair-fed		
Harris and Chase[29]	Long Evans rat	Prior to and during pregnancy	5.5% in liquid diet (13 g/kg/day)	Yes	→	—
Henderson and Schenker[3]	Sprague-Dawley rat	Prior to and during pregnancy day 1–20	6% w/v in liquid diet (67–150 mg%)	Yes	—	—
Lee et al.[31]	Long Evans rat	Pregnancy day 1–2 3–4 5–21	17% EDC 25% EDC 35% EDC	Yes	→	—
Leichter and Lee[32]	Sprague-Dawley rat	Prior to and during pregnancy	10–20% v/v in water prior to and 30% v/v during pregnancy	Yes	→	—
Lochry et al.[33]	Long Evans rat	Pregnancy day 5–20	(12.4 g/kg) 35% EDC 17% EDC (0–112 mg%)	Yes	— →	— —
Martin et al.[34]	Sprague-Dawley rat	Pregnancy	20% v/v in water plus 1 g/kg/day (approx. 13.8 g/kg/day)	Yes	—	—
Oisund et al.[35]	Wistar rat	Prior to and during pregnancy	12% v/v in sucrose solution (33–75 mg%)	fluid, not food	—	—
Papara-Nicholson and Telford[36]	Guinea pig	Pregnancy	3 cc/kg (concentration not specified)	No	→	—

(continued)

Table 16. (*Continued*)

Source	Species and strain	Duration of exposure	Amount consumed or administered (B.A.C. Levels)	Pair-fed	Litter size	Body weight (g)
Pilstrom and Kiessling[37]	Wistar rat	Prior to and during pregnancy	15% v/v in water	Yes	—	↓
Rider[38]	McCollom rat	4 days prior to and during pregnancy	11% w/v	No	↓	—
Riley et al.[39]	Long Evans rat	Pregnancy day 6–20	6.6% v/v 3.3% v/v liquid diet (20–250 mg%)	Yes	—	↓
Swanberg and Crumpacker[40]	LS and SS mouse	Pregnancy day 1–10 11–20 1–20	10% v/v (approx. 19.0 g/kg/day for SS 17.5 g/kg/day for LS)	No	—	—
Skosyreva[41]	Rat	Pregnancy day 8–14	1.5 g/kg (40% v/v)	No	—	↓
Tittmar[42]	Wistar rat	Pregnancy day 5–19	10% v/v	Partial	—	—
Tze and Lee[43]	Sprague-Dawley rat	Prior to and during pregnancy	30% v/v in water (61 mg%)	Yes	↓	↓
Volk[44]	Wistar rat	Prior to and during pregnancy	12% w/v	No	—	↓
Yanai and Ginsburg[45]	G57 BL 10 Bg DBA/1 Bg mouse	Prior to and during pregnancy	10% v/v (20–45mg%)	No	— —	←→

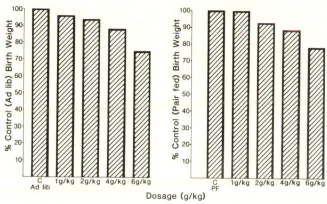

Figure 6. Mean percentage body weight of rats prenatally exposed to alcohol compared to *ad libitum*-fed controls and pair-fed controls.

or 2 g/kg/day. These doses correspond to blood alcohol levels of less than 100 mg%. The threshold for a significant decrease in birth weight lies somewhere between 2 and 4 g/kg/day of alcohol. This corresponds to a range in blood alcohol levels of 90 mg% to 150 mg%.

To examine the period during gestation when alcohol exerts its greatest impact on birth weight, Abel intubated pregnant rats with 6 g/kg/day of alcohol during gestation days 1–7, 8–14, 15–21, or 1–21, inclusive. Control animals were either pair-fed with those in the 1–21 group or were fed *ad lib*. The results are shown in Figure 7.

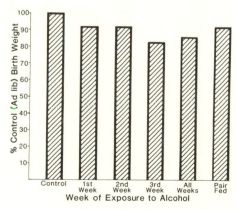

Figure 7. Mean percentage body weights of rats prenatally exposed to alcohol during different weeks of gestation compared to *ad libitum*-fed controls.

As indicated by the figure, animals exposed during the 3rd gestation week or throughout gestation were depressed in birth weight the most, whereas exposure during the 1st or 2nd gestation week had minimal effects on birth weight. Similar findings have now been reported for mice.[46] These results support clinical observations noting a beneficial effect on birth weight among alcoholic women who are able to reduce their drinking during the third trimester of pregnancy.[12]

Although the effects of prenatal alcohol exposure on postnatal weight in adults has not been systematically studied in humans, most clinical reports indicate that children with fetal alcohol syndrome are growth-retarded after birth and fail to exhibit "catch-up" growth. Studies in animals indicate that depending on the amount of *in utero* alcohol exposure, postnatal growth retardation may indeed be permanent.[22,47]

For example, Figure 8 illustrates the body weights of animals at 21 days of age that were prenatally exposed to alcohol. (These are the same animals described in Figure 7.) As indicated by Figure 8, animals exposed to doses of 1, 2, or 4 g/kg exhibited catch-up growth by this age, whereas animals exposed to the 6-g/kg dose weighed considerably less than controls.

In Figure 9, the body weights of animals exposed to the 4- and 6-g/kg doses are shown at 5 months of age. As evident from the figure, body weights of animals exposed to the higher dose are still depressed relative to control animals, suggesting that the depressed body weight of these animals noted at birth is permanent.

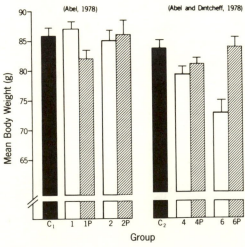

Figure 8. Mean body weights of rats prenatally exposed to 1, 2, 4, or 6 g/kg/day of alcohol at 21 days of age. P = pair-fed; C = *ad libitum*-fed.

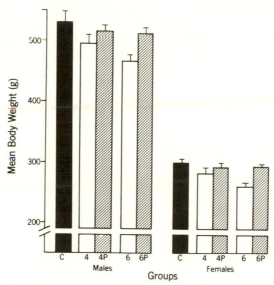

Figure 9. Mean body weights of male and female rats at 5 months of age that were prenatally exposed to 4 or 6 g/kg/day of alcohol. P = pair-fed; C = *ad libitum*-fed.

Although alcohol has been definitely implicated as the etiological agent responsible for fetal alcohol effects and fetal alcohol syndrome, there is still the possibility that congeners present in alcoholic beverages may contribute in some way to some of these effects and that some beverages may pose a greater danger than others to the developing fetus (see above).

In the only series of studies comparing beverage alcohol with ethanol reported thus far,[15,48,49] fetuses exposed to beer and wine weighed less than ethanol, whiskey, or control fetuses when examined on gestation day 20.[48] In this study, pregnant rats were intubated with the equivalent of 3 g/kg of ethanol twice daily in the form of beer (Budweiser), wine (Almaden Rosé), whiskey

Table 17. Effects of Beer, Wine, Whiskey, and Ethanol on Fetal Weight (Gestation Day 20) in Rats ($\bar{X}$ ± standard error)[a,b]

	Beer	Wine	Whiskey	Ethanol	Control
Maternal blood Alcohol level (mg%)	172 ± 21	206 ± 21	204 ± 14	204 ± 111	
Fetal weight (g)	3.5 ± .11	3.2 ± .07	3.8 ± .04	4.1 ± .04	4.4 ± .07

[a]Dose = 3 g/kg/twice daily; concentration = 8% v/v for all solutions.
[b]Data from Abel.[48]

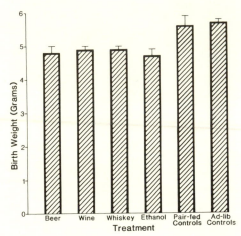

Figure 10. Mean birth weights of rats prenatally exposed to the equivalent of 3 g/kg/twice daily of ethanol in the form of beer, wine, whiskey, or ethanol, compared to pair-fed and *ad libitum*-fed controls.

(Hiram Walker Blended), or ethanol (U.S.P.). All beverages were given at the same concentration and same volume of administration. Blood alcohol levels in the dams and the fetal weights of animals in the various treatment groups are shown in Table 17.

However, when another group of dams was allowed to deliver offspring at birth, weights at birth were not significantly different among offspring exposed to beverage alcohol or ethanol (although all weighed less than controls),[15] as indicated in Figure 10.

In summary, decreased birth weight is one of the most common consequences of *in utero* exposure to alcohol. This effect is dose-related to the amount of alcohol exposure and occurs primarily when exposure is during the latter part of pregnancy.

There have been several attempts to determine how this decrease in birth weight arises. Among the more likely possibilities examined so far are that the decrease arises due to preterm delivery, unresponsiveness to growth-promoting hormones, and intrauterine growth retardation due to interference with cellular accretion.

Preterm Delivery

A basic reason that children with fetal alcohol syndrome weigh considerably less at birth than other children is that they are premature, i.e., they are born with a gestational age of less than 37 weeks. Because of this shortened gestational age they would not have had time to develop to the same extent as full-term infants. Children with low birth weight (<2500 grams) who also have a shorter age of gestation tend to have a neonatal mortality rate that is twice as high as those infants who are also low birth weight but of normal gestation age.[50] Prematurity is also one of the major causes of neonatal morbidity.[51] Premature birth is associated with several known factors, such as race, twin births, pregnancy complications, or maternal smoking, and conceivably could account for the lower birth weight of fetal alcohol syndrome infants.

To examine the question of preterm births among children with fetal alcohol syndrome, a retrospective analysis of 358 cases was conducted.[1] Birth age was described for only 220 cases, and exactly half of these were preterm births. However, even when preterm infants were excluded from the analysis, birth weight was far below normal (average = 2178 grams for 110 infants for whom both gestational age and birth weight are recorded).

Epidemiological studies in which gestational age has been studied have not found consistent effects of drinking on term delivery.

Sokol and his co-workers[10] did not find any significant increase in the incidence of preterm delivery among alcohol abusers. Kaminski and her co-workers[14,52] also failed to find a significant relationship between alcohol consumption and preterm delivery in their prospective studies. However, in a retrospective study conducted by these investigators, the incidence of preterm delivery was increased among heavy drinkers. A small but significant increase in preterm delivery associated with alcohol consumption has also been noted by Tennes and Blackard, but this could have been due to various maternal and obstetric factors not examined by the authors, e.g., maternal age, race, pregnancy complications.

Hingson and his co-workers[53] reported that maternal drinking prior to, but not during pregnancy was associated with shortened gestation. However, drinking was not significantly related to infant growth.

In a case control study of 175 mothers of singleton preterm infants and 313 mothers of singleton term infants, Berkowitz[54] found that consumption of alcohol prior to the third trimester of pregnancy was significantly related to shortened gestation, even when other risk factors were controlled statistically. In this study, average daily consumption of alcohol for controls was 2.4 drinks per week per trimester compared to 1.9 drinks for controls. However, almost twice as many women with preterm delivery reported drinking 7 or more drinks per week for the second trimester. In a subsequent study, Berkowitz and co-workers[55] found that there was no increased risk for a preterm delivery if women consumed less than 14 drinks per week or 2 drinks per day.

While both the Berkowitz studies and the Hingson study are suggestive of an effect of drinking on preterm delivery, the data upon which these studies base their conclusions were obtained retrospectively, and the number of women drinking the higher amounts of alcohol were few. As noted by the authors, in such retrospective studies, recall of drinking activity may have been heightened for women who gave birth to preterm infants, or alternatively, it might be under-reported to avoid possible guilt feelings. In terms of sample size, there were only 8 heavy drinkers out of the 166 cases studied.

Because of these limitations in terms of sample gathering and size, these data suggesting that alcohol consumption during pregnancy may be related to preterm delivery should be regarded only as tentative. As noted earlier, even when term delivery is taken into account in the case of children with fetal alcohol syndrome, these children still weigh significantly less than other children.

Studies in animals likewise indicate that the reduction in birth weight associated with maternal alcohol exposure cannot be accounted for in terms of preterm delivery. In most cases, delivery is at term or slightly longer than usual.[22,30,31–34,56]

Hormonal Factors in Growth

Although hormones are involved in postnatal growth and development, their role in fetal growth is still unclear, and hypotheses about their involvement generally involve extrapolations from the postnatal to the prenatal period.

For example, whereas growth hormone is required for general growth and especially growth of bones, it does not appear to be needed for growth *in utero* or for prenatal differentiation or morphogenesis. In fact, the human fetus seems able to grow at a normal rate in the complete absence of growth hormone.[57] Tze and his co-workers[58] measured gorwth hormone secretion following insulin-induced hypoglycemia or arginine infusion in five fetal alcohol syndrome patients and found no evidence for lowered levels of growth hormone. In fact, some of these patients exhibited hypersecretion of growth hormone. Majewski[59] likewise did not detect any significant decreases in growth hormone in fetal alcohol syndrome children. Root and his co-workers[60] failed to find any evidence for decreased levels of growth hormone in four children born to an alcoholic mother. Castells and his co-workers[61] did not find any differences in basal plasma growth hormone in seven patients with fetal alcohol syndrome who were referred to them because of growth failure. However, peak plasma levels during insulin-induced hypoglycemia were higher in five of these patients than in a control group matched for age and sex. This increase was interpreted as possibly suggestive of peripheral resistance to the actions of this hormone.

A study in animals also found increased growth hormone in offspring prenatally exposed to alcohol. In this study, dams received a liquid alcohol diet beginning on day 13. Control animals were pair-fed. At birth, offspring were cross-fostered, and half the dams continued to receive alcohol postnatally. Twenty-day-old fetuses and 2- and 3-day-old newborns that had been prenatally exposed to alcohol had significantly higher growth hormone levels compared to controls. At 11 and 13 days of age, growth hormone levels in these animals were significantly depressed but were significantly increased once again at postnatal day 20.[62]

Thyroid hormone function has also been examined in conjunction with fetal alcohol exposure as a possible underlying mechanism associated with decreased birth weight. Although normal thyroid function is essential for cellular metabolism, hypothyroid human fetuses are not growth-retarded,[63] nor are animal fetuses that have had their thyroids removed *in utero*.[63] Higher than normal levels of thyroid hormone can even be growth-retarding.[64]

In contrast to the relative absence of any effect of thyroid activity on body weight, however, decreased thyroid activity in the pregnant woman or the fetus may be associated with decreased synthesis of protein in the brain.[65]

Decreased basal thyroid hormone levels have not been reported in any children with fetal alcohol syndrome.[58,60,61] Rose and his co-workers[66] also observed normal basal levels of thyroid in lamb fetuses. But after a challenge dose of thyrotropin-releasing hormone, fetuses of mothers treated daily with alcohol had considerably lower levels of thyroxine (T_4) and triodothyronine (T_3) than did fetuses of control mothers. In this study, fetuses were cannulated prior to treatment and mothers were infused with alcohol daily. Control ewes were infused with dextrose and were pair-fed with alcohol-treated ewes. This is an important study since, unlike those in the previously mentioned clinical reports, these data were obtained from the fetus and therefore more closely reflect thyroid events during *in utero* exposure to alcohol. Whether or not the decreased responsiveness to thyroid-stimulating hormone is of sufficient nature to account for any of the effects associated with fetal alcohol exposure, however, remains to be determined since, as previously noted, hypothyroid activity in the human fetus does not necessarily result in decreased birth weight.

There have also been some pertinent studies of insulin response and blood glucose determinations in offspring of chronic alcoholics and of animals chronically fed alcohol during pregnancy.

Insulin exerts a major role in fetal development. Although the placenta is not permeable to insulin,[67] the fetus does respond to changes in maternal insulin levels that can affect fetal glucose levels and transport of other nutrients across the placenta.[68] Since glucose is a major fetal nutrient,[69] maternal and fetal hypoglycemia could result in decreased birth weight. In fact, Liggins,[70] in his review of the various hormonal factors affecting fetal growth, regards insulin as "the most important 'growth hormone' of the fetus." The reason for this view is that fetal insulin secretion is associated with a wider range in birth weight than any other factor. For example, birth weights of as much as 6 kg are occasionally found in women diabetics whose condition has not been adequately controlled, whereas birth weights at term of as little as 1250 grams have been found for infants of diabetics receiving adequate treatment.[70]

Clinical evidence of hypoglycemia in fetal alcohol syndrome children has been reported in some instances,[71,72] but not always[60,73–75] when it has been looked for. The difficulty with evaluating these reports is that tests have not been routine, nor have they been conducted shortly after birth when such evidence would be most valuable and least confounded with postnatal treatments. Results of glucose tolerance tests have also been ambiguous. Castells and co-workers[61] reported that three out of seven patients with fetal alcohol syndrome had abnormal reactions in oral glucose tolerance tests with higher than normal glucose values and significantly elevated plasma insulin levels. Root and co-workers,[60] however, did not observe abnormal glucose response in the same test. Fitze and his co-workers[72] did not observe an abnormal glucose response in the glucose tolerance test but found a less than normal response to insulin administration in a fetal alcohol syndrome patient. The same test resulted in a normal glucose response in another patient.[76]

Surprisingly, there is very little information available concerning insulin and glucose levels in animals prenatally exposed to alcohol. Tanaka and his co-workers[77] have reported decreased serum insulin levels in rat dams consuming alcohol at gestation day 15 and decreased blood glucose levels at gestation days 18 and 21, along with decreased blood glucose levels in fetuses of these dams on gestation day 21. Alcohol was administered via the drinking water in this study and control animals were not pair-fed, so that these results should be regarded only as suggestive of maternal and fetal hypoglycemia. Such studies, however, are of considerable importance since they are a better reflection of events *in utero*.

Since pregnant women that have been treated with corticosteroids have increased incidences of spontaneous abortions and their children have increased incidences of intrauterine growth retardation, congenital anomalies, and CNS dysfunction,[78] it is conceivable that some of the effects associated with fetal alcohol exposure may be mediated by alcohol's effects on the maternal/fetal pituitary axis.

In his review of alcohol's effects on endocrine function, Anderson[78] noted that alcohol-induced activation of adrenocortical activity is frequently associated with thymus regression and could result in a poorly developed immune system in the developing fetus. Immune deficiency has, in fact, been noted in connection with fetal alcohol syndrome[79] and with *in utero* alcohol exposure in animals.[80,81] This observation thus likewise supports the possible involvement of the pituitary-adrenal axis in fetal alcohol effects.

More direct evidence of such involvement comes from studies in animals in which rats exposed to alcohol prenatally and for the first 24 hours after birth were found to have significantly higher brain corticosterone levels and enlarged adrenal glands compared to pair-fed controls.[82] Taylor[83] reported that at 75–90 days of age, rats prenatally exposed to alcohol had significantly higher corticosterone responses to a challenge dose of alcohol than did pair-fed controls. Basal levels prior to alcohol challenge were not significantly different. In a previous study from Taylor's group,[84] rats prenatally exposed to alcohol did not exhibit the increase in corticosterone levels normally associated with the circadian rhythm at 15–21 days of age, suggesting a possible delay in maturation of the pituitary-adrenal axis.

Amino Acids, DNA, Protein

Amino Acids

Transfer of amino acids across the placenta is essential for fetal protein synthesis.[85] Inhibition of such transfer to the fetus may result in a biologically significant decrease in protein accrual, which in turn could result in fetal growth retardation. Because of these relationships involving amino acids, protein, and growth, considerable attention has been devoted to the effects of alcohol on both amino acid transport and protein accretion in the fetus.

Some amino acids are transferred passively according to the maternal-placental concentration gradient. Other amino acids rely on active transport processes to transfer them against a concentration gradient. Any inhibition of these transport processes could result in decreased amino acid availability for protein accretion and hence decreased growth and development.

In vivo and *in vitro* studies have shown that alcohol may affect both passive and active transport processes. Passive transport is affected as a result of decreases in placental blood flow following alcohol ingestion. This effect was demonstrated by Jones and co-workers[86] in rats that had consumed alcohol in their drinking water (30% v/v) during pregnancy. On gestation day 20, pregnant rats were injected with a radioactive marker, and radioactivity was subsequently determined in blood and various other maternal and fetal tissues. Cardiac output was not affected, nor was blood flow to the kidneys. However, blood flow to the placentas of alcohol-ingesting rats was significantly reduced compared to that of pair-fed controls, which in turn was lower than that in nontreated controls. These data are shown in Table 18.

These results may, however, have been the result of differences in water consumption between alcohol and control animals. Although one group of animals was pair-fed, this same group was not pair-watered. Since alcohol reduces water consumption as well as food consumption, it is important to control for this contingency as well.[87] In this study, moreover, alcohol-consuming animals had

Table 18. Effects of consumption of Alcohol During Pregnancy on Fetal Size and Blood Flow to the Kidney and Placenta[a]

Treatment	Fetal body weight (g)	Maternal kidney blood flow (% cardiac output)	Placental blood flow (ml/min/placenta)
Alcohol	2.04	13.2	.170
Pair-fed	2.38	10.9	.260
Ad lib control	2.62	11.6	.357

[a]Data from Jones et al.[86]

significantly higher plasma osmolalities, and therefore, alcohol-related dehydration may have affected these observations. In another study in which alcohol was acutely administered to pregnant rats, no decrease in placental blood flow was observed.[88] While alcohol-related decreased blood flow could account for decreased transport of some amino acids, evidence for this possibility is still equivocal at this time.

On the other hand, there is considerably more evidence indicating that alcohol affects active transport of amino acids across the placenta. Lin[89] reported that transport of alpha-aminoisobutyric acid—a nonmetabolizable amino acid—across the rat placenta was inhibited in rats on gestation day 21 if they had consumed a liquid alcohol diet (4.3% v/v) on gestation days 6 to 21. Distribution of this amino acid in maternal plasma or liver was not affected, whereas concentration in placenta and fetal tissues was reduced by 20% to 40% relative to pair-fed controls. Decreased uptake of this same amino acid by placental tissue in rats has also been reported by Henderson and his associates[90] and by Gordon and her co-workers.[91]

In an extensive series of studies, Henderson and co-workers[92] have also reported an alcohol-related decrease in placental uptake of the amino acid valine that is also actively transported. Acute exposure to alcohol by intubation (4 g/kg) 2 hours before sacrifice of pregnant rats on gestation days 16 and 20 depressed subsequent in vitro placental valine uptake by 31% and 40%, respectively. When rats consumed a liquid alcohol diet for 30 days prior to and during gestation, valine uptake was decreased by 44% on gestation day 20. Alcohol was also found to exert an effect on valine uptake several days after exposure. Treatment with alcohol (4 g/kg/twice daily, p.o.) on gestation days 8 to 10 did not affect placental valine uptake. However, treatment on days 11 to 13 or 14 to 16, resulted in a decrease in valine uptake on gestation day 20 of 24% and 28%, respectively. In yet another study contained in this report, in vitro exposure of placental tissue to alcohol at concentrations of 100–300 mg% produced a 26–36% inhibition of valine uptake (cf., however, references 93 and 94).

In an extension of this study using similar methods, Henderson and co-workers[95] found that chronic alcohol intake for 30 days prior to pregnancy and during gestation resulted in decreased uptake for other amino acids as well, including alpha-aminoisobutryric acid, cycloleucine, l-alanine, l-leucine, and l-lysine.

Levels of acetaldehyde (450 μM) that produced a comparable effect on valine uptake were far above those normally encountered *in vivo,*[92] suggesting that any effect of alcohol on valine transport *in vivo* are probably due to alcohol itself and not to its metabolite.

In yet another study, this time using the monkey as the "animal model," Fisher and his co-workers[96] likewise found that placentas from monkeys fed a liquid alcohol diet had depressed uptake of alpha-aminoisobutyric acid.

These data are thus very consistent in showing that consumption of alcohol can result in decreased uptake of amino acids by placental tissue and decreased transmission of amino acids across the placenta.

While amino acid uptake and transport may be impaired by alcohol, nutrient transport may still be adequate enough to supply the needs of the developing fetus. Preliminary studies of this issue have involved measurement of amino acid levels in the fetus. In one such study, Lin[97] found that only fetal plasma levels of histidine, out of 16 amino acids examined, were significantly decreased in the rat in conjunction with maternal alcohol exposure.

Protein Synthesis and Accretion

Protein synthesis is controlled by nucleic acids. RNA is synthesized in the nucleus by DNA and is then extruded into the cytoplasm. In the cytoplasm RNA is acylated in the presence of ATP and then attaches to ribosomes to provide material for amino acids to form into protein.

Alcohol has been found to inhibit this formation of amino acids into protein. Rawat reported that chronic alcohol consumption by pregnant and lactating rats resulted in a 30% decrease in incorporation of leucine into cerebral ribosomes in fetal rats and a 60% decrease in sucklings.[98,99] Maternal consumption of alcohol in rats also resulted in decreased leucine incorporation into fetal and neonatal cardiac and hepatic protein[99,100] (cf. also references 101 and 102). Fisher and his co-workers[103] recently reported an *in vivo* demonstration of alcohol-related inhibition of leucine into fetal protein. In this study, pregnant rats were injected (i.p.) with alcohol (47.5% v/v) on gestation day 19. One hour after the first injection, the animals were lightly anesthetized and the abdomen was opened. The uterus was then exposed and leucine was administered into the amnion. A second alcohol injection was given 1 hour later, resulting in a total dose of about 3 g/kg for the high-dose group and 1.5 g/kg for the low-dose group. Three hours after the intraamniotic injection of leucine, animals were sacrificed.

Blood alcohol levels were about 300 mg% and 95 mg%, respectively, for the two doses. Tissue uptake and incorporation into protein were both decreased in the brain for fetuses exposed to the high dose of alcohol. Incorporation of leucine into protein in the liver was also depressed, but tissue uptake was not affected.

These studies thus demonstrate that alcohol reduces the availability of amino acids to the developing fetus by affecting placental uptake and transport processes and by inhibiting protein synthesis by interfering with tissue uptake and synthesizing processes.

Decreased production of protein will be reflected in growth retardation since accretion of protein is essential for growth. Intrauterine growth retardation is, of course, one of the most reliable consequences of *in utero* alcohol exposure, so it is not surprising that decreased protein content in bodily organs has been reported in conjunction with prenatal alcohol exposure.

Decreases in protein content, however, may be due to either small cell size or fewer total cells, or both. By determining DNA content in a sample of tissue it is possible to estimate cell number because the DNA content per cell in many mammalian cells is constant. By determining the ratio of protein (which increases as cell size increases) to DNA, it is possible to estimate cell size. RNA content is an index of protein synthesis.

Decreased fetal organ DNA content as a consequence of prenatal alcohol exposure has been noted in several studies.[98–100,104–107] The long-range implications of this finding are that growth retardation will be permanent since, once cell division has been halted, it cannot be compensated for by later cellular increases. This observation thus accounts for the failure of many fetal alcohol syndrome children to exhibit catch-up growth despite all efforts to give them extra feedings.

In vitro studies have also shown that alcohol can inhibit multiplication of cells.[108–110] In a study by Brown and co-workers,[109] rat embryos were removed from the uterus and were placed in a culture medium to which alcohol was added at 300 mg% or 150 mg%. Control embryos received the same kinds of solutions except for the presence of alcohol. Forty-eight hours later, embryos cultured in the presence of alcohol were significantly smaller in size and had less DNA and protein content. The ratio of DNA to total protein, however, was not significantly different between alcohol and control embryos, suggesting that cell size was not reduced. These data are presented in Table 19.

Since the rat embryo has no alcohol-oxidizing ability and does not have any alcohol dehydrogenase activity, these observations have been interpreted as evidence that the growth-retarding effects of alcohol *in vivo* do not have to be mediated by acetaldehyde, the primary metabolite of alcohol.

Yet another means by which protein synthesis may be inhibited is by affecting enzymes involved in protein production. Thadani and her co-workers,[111,112]

Table 19. Effects of *in Vitro* Exposure to Alcohol on 9½-Day
Rat Embryos[a]

Development 48-hours after incubation	Length (mm)	DNA content (g)	Protein content (g)
Alcohol (300 mg%)	3.78	22.7	223.4
Alcohol (150 mg%)	4.29	31.9	295.4
Control	4.54	33.4	333.3

[a]Data from Brown *et al.*[109]

for example, have reported that *in utero* alcohol exposure affects ornithine decarboxylase (ODC) levels in neonatal rat brain. This enzyme is involved in polyamine synthesis, beginning with the metabolism of the amino acid ornithine. Changes in the activity of this enzyme could thus affect protein synthesis. However, there is no clear pattern to the changes in ODC associated with prenatal alcohol exposure. Activity of ODC is also affected by many nonspecific variables,[113] so that, as yet, no unequivocal relationship between the reported changes in ODC and alcohol-induced prenatal growth retardation has been determined.

Trace Elements

Chronic alcohol ingestion is associated with deficiencies in many trace elements such as zinc, magnesium, and calcium.[114] Such deficiencies are potentially of importance to the developing fetus since these and other electrolytes are essential for normal growth and development. Zinc and magnesium, for example, are intimately involved in DNA and protein synthesis. Deficiencies in these trace elements could thus result in growth retardation and congenital abnormalities.[115,116]

Not much attention has as yet been devoted to alcohol's effects on fetal mineral metabolism, with the possible exception of zinc. Zinc excretion is increased in alcoholics,[117] and concentrations of zinc in the serum and hair of alcoholic women of childbearing age have been found to be lower compared to those in other women.[118,119] Flynn and his co-workers[120] reported decreased serum zinc levels in alcohol-abusing women at time of delivery and decreased newborn cord blood levels of zinc in their offspring. On the basis of these observations, they have speculated that alcohol-related decreases in maternal zinc levels may underlie many fetal alcohol effects. However, the zinc levels of all women in the Flynn *et al.* study were lower than normal, and there was a relatively high incidence of abnormalities among control women as well as alcohol abusers. If zinc status were involved in fetal alcohol effects, the Flynn study[120] could be interpreted as suggesting that it is the interaction of underlying poor zinc status plus alcohol, rather than alcohol *per se,* that is the critical factor. This possibility is also suggested by a study in animals reported by Ruth and Goldsmith (see below).

Horrobin[121] has also proposed that alcohol-related zinc deficiencies may underlie some fetal alcohol effects and has advanced a specific mechanism whereby this could occur. Horrobin's hypothesis contends that by the depletion of zinc levels, the enzyme activity of delta-6-desaturase is adversely affected, since zinc is a cofactor for this enzyme. This enzyme is in turn responsible for conversion of linoleic acid—a major essential fatty acid—into gamma-linoleic acid, which eventually is converted into prostaglandin $E_1(PGE_1)$. Horrobin points out that many of the symptoms associated with decreased PGE_1 and zinc levels are similar to those reported in conjunction with fetal alcohol syndrome. He also points out that diphenylhydantoin, which also prevents conversion of linoleic acid to PGE_1, produces a pattern of defects in the human fetus that is very similar to fetal alcohol syndrome.

Although these possibilities are plausible, direct studies of zinc levels or studies in which zinc supplementation to the diet has been used have been only partially supportive. In one series of studies, for instance, Ghishan and his co-workers[122] reported that intubation of pregnant rats on gestation day 20 with alcohol (4 g/kg, 25% w/v) resulted in a 40% decrease in placental uptake of ^{65}Zn compared to controls. Consumption of liquid alcohol diet on gestation days 4 to 20 also resulted in a 40% decrease in placental uptake and a 30% decrease in fetal ^{65}Zn uptake. Total body zinc levels in fetuses were also reduced. Comparable effects were not found by Jones and his co-workers.[123]

Administration of alcohol to pregnant rats did not affect zinc levels in maternal femur or liver, but it increased levels in fetal carcass.[124] In a second study from the same laboratory, consumption of alcohol in drinking water during pregnancy resulted in decreased maternal and fetal zinc levels.[125] Three other studies found no evidence for zinc deficiency associated with *in utero* alcohol exposure in animals.[104,126,127] In zinc-deficient pregnant rats, a single intraperitoneal injection of alcohol (1.4, 1.9, or 2.4 g/kg, 24% w/v) on gestation day 10 exacerbated the existing condition and resulted in increased resorptions.[128]

In an attempt to attenuate the effects of alcohol on the developing fetus, Leitch[129] supplemented the drinking water of mice with zinc prior to and during pregnancy. Supplementation did not affect pregnancy outcome or fetal weight. In a brief abstract report, however, Tanaka[130] reported that zinc supplementation resulted in decreased resorption rate and higher fetal weights.

Using the "pup in the cup" model, in which neonatal rats are artificially reared in the laboratory, Samson and Diaz[131] supplemented the milk formula provided to alcohol and control rats with zinc. Zinc supplementation did not prevent the alcohol-induced microcephaly that occurred in alcohol-treated animals.

Magnesium levels in rat fetal carcasses were not significantly affected by *in utero* alcohol exposure in two studies[124,126] but were increased in fetal liver in another study.[125]

Poor ossification in fetal bone structure resulting from *in utero* alcohol exposure has been reported in animals,[132] and there are reports of transient hypocalcemia in children with fetal alcohol syndrome.[71,133] No evidence for fetal hypocalcemia was found in a study in which pregnant rats were chronically treated with alcohol.[126]

Streissguth and her co-workers[134] reported that serum iron levels in pregnant women were not associated with drinking. Serum iron levels were also unaffected by alcohol exposure during pregnancy in mothers or fetuses.[126]

Increased fetal sodium and fetal sodium:water ratios were noted in one study in conjunction with prenatal alcohol exposure,[126] but thus far this remains an isolated report. Fetal body water content was also significantly increased, and this increase occurred even after a single administration of alcohol to pregnant rats.[135] This increase in body water is suggestive of a delay in fetal development since fetal body water content decreases as growth progresses.

Postnatal Growth Retardation

Although the effects of *in utero* alcohol exposure on postnatal weight in adults has not been systematically studied in humans, clinical studies are very consistent in their reports of "failure to thrive." This "failure to thrive" in some cases may be due to weak sucking ability in fetal alcohol infants.[136,137] Van Dyke and his co-workers[137] reported a case study of three fetal alcohol syndrome infants who required prolonged hospitalization for nutritional and growth problems due to feeding dysfunction. All three had delayed oral motor development, which resulted in limited suck patterns and early tiring of sucking. As a result, they required gastronomic or nasogastric feeding for several months and were not successfully placed on oral feeding until 14–18 months of age. In animals, Chen and his co-workers[138] found that rat pups prenatally exposed to alcohol took longer to attach to a nipple than control rat pups. The authors suggest a possible relation between this increased latency to attachment and decreased weight gain. Although it is quite likely that impairment of sucking contributes to the "failure to thrive" of fetal alcohol patients, it is unlikely that this impairment is responsible for the postnatal growth retardation observed in the majority of such cases.

Studies in animals indicate that the growth retardation associated with prenatal alcohol exposure also need not be permanent. For example, animals whose dams were intubated with 1, 2, or 4 g/kg of alcohol exhibit catch-up growth by about 21 days of age,[20] whereas animals whose dams received 6 g/kg weigh consistently less than pair-fed controls at this age and continue to weigh less at a later age.[47,136]

As suggested by the data cited in the previous section, a major reason for this "failure to thrive" and permanent growth deficit is alcohol's effects on protein and DNA accretion (indices of cell size and cell number, respectively) in the fetus, which are both decreased during development by alcohol. Although decreases in cell size are reversible, decreases in cell number are not, and this decreased cell number is a likely explanation for the growth retardation that occurs in conjunction with fetal alcohol exposure.

Other studies in animals have shown that the failure to thrive in alcohol-exposed offspring is not due to postnatal metabolic deficiencies in assimilation or utilization of food[140] or in intestinal protein malabsorption.[141] Attempts to "fatten" alcohol-exposed offspring by raising them in small litters, thus making more milk available, have also had little effect on postnatal weight gain.[142]

Summary

In summary, intrauterine and postnatal growth retardation are two of the most consistently observed effects of *in utero* alcohol exposure in both humans and animals. This effect is dose-related, and the period of development when this impact is greatest is during the last third of gestation. The most likely explanation for this effect is cellular hypoplasia. As a result of this reduction in cell number, alcohol-exposed offspring tend to be growth-retarded after birth, and attempts to overcome their "failure to thrive" are unlikely to succeed. Although some attempts have been made to assess the role of congeners present in beverage alcohol on fetal and neonatal growth, these studies are still inconclusive.

References

1. Abel, E. L. *Marihuana, tobacco, alcohol and reproduction.* Boca Raton: CRC Press, 1983.
2. Querec, L. J. *Characteristics of births. Vital and health statistics. Series 21. Data From the National Vital Statistics Systems.* Hyattsville, Md.: U.S. Department of Health, Education, and Welfare, 1978.
3. Lee, K., Paneth, N., Gartner, L., and Pearlman, M. The very low-birth weight rate: Principal predictor of neonatal mortality in industrialized populations. *Journal of Pediatrics,* 1980, *97,* 759–764.
4. Peacock, W. G., and Hirata, T. Outcome in low-birth weight in infants (750 to 1,500 grams): A report of 164 cases managed at Children's Hospital, San Francisco, California. *American Journal of Obstetrics and Gynecology,* 1981, *140,* 165–172.

5. Bjerre, I. Physical growth of 5-year-old children with low birthweight. *Acta Paediatrica Scandinavica*, 1975, *64*, 33–43.
6. Fitzhardinge, P. M., and Steven, E. M. The small-for-date infant. II. Neurological and intellectual sequelae. *Pediatrics*, 1972, *50*, 50–57.
7. Als, H., Tronick, E., Adamson, L., and Brazelton, T. B. The behavior of the full-term but underweight newborn infant. *Developmental Medicine and Child Neurology*, 1976, *18*, 590–602.
8. Drillien, C. M. Growth and development in a group of children of very low birth weight. *Archives of Disease in Childhood*, 1958, *33*, 10–15.
9. Little, R. E. Moderate alcohol use during pregnancy and decreased infant birth weight. *American Journal of Public Health*, 1977, *67*, 1154–1156.
10. Sokol, R. J., Miller, S. I., and Reed, G. Alcohol abuse during pregnancy. An epidemiological study. *Alcoholism: Clinical and Experimental Research*, 1980, *4*, 135–145.
11. Ouelette, E. M., Rosett, H. L., Rosman, N. P., and Weiner, L. Adverse effects on offspring of maternal alcohol abuse during pregnancy. *New England Journal of Medicine*, 1977, *297*, 528–530.
12. Rosett, H. L., Ouellette, E. M., Weiner, L., and Owens, E. Therapy of heavy drinking during pregnancy. *American Journal of Obstetrics and Gynecology*, 1978, *51*, 41–46.
13. Kuzma, J. W., and Sokol, R. J. Maternal drinking behavior and decreased intrauterine growth. *Alcoholism: Clinical and Experimental Research*, 1982, *6*, 396–402.
14. Kaminski, M., Rumeau-Rouquette, C., and Schwartz, D. Alcohol consumption in pregnant women and the outcome of pregnancy. *Alcoholism: Clinical and Experimental Research*, 1978, *2*, 155–163.
15. Abel, E. L., Dintcheff, B. A., and Bush, R. Effects of beer, wine, whiskey, and ethanol on pregnant rats and their offspring. *Teratology*, 1981, *23*, 217–222.
16. Bottoms, S. F., Judge, N. E., Kuhnert, P. M., and Sokol, R. J. Thiocyanate and drinking during pregnancy. *Alcoholism: Clinical and Experimental Research*, 1982, *6*, 391–395.
17. Meberg, A., Sande, H., Foss, O. P., and Stenwig, J. T. Smoking during pregnancy—Effects on the fetus and on thiocyanate levels in mother and baby. *Acta Paediatrica Scandinavica*, 1979, *68*, 547–552.
18. Pettigrew, A. R., Logan, R. W., and Willocks, J. Smoking in pregnancy—Effects on birth weight and on cyanide and thiocyanate levels in mother and baby. *British Journal of Obstetrics and Gynaecology*, 1977, *84*, 31–34.
19. Abel, E. L. Effects of ethanol on pregnant rats and their offspring. *Psychopharmacology*, 1978, *57*, 5–11.
20. Abel, E. L., and Dintcheff, B. A. Effects of prenatal alcohol exposure on growth and development in rats. *Journal of Pharmacology and Experimental Therapeutics*, 1978, *207*, 916–921.
21. Abel, E. L., Dintcheff, B. A., and Day, N. Effects of in utero exposure to alcohol, nicotine, and alcohol plus nicotine, on growth and development in rats. *Neurobehavioral Toxicology*, 1979, *1*, 153–159.
22. Abel, E. L. Effects of ethanol exposure during different gestation weeks of pregnancy on maternal weight gain and intauterine growth retardation in the rat. *Neurobehavioral Toxicology*, 1979, *1*, 145–151.
23. Buttar, H. S. Effects of the combined administration of ethanol and chlordiazepoxide on the pre- and postnatal development of rats. *Neurobehavioral Toxicology*, 1980, *2*, 217–225.
24. Chen, J. J., and Smith, E. R. Effects of perinatal alcohol on sexual differentiation and open-field behavior in rats. *Hormones and Behavior*, 1979, *13*, 219–231.
25. Detering, N., Reed, W. P., Ozand, P. T., and Karahasan, A. The effects of maternal ethanol consumption in the rat on the development of their offspring. *Journal of Nutrition*, 1979, *109*, 999–1009.

26. Dexter, J. D., Tumbleson, M. E., Decker, J. D., and Middleton, C. C. Fetal alcohol syndrome in Sinclair (s-1) miniature swine. *Alcoholism: Clinical and Experimental Research*, 1980, *4*, 146–151.

27. Druse-Manteuffel, M. J., and Hofteig, J. H. The effect of chronic maternal alcohol consumption on the development of central nervous system myelin subfractions in rat offspring. *Drug and Alcohol Dependence*, 1977, *2*, 421–429.

28. Ellis, F. W., and Pick, J. R. An animal model of the fetal alcohol syndrome in beagles. *Alcoholism: Clinical and Experimental Research*, 1980, *4*, 123–134.

29. Harris, R. A., and Chase, J. Effects of maternal consumption of ethanol, barbital, or chlordiazepoxide on the behavior of offspring. *Behavioral and Neural Biology*, 1979, *26*, 234–247.

30. Henderson, G. I., and Schenker, S. The effects of maternal alcohol consumption on the viability and visceral development of the newborn rat. *Research Communications on Chemical Pathology and Pharmacology*, 1977, *16*, 15–32.

31. Lee, M. H., Haddad, R., and Rabe, A. Developmental impairments in the progeny of rats consuming ethanol during pregnancy. *Neurobehavioral Toxicology*, 1980, *2*, 189–198.

32. Leichter, J., and Lee, M. Effects of maternal ethanol administration on physical growth of the offspring in rats. *Growth*, 1979, *43*, 288–297.

33. Lochry, E. A., Shapiro, N. R., and Riley, E. P. Growth deficits in rats exposed to alcohol in utero. *Journal of Studies on Alcohol*, 1980, *41*, 1031–1039.

34. Martin, J. C., Martin, D. C., Sigman, P., and Radow, B. Offspring survival, development, and operant performance following maternal ethanol consumption. *Developmental Psychobiology*, 1977, *10*, 435–445.

35. Oisund, J. F., Fjorden, A. E., and Morlund, J. Is moderate ethanol consumption teratogenic in the rat? *Acta Pharmacologica et Toxicologica*, 1978, *43*, 145–155.

36. Papara-Nicholson, D., and Telford, I. R. Effects of alcohol on reproduction and fetal development in the guinea pig. *Anatomical Record*, 1957, *127*, 438–439.

37. Pilstrom, L., and Kiessling, K. H. Effects of ethanol on the growth and on the liver and brain mitochondrial functions of the offspring of rats. *Acta Pharmacologica et Toxicologica*, 1967, *25*, 225–232.

38. Rider, A. A. Adaptation to moderate ethanol intake as reflected in reproductive performance in the rat. *Nutrition Reports International*, 1979, *19*, 765–772.

39. Riley, E. P., Lochry, E. A., and Shapiro, N. R. Lack of response inhibition in rats prenatally exposed to alcohol. *Psychopharmacology*, 1979, *62*, 47–52.

40. Swanberg, K. M., and Crumpacker, D. W. Genetic differences in reproductive fitness and offspring viability in mice exposed to alcohol during gestation. *Behavioral Biology*, 1977, *20*, 122–127.

41. Skosyreva, A. M. Vliyaniye etilovogo spirta na razvitie embrionov stadii organogeneza. *Akusherstvo i Ginekologiya*, 1973, *4*, 15–18.

42. Tittmar, H. G. Some effects of ethanol, presented during the prenatal period, on the development of rats. *British Journal of Alcohol and Alcoholism*, 1977, *12*, 71–83.

43. Tze, W. J., and Lee, M. Adverse effects of maternal alcohol consumption on pregnancy and foetal growth in rats. *Nature*, 1975, *257*, 479–480.

44. Volk, B. Verzogerte Kleinhirnentwicklung im Rahmen des "Embryofetalen Alkoholsyndroms." Lichtoptische Untersuchungen am Kleinhirn der Ratte. *Acta Neuropathologica*, 1977, *39*, 157–163.

45. Yanai, J., and Ginsburg, B. E. A developmental study of ethanol effect on behavior and physical development in mice. *Alcoholism: Clinical and Experimental Research*, 1977, *1*, 325–333.

46. Lochry, E. A., Randall, C. L., Goldsmith, A. A., and Sutker, P. B. Effects of acute alcohol exposure during selected days of gestation in C_3H mice. *Neurobehavioral Toxicology and Teratology*, 1982, *4*, 15–19.

47. Monjan, A. A., and Mandell, W. Fetal alcohol and immunity: Depression of mitogen-induced lymphocyte blastogenesis. *Neurobehavioral Toxicology,* 1980, *2,* 213–215.

48. Abel, E. L. Prenatal effects of beverage alcohol on fetal growth. In F. S. Messiha and G. S. Tyner (Eds.), *Progress in biochemical pharmacology.* Basel, Switzerland: S. Karger, 1981. pp. 111–114.

49. Abel, E. L., Dintcheff, B. A., and Bush, R. Behavioral teratology of alcoholic beverages compared to ethanol. *Neurobehavioral Toxicology and Teratology,* 1981, *3,* 339–342.

50. National Center for Health Statistics. *Factors associated with low birth weight.* Hyattsville, Md.: U.S. Department of Health, Education, and Welfare, 1980.

51. Chase, H. Perinatal mortality: Overview and current trends. *Clinical Perinatology,* 1974, *1,* 3–17.

52. Kaminski, M., Franc, M., Lebouvier, M., Du Mazaubrun, C., and Rumeau-Ruoquette, C. Moderate alcohol use and pregnancy outcome. *Neurobehavioral Toxicology and Teratology,* 1981, *3,* 173–181.

53. Hingson, R., Alpert, J. J., Day, N., Dooling, E., Kayne, H., Morelock, S., Oppenheimer, E., and Zuckerman, B. Effects of maternal drinking and marijuana use on fetal growth and development. *Pediatrics,* 1982, *70,* 539–546.

54. Berkowitz, G. S. An epidemiologic study of preterm delivery. *American Journal of Epidemiology,* 1981, *113,* 81–92.

55. Berkowitz, G. S., Holford, T. R., and Berkowitz, R. L. Effects of cigarette smoking, alcohol, coffee and tea consumption on preterm delivery, in press.

56. Bond, N. W. Prenatal exposure to ethanol: Association between increased gestational length and offspring mortality. *Neurobehavioral Toxicology and Teratology,* 1982, *4,* 501–503.

57. Liggins, G. C. The influence of the fetal hypothalamus and pituitary on growth. In K. Elliott and J. Knight (Eds.), *Size at birth.* Amsterdam: Associated Scientific Publishers, 1974. pp. 165–183.

58. Tze, W. G., Friesen, H. G., and MacLeod, P. M. Growth hormone response in fetal alcohol syndrome. *Archives of Disease in Childhood,* 1976, *51,* 703–706.

59. Majewski, F. Untersuchungen zur Alkohol-Embryopathie. *Fortschritte der Medizin,* 1978, *96,* 2207–2213.

60. Root, A. W., Reiter, E. O., Andriola, M., and Duckett, G. Hypothalamic-pituitary function in the fetal alcohol syndrome. *Journal of Pediatrics,* 1975, *87,* 585–587.

61. Castells, S., Mark, E., Abaci, F., and Schwartz, E. Growth retardation in fetal alcohol syndrome. Unresponsiveness to growth-promoting hormones. *Developmental Pharmacology and Therapeutics,* 1981, *3,* 232–241.

62. Thadani, P. V., and Schanberg, S. M. Effect of maternal ethanol ingestion on serum growth hormone in the developing rat. *Neuropharmacology,* 1979, *18,* 821–826.

63. Andersen, H. J. Studies of hypothyroidism in children. *Acta Paediatrica,* 1961, *50*(Suppl. 125), 1–150.

64. Samsamy, B., Jethwa, A. K. N., and Ferriman, D. Congenital thyrotoxicosis. *Proceedings of the Royal Society of Medicine,* 1970, *63,* 577–578.

65. Holt, A. B., Cheek, D. B., and Kerr, G. R. Prenatal hypothyroidism and brain composition in a primate. *Nature,* 1973, *243,* 243–415.

66. Rose, J. C., Meis, P. J., and Castro, M. I. Alcohol and fetal endrocrine function. *Neurobehavioral Toxicology and Teratology,* 1981, *3,* 105–110.

67. Buse, M. G., Roberts, W. J., and Buse, J. The role of the human placenta in the transfer and metabolism of insulin. *Journal of Clinical Investigation,* 1962, *41,* 29–41.

68. Picon, L. Effect of insulin on growth and biochemical composition of the rat fetus. *Endocrinology,* 1967, *81,* 1419–1421.

69. Silver, M. Fetal energy metabolism. In R. W. Beard and P. W. Nathanielsz (Eds.), *Fetal physiology and medicine.* Philadelphia: Saunders, 1976. pp. 173–193.

70. Liggins, G. C. The drive to fetal growth. In R. W. Beard and P. W. Nathanielsz (Eds.), *Fetal physiology and medicine*. Philadelphia: Saunders, 1976. pp. 254–270.

71. Van Biervliet, J. P. The foetal alcohol syndrome. *Acta Paediatrica Belgica*, 1977, *30*, 113–116.

72. Fitze, F., Spahr, A., and Pescia, G. Familienstudie zum Problem des Embryofotalen Alkohol-syndroms. *Schweizerische Rundschau Medizin*, 1978, *67*, 1338–1354.

73. Walpole, I. R., and Hockey, A. Fetal alcohol syndrome: Implications to family and society in Australia. *Australian Pediatric Journal*, 1980, *16*, 101–105.

74. Beyers, N., and Moosa, A. The fetal alcohol syndrome. *South African Medical Journal*, 1978, *54*, 575–578.

75. McClure, J. P., and Stephenson, J. B. P. Fetal alcohol syndrome—Case presentations. In J. S. Madden, R. Walker, and W. H. Kenyon (Eds.), *Aspects of alcohol and drug dependence*. Kent, England: Pitman Medical, 1980. pp. 368–371.

76. Barry, R. G. G., and O'Nuallain, S. Foetal alcoholism. *Irish Journal of Medical Science*, 1975, *144*, 286–288.

77. Tanaka, H., Suzuki, N., and Arima, M. Hypoglycemia in the foetal alcohol syndrome in rat. *Brain and Development*, 1982, *4*, 97–103.

78. Anderson, R. A. Endocrine balance as a factor in the etiology of the fetal alcohol syndrome. *Neurobehavioral Toxicology and Teratology*, 1981, *3*, 89–104.

79. Johnson, S., Knight, R., Marmer, D. J., and Steele, R. W. Immune deficiency in fetal alcohol syndrome. *Pediatric Research*, 1981, *15*, 908–911.

80. Monjan, A. A., and Mandell, W. Fetal alcohol and immunity: Depression of mitogen-induced lymphocyte blatogenesis. *Neurobehavioral Toxicology*, 1980, *2*, 213–215.

81. Haughton, G., Mohr, K., and Ellis, F. Increased susceptibility to induction of primary rous sarcoma in C57BL/10ScSn mice following perinatal exposure to dietary ethanol. *Alcoholism: Clinical and Experimental Research*, 1981, *5*, 347.

82. Kakihana, R., Butte, J. C., and Moore, J. A. Endocrine effects of maternal alcoholization: Plasma and brain testosterone, dihydrotestosterone, estradiol, and corticosterone. *Alcoholism: Clinical and Experimental Research*, 1981, *5*, 237–246.

83. Taylor, A. N., Branch, B. J., Liu, S. H., Wiechmann, A. F., Hill, M. A., and Kokka, N. Fetal exposure to ethanol enhances pituitary-adrenal and temperature responses to ethanol in adult rats. *Alcoholism: Clinical and Experimental Research*, 1981, *5*, 237–246.

84. Cooley-Mathews, B., and Taylor, A. N. Exposure to ethanol in utero may delay maturation of hypothalamo-pituitary function in the rat. *Neuroscience Abstracts*, 1978, *4*, 110.

85. Dancis, J., Money, W., Springer, D., and Levitz, M. Transport of amino acids by placenta. *American Journal of Obstetrics and Gynecology*, 1968, *15*, 820–829.

86. Jones, P. J. H., Leichter, J., and Lee, M. Placental blood flow in rats fed alcohol before and during gestation. *Life Sciences*, 1981, *29*, 1153–1159.

87. Abel, E. L. Procedural considerations in evaluating prenatal effects of alcohol in animals. *Neurobehavioral Toxicology*, 1980, *2*, 167–174.

88. Cotaescu, I., Deutsch, G., and Dreichlinger, O. The influence of caffeine, nicotine and ethanol on rat placentary blood circulation established by means of Rb^{86} uptake. *Revue Roumaine d'Embryologie et de Cytologie, Séries d'Embryologie*, 1965, *2*, 31–35.

89. Lin, G. W. J. Effect of ethanol feeding during pregnancy on placental transfer of alpha-aminoisobutyric acid in the rat. *Life Sciences*, 1981, *28*, 595–601.

90. Henderson, G. I., Hoyumpa, A., Patwardhan, R., and Schenker, S. Effect of acute and chronic ethanol exposure on placental uptake of amino acids. *Alcoholism: Clinical and Experimental Research*, 1981, *5*, 153.

91. Gordon, B. H. J., Durandin, R. M., Rosso, P., and Winick, M. Placental amino acid transport in alcohol fed rats. *Federation Proceedings*, 1982, *41*, 946.

92. Henderson, G. I., Turner, D., Patwardhan, R. V., Lumeng, L., Hoyumpa, A., and Schenker, S. Inhibition of placental valine uptake after acute chronic maternal ethanol consumption. *Journal of Pharmacology and Experimental Therapeutics,* 1981, *216,* 465–472.

93. Fisher, S. E., Atkinson, M. B., Holzman, I. R., David, R., and Van Thiel, D. H. Ethanol-associated inhibition of human placental amino acid uptake: A new concept in the fetal alcohol syndrome. *Alcoholism: Clinical and Experimental Research,* 1981, *5,* 149.

94. Durandin, R. M., and Rosso, P. In vitro effects of ethanol in human placental transport of amino acids. *Obstetrics and Gynecology,* 1976, *4,* 439.

95. Henderson, G. I., Patwardhan, R. V., McLeroy, S., and Schenker, S. Inhibition of placental amino acid uptake in rats following acute and chronic ethanol exposure. *Alcoholism: Clinical and Experimental Research,* 1982, *6,* 495–505.

96. Fisher, S. E., Burnap, J. K., Jacobson, S., Sehgal, P. K., Scott, W., and Van Thiel, D. H. Ethanol-associated selective fetal malnutrition: A contributing factor in the fetal alcohol syndrome. *Alcoholism: Clinical and Experimental Research,* 1982, *6,* 197–201.

97. Lin, G. W. J. Fetal malnutrition: A possible cause of the fetal alcohol syndrome. *Progress in Biochemical Pharmacology,* 1981, *18,* 115–121.

98. Rawat, A. K. Ribosomal protein synthesis in the fetal and neonatal rat brain as influenced by maternal ethanol consumption. *Research Communications in Chemical Pathology and Pharmacology,* 1975, *12,* 723–732.

99. Rawat, A. K. Effect of maternal ethanol consumption on foetal and neonatal rat hepatic protein synthesis. *Biochemical Journal,* 1976, *160,* 653–661.

100. Rawat, A. K. Derangement in cardiac protein metabolism in fetal alcohol syndrome. *Research Communications in Chemical Pathology and Pharmacology,* 1979, *25,* 365–375.

101. Tewari, S., and Carin, S. Ethanol induced changes on *in vitro* protein synthesis during the development and maturation of brain tissue. In R. G. Thurman (Ed.), *Alcohol and aldehyde metabolizing systems—IV.* New York: Plenum Press, 1980. pp. 813–821.

102. Dreosti, I. E., Ballard, J., Belling, B., Record, I. R., Manuel, S. J., and Hetzel, B. S. The effect of ethanol and acetaldehyde on DNA synthesis in growing cells and on fetal development in the rat. *Alcoholism: Clinical and Experimental Research,* 1981, *5,* 357–362.

103. Fisher, S. E., Barnicle, M. A., Steis, B., Holzman, I., and Van Thiel, D. H. Effects of acute ethanol exposure upon in vivo leucine uptake and protein synthesis in the fetal rat. *Pediatric Research,* 1981, *15,* 335–339.

104. Henderson, G. I., Hoyumpa, A. M., Rothschild, M. A., and Schenker, S. Effect of ethanol and ethanol-induced hypothermia on protein synthesis in pregnant and fetal rats. *Alcoholism: Clinical and Experimental Research,* 1980, *4,* 165–177.

105. Woodson, P. M., and Ritchey, S. J. Effect of maternal alcohol consumption on fetal brain cell number and cell size. *Nutrition Reports International,* 1979, *20,* 225–228.

106. Suzuki, N., Tanaka, H., and Arima, M. Fetal and postnatal biochemical development in the fetal alcohol syndrome of the rat. *Brain and Nerve,* 1980, *32,* 1136–1142. (In Japanese)

107. Sorette, M. P., Maggio, C. A., Starpoli, A., Boissevain, A., and Greenwood, M. R. C. Maternal ethanol intake affects rat organ development despite adequate nutrition. *Neurobehavioral Toxicology,* 1980, *2,* 181–188.

108. Skosyreva, A. M. Vliyaniye etiolovogo spirta na razvitie embrionov stadii organogeneza. *Akusherstvo i Ginekologiya,* 1973, *4,* 15–18.

109. Brown, N. A., Goulding, E. H., and Fabro, S. Ethanol embryotoxicity: Direct effects on mammalian embryos *in vitro. Science,* 1979, *206,* 573–575.

110. Popov, V. B., Vaisman, B. L., Puchkov, V. F., and Ignat'eva, T. V. Toxic action of ethanol and its biotransformation products on postimplantation rat embryos in culture. *Byulleten Eksperimental'noi Biologii i Meditsiny,* 1981, *92,* 725–728.

111. Thadani, P. V., Lau, C., Slotkin, T. A., and Schanberg, S. M. Effect of maternal ethanol

ingestion on neonatal rat brain and heart ornithine decarboxylase. *Biochemical Pharmacology*, 1977, *26*, 523–527.

112. Thadani, P. V., Slotkin, T. A., and Schanberg, S. M. Effects of late prenatal or early postnatal ethanol exposure on ornithine decarboxylase activity in brain and heart of developing rats. *Neuropharmacology*, 1977, *16*, 289–293.

113. Henderson, G. I., Patwardhan, R. V., Hoyumpa, A. M., and Schenker, S. Fetal alcohol syndrome: Overview of pathogenesis. *Neurobehavioral Toxicology and Teratology*, 1981, *3*, 73–80.

114. Roe, D. A. *Alcohol and the diet*. Westport, Conn.: Avi, 1979.

115. Hurley, L. S., Gowan, J., and Swenerton, H. Teratogenic effects of short term and transitory zinc deficiency in rats. *Teratology*, 1971, *4*, 199–204.

116. Prasad, A. S. Clinical, biochemical and pharmacological role of zinc. *Annual Review of Pharmacology and Toxicology*, 1979, *19*, 393–426.

117. Sullivan, J. E., and Lankford, J. E. Zinc metabolism and chronic alcoholism. *American Journal of Clinical Nutrition*, 1965, *17*, 57–63.

118. Breskin, M. W., Clarren, S. K., and Little, R. E. Zinc concentrations in serum and hair and dietary zinc content of alcoholic women of child-bearing age compared with suitable controls. *Alcoholism: Clinical and Experimental Research*, 1981, *5*, 144.

119. Castro-Magana, M., Collip, P. J., and Chen, S. Y. Zinc levels in one case of fetal alcohol syndrome. *Pediatric Research*, 1978, *12*, 515.

120. Flynn, A., Miller, S. I., Martier, S. S., Golden, N. I., Sokol, R. J., and Del villano, B. C. Zinc status of pregnant alcoholic women: A determinant of fetal outcome. *Lancet*, 1981, *1*, 572.

121. Horrobin, D. F. A biochemical basis for alcoholism and alcohol-induced damage including the fetal alcohol syndrome and cirrhosis: Interference with essential fatty acid and prostaglandin metabolism. *Medical Hypotheses*, 1980, *6*, 929–942.

122. Ghishan, F. K., Patwardhan, R., and Greene, H. L. Fetal alcohol syndrome: Inhibition of placental zinc transport as a potential mechanism for fetal growth retardation in the rat. *Journal of Laboratory and Clinical Medicine*, 1982, *100*, 45–52.

123. Jones, P. J. H., Leichter, J., and Lee, M. Uptake of zinc, folate and analogs of glucose and amino acid by the rat fetus exposed to alcohol *in utero*. *Nutrition Reports International*, 1981, *24*, 75–83.

124. Mendelson, R. A., and Huber, A. M. The effect of duration of alcohol administration on the deposition of trace elements in the fetal rat. *Advanced in Experimental Medicine and Biology*, 1980, *132*, 295–304.

125. Mendelson, R. A., and Huber, A. M. Maternal alcohol consumption: Effect of alcohol on trace element deposition in the fetus. *Alcoholism: Clinical and Experimental Research*, 1979, *3*, 186.

126. Abel, E. L., and Greizerstein, H. B. Ethanol-induced prenatal growth deficiency: Changes in fetal body composition. *Journal of Pharmacology and Experimental Therapeutics*, 1979, *211*, 668–671.

127. Greizerstein, H. B., and Abel, E. L. Acute effects of ethanol on fetal body composition and electrolyte content in the rat. *Bulletin of the Psychonomic Society*, 1979, *14*, 355–356.

128. Ruth, R. E., and Goldsmith, S. K. Interaction between zinc deprivation and acute ethanol intoxication during pregnancy in rats. *Journal of Nutrition*, 1981, *111*, 2034–2038.

129. Leitch, G. L. Failure of zinc supplement to reverse the teratogenic effects of *in utero* ethanol. *Alcoholism: Clinical and Experimental Research*, 1981, *5*, 159.

130. Tanaka, H. Congenital anomalies induced by maternal alcohol and caffeine. *Teratology*, 1982, *26*, 6A.

131. Samson, H. H., and Diaz, J. Altered development of brain by neonatal ethanol exposure: Zinc

levels during and after exposure. *Alcoholism: Clinical and Experimental Research,* 1981, *5,* 563–569.

132. Haddad, R., Canlon, B., Dumas, R., Lee, M., and Rabe, A. *Maternal ethanol consumption during pregnancy affects fetal skeletal development in the rat.* Paper presented at the Laboratory Animal Science Meeting, Atlanta, 1979.

133. Jones, K. L., and Smith, D. W. Recognition of the fetal alcohol syndrome in early infancy. *Lancet,* 1973, *2,* 999–1001.

134. Streissguth, A. P., Barr, H. M., Smith, J. R., Labbe, R. F., Darby, B. L., Smith, N. J., Martin, D. C., and Doan, R. N. Alcohol use and iron status in pregnant women. *Alcoholism: Clinical and Experimental Research,* 1982, *6,* 154.

135. Greizerstein, H. B., and Abel, E. L. Acute effects of ethanol on fetal body composition and electrolyte content in the rat. *Bulletin of the Psychonomic Society,* 1979, *14,* 355–356.

136. Martin, D. C., Martin, J. C., Streissguth, A. P., and Lund, C. A. Sucking frequency and amplitude in newborns as a function of maternal drinking and smoking. In M. Galanter (Ed.), *Currents in alcoholism.* Grune and Stratton: New York, 1979, pp. 359–364.

137. Van Dyke, D., Mackay, L., and Ziaylek, E. N. Management of severe feeding dysfunction in children with fetal alcohol syndrome. *Clinical Pediatrics,* 1982, *21,* 336–339.

138. Chen, J. S., Riley, E. P., and Driscoll, C. D. Ontogeny of suckling in rat pups prenatally exposed to ethanol. *Alcoholism: Clinical and Experimental Research,* 1981, *5,* 145.

139. Abel, E. L. Prenatal effects of alcohol on adult learning in rats. *Pharmacology, Biochemistry and Behavior,* 1979, *10,* 239–243.

140. Abel, E. L. Prenatal exposure to beer, wine, whiskey and ethanol: Effects on postnatal growth and food and water consumption. *Neurobehavioral Toxicology and Teratology,* 1981, *3,* 49–51.

141. Ghishan, F. K., Henderson, G., and Meneely, R. Intestinal function in infant rats: Effect of maternal chronic ethanol ingestion. *Journal of Nutrition,* 1981, *111,* 1124–1127.

142. Lee, M., and Leichter, J. Effect of litter size on the physical growth and motivation of the offspring of rats given alcohol during gestation. *Growth,* 1980, *44,* 327–335.

CHAPTER 8

Head and Facial Abnormalities

Although there is considerable variation in individual craniofacial features, the overall pattern of these features is often distinctive enough to provide a basis for a diagnosis of fetal alcohol syndrome. Clarren and Smith[1] regard short palpebral fissures, hypoplastic upper lip with thinned vermilion, and diminished to absent philtrum as key facial features. Majewski[2] also considers the philtrum and upper lip as key features but minimizes the importance of palpebral fissures. Instead, he emphasizes the short, upturned nose. Other facial features are listed in Table 13. Some of these facial features are evident in Figures 11a–11e.

Whereas these facial features have been regarded as being as distinctive as those associated with Down's syndrome,[3] Neugut[4] has questioned this assertion. Neugut points out that Down's syndrome was described and diagnosed a hundred years prior to the discovery of the underlying chromosomal anomaly responsible for the disorder. The diagnosis was therefore based solely on physical features. By contrast, fetal alcohol syndrome as an entity and its relation to maternal· alcohol consumption were recognized simultaneously.

The examples presented in Figures 11a–11e are, in fact, hardly as distinctive as those that could be presented in connection with Down's syndrome. Furthermore, the facial features of fetal alcohol syndrome are almost identical to those of fetal hydantoin syndrome.[5] Without foreknowledge of maternal drinking or hydantoin histories, it would be very difficult to differentiate between the diagnoses. It is only when there is evidence of maternal drinking that a diagnosis of fetal alcohol syndrome can be reasonably certain.

As indicated in Table 13, there are a number of facial anomalies associated with fetal alcohol exposure, and these anomalies are in turn associated with function deficits of sensory organs.

Anomalies of the eye, apart from shortened palpebral fissures, include ptosis, strabismus, epicanthic folds, and microphthalmia. Blepharophimosis is also frequently cited in conjunction with fetal alcohol syndrome and refers to

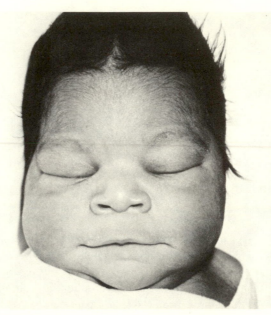

Figure 11a. Infant girl. Frontal view showing characteristic facial features including short, upturned nose, posterior rotation of ear, hypoplastic philtrum, thin upper vermilion border of lip, and micrognathia. Note also hirsutism. Photo courtesy Dr. Robert Sokol.

shortened palpebral size. However, Miller and her associates[6] comment that this term can have a variety of meanings related to palpebral fissures and has not been specifically defined in most reports. The size of the palpebral fissure, they point out, is affected by the position of the canthus. This is of more than academic concern since a shortened palpebral fissure could be a reflection of decreased eye growth or abnormal eyelid development, the former being the more severe disturbance.

Rabinowicz (quoted by Gonzalez)[7] regards arterial or venous tortuosity of the retinal vessels as one of the most common ocular disorders associated with fetal alcohol exposure. This opinion is based on a study of 17 cases of fetal alcohol syndrome in which 16 patients all had the disorder. Tortuous retinal vasculature has also been noted in 3 out of 4 fetal alcohol patients by Root.[8] This anomaly has also been noted in such patients by Miller[6] and by Hanson and his co-workers[9] and is possibly more common than previously noted because it is not readily apparent unless one is looking for it.

Strabismus is commonly noted in conjunction with fetal alcohol syndrome (see, e.g., references 9 through 14). In this condition, one of the eyes deviates so that only one of the eyes fixes on an object. Esotropia is also found in conjunc-

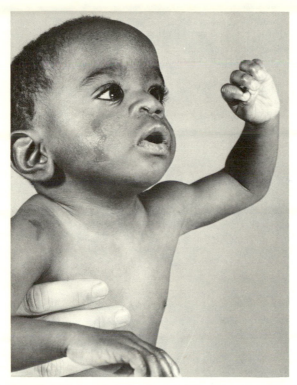

Figure 11b. Infant boy. Facial features include epicanthic folds, low-set ears, hypoplastic philtrum, low nasal bridge. Photo courtesy Dr. Carrie Randall.

tion with the syndrome,[6,7] and in this case both eyes converge. This condition is more commonly known as "cross-eyes." In some patients, estropia only occurs when the subject is looking downward[7] and may require exact surgery to prevent development of a permanent abnormal head position.[7]

Myopia has also been frequently noted in fetal alcohol syndrome patients[1,6,7] and may also be more common than previously noted.[7] Corneal opacity has been noted in some reports[7,15] but does not appear to be a common feature of the syndrome.

The nose is often short and upturned, with a low and broad bridge. The upturned nose may give the false impression that the distance between the nose and upper lip is elongated. Johnson[16] reported a case of persistent rhinorrhea associated with a small nose and small nasal canals in connection with the syndrome, and this condition may occur more often than this single report suggests.

The ears are sometimes large, low-set, and rotated posteriorly. Conchal

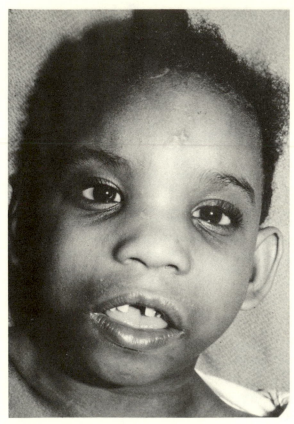

Figure 11c. Young girl. Frontal view showing short palpebral fissures, low-set ears, hypoplastic philtrum. Photo courtesy Dr. Phillip Spiegel.

shape is also altered on occasion. Otitis media (inflammation of the inner ear) has also been noted[16] and may be more common than previously reported.

The upper and lower jawbones are frequently underdeveloped. A short midface and maxillary hypoplasia often give the patient's face a concave appearance in profile. These craniofacial anomalies may result in subsequent dental problems.[17] Frias and his co-workers,[18] however, point out that while many fetal alcohol syndrome patients are black, authors have used standards based on whites, and therefore their assessment of various facial features, including maxillary hypoplasia, may be biased. On the basis of facial radiographs of patients with fetal alcohol syndrome, they observed that the midfacial deficiency associated with the syndrome is not due to true maxillary hypoplasia but to retrusion of the maxilla (backward movement of the maxilla). Frias and co-workers[18] at-

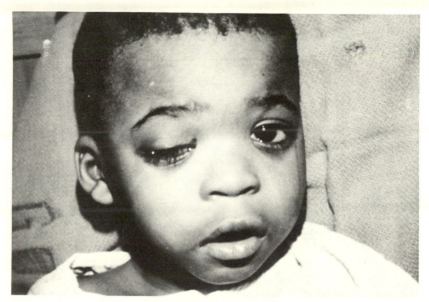

Figure 11d. Young male with ptosis, epicanthic folds, hyperteleorism, hypoplastic nasal bridge, hypoplastic philtrum. Photo courtesy Dr. Phillip Spiegel.

tribute this restricted growth of the face to abnormal growth of the brain, which in turn results in a subsequent shortening of the lower front part of the head.

Cleft palate has also been noted in some patients with fetal alcohol syndrome (see, e.g., references 19 through 26), but this is not a frequently occurring effect of prenatal alcohol exposure. Other abnormal craniofacial features that have been noted are thin epiglottis and small trachea.[19,25] Finucane[25] reported that because of their small tracheas, it was difficult to intubate two fetal alcohol syndrome patients so that they could be anesthetized.

Abnormal facial features have also been noted in rodents prenatally exposed to alcohol, such as low-set, or absent ears,[27,28] maxillary or mandibular hypoplasia,[28] shortening of the nose,[26] and cleft lip or palate.[28–30] Sulik and her co-workers[31] were able to produce abnormal facial features in mouse embryos by administering two relatively large doses of alcohol on gestation day 7. The facial anomalies resembled those seen in fetal alcohol syndrome in humans and consisted of eye malformations such as microphthalmia, coloboma of the iris, and shortened palpebral fissures. There were also nasal and upper lip abnormalities, including the equivalent of a deficient philtrum, small nose, and long upper lip (see Figure 11f).

The Sulik study is interesting for a number of reasons, apart from the fact that it provides another model for studying fetal alcohol effects in animals. For

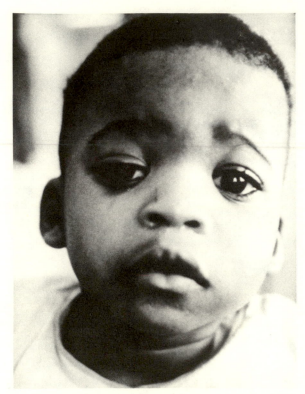

Figure 11e. Young male with slight ptosis, epicanthic folds, short palpebral fissures, hypoplastic nasal bridge, low-set ears. Photo courtesy Dr. Phillip Spiegel.

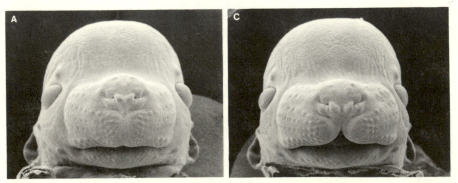

Figure 11f. 14-day-old mouse fetuses from alcohol-exposed (A) and control (C) mothers. Note the shorter distance between nostrils, long upper lip, and absence of philtrum in A. Facial characteristics were induced by acute alcohol exposure at a time corresponding to 3rd week of human gestation. Photo courtesy Dr. Kathy Sulik.

one thing, the finding that these malformations were evident after only two administrations of alcohol on a single day suggests that something comparable could occur in the human as a result of "binging" during early pregnancy (although 1 day of pregnancy in the mouse is not equal to 1 day of human pregnancy). The second point is that some of these malformations, e.g., diminished philtrum, either are not present at birth or are very difficult to distinguish at birth. This suggests that there may be some recovery from the insult associated with *in utero* alcohol exposure. There are also some methodological problems associated with this study that should be noted since it is potentially an important contribution to this area of research. Some of these problems are the administration of alcohol intraperitoneally, in a rather high concentration (25% v/v), absence of "blind" teratological examination of embryos, and absence of nutritional controls. The blood alcohol levels associated with injection were about 200 mg%, which is considerable and hardly qualifies as "social" drinking, as suggested by the authors. Nevertheless, this is a very important report and offers further evidence and corroboration of alcohol's teratogenic effects on facial development.

Using another model, the zebra fish (*Brachydanio rerio*), Schmatolla[32] reported that immersion of blastula stage eggs in a 3% alcohol solution for 2 hours resulted in various abnormalities of the eyes, including cyclopia (fusion of the two eyes into one). Optic nerves developed within the retinas of all cyclopic embryos but did not leave the eyes in half the cases.

As noted above, cleft palate occurs in rodents prenatally exposed to alcohol.[28-30] This anomaly has also been reported in dogs both by Ellis and Pick[33] and by Rahwan and his co-workers.[34]

Clarren and Bowden[35] reported facial anomalies similar to those occuring in human fetal alcohol syndrome in monkeys prenatally exposed to alcohol. In this study, alcohol was administered only once a week from 30 to 40 days after conception. Three pregnant females received 2.5 g/kg and one received 4.1 g/kg. One of three females receiving the lower dose aborted. Peak blood alcohol levels for the two doses were 200–300 mg% and 300–450 mg%, respectively. The facial abnormalities were observable only in the infants born to the mother receiving the high dose and included a wide nose, flattened philtrum, small ears that were posteriorly rotated, and a short and retrusive maxilla. These results, like those reported by Sulik, suggest that "binging" during pregnancy could produce facial anomalies in the developing fetus. As in the Sulik study, however, it appears that such anomalies occur only after relatively high alcohol exposure (e.g., in this study, over 300 mg%). Also, like the Sulik study, the Clarren and Bowden study suffers from some possible confounding factors. For example, while control animals were physically restrained during pregnancy, they were not intubated with placebos. Since it is likely that animals receiving intubation would have reacted more intensely to the restraint needed to intubate them, this could have affected stress-related mechanisms to a greater extent, e.g., adrenocorticosteroid response. Control animals were also not bled, as were dams receiving alcohol, which could also have contributed to increased stress. Nor was there any attempt to pair-feed controls. Despite these criticisms, the results of this study are in keeping with the human fetal alcohol syndrome data and indicate that comparable effects can and do occur in primates exposed to relatively large amounts of alcohol for even a brief period during gestation.

In summary, various facial anomalies are associated with prenatal alcohol exposure in both humans and animals. None of these individual anomalies, however, is solely characteristic of *in utero* alcohol exposure. Recognition of these anomalies also requires some experience since the pattern is much less distinctive than other patterns, such as that occurring in Down's syndrome. While there is some evidence in animals that a single "binging" experience may produce kinds of facial abnormalities similar to those occurring in fetal alcohol syndrome, the shorter duration of pregnancy in animals must be taken into consideration in extrapolating this finding to humans.

References

1. Clarren, S. K., and Smith, D. W.The fetal alcohol syndrome: A review of the world literature. *New England Journal of Medicine*, 1978, *298*, 1063–1067.
2. Majewski, F. Alcohol embryopathy: Some facts and speculations about pathogeneses. *Neurobehavioral Toxicology and Teratology*, 1981, *3*, 129–144.
3. Streissguth, A. P. Fetal alcohol syndrome: An epidemiologic perspective. *American Journal of Epidemiology*, 1978, *107*, 467–478.
4. Neugut, R. H. Epidemiological appraisal of the literature on the fetal alcohol syndrome in humans. *Early Human Development*, 1981, *5*, 411–429.
5. Gordon, N. Fetal drug syndromes. *Postgraduate Medical Journal*, 1978, *54*, 796–798.
6. Miller, M., Israel, J., and Cuttone, J. Fetal alcohol syndrome. *Journal of Pediatric Ophthalmology and Strabismus*, 1981, *18*, 6–15.
7. Gonzalez, E. R. New ophthalmic finding in fetal alcohol syndrome. *Journal of the American Medical Association*, 1981, *245*, 108.
8. Root, A. W., Reiter, E. O., Andriola, M., and Duckett, G. Hypothalamic-pituitary function in the fetal alcohol syndrome. *Journal of Pediatrics*, 1975, *87*, 585–588.
9. Hanson, J. W., Streissguth, A. P., and Smith, D. W. The effect of moderate alcohol consumption during pregnancy on fetal growth and morphogenesis. *Journal of Pediatrics*, 1978, *92*, 457–460.
10. Altman, B. Fetal alcohol syndrome. *Journal of Pediatric Ophthalmology*, 1978, *13*, 255–257.
11. Collins, E., and Turner, G. Six children affected by maternal alcoholism. *Medical Journal of Australia*, 1978, *2*, 606–608.
12. DeBeukelaer, M. M., Randall, C. L., and Stroud, D. R. Renal anomalies in the fetal alcohol syndrome. *Journal of Pediatrics*, 1977, *91*, 759–760.
13. Hayden, M. R., and Welson, M. M. The fetal alcohol syndrome. *South African Medical Journal*, 1978, *54*, 571–574.

14. Mulvihill, J. J., Klimas, J. T., Stokes, D. C., and Risemberg, H. M. Fetal alcohol syndrome: Seven new cases. *American Journal of Obstetrics and Gynecology,* 1976, *125,* 937–941.
15. Goldstein, F., and Arulananthan, K. Neural tube defects and renal anomalies in a child with fetal alcohol syndrome. *Journal of Pediatrics,* 1978, *93,* 636–637.
16. Johnson, K. G. Fetal alcohol syndrome: Rhinorrhea, persistent otitis media, choanal stenosis, hypoplastic sphenoids and ethmoid. *Rocky Mountain Medical Journal,* 1979, *76,* 64–65.
17. Wood, R. E. Fetal alcohol syndrome: Its implications for dentistry. *Journal of the American Dental Association,* 1977, *95,* 596–599.
18. Frias, J. L., Wilson, A. L., and King, G. J. A cephalometric study of fetal alcohol syndrome. *Journal of Pediatrics,* 1982, *101,* 870–873.
19. Lindor, E., McCarthy, A. M., and McRae, M. G. Fetal alcohol syndrome: A review and case presentation. *Journal of Gynecological Nursing,* 1980, *9,* 222–223, 225–228.
20. Spiegal, P. G., Pekman, W. M., Rich, B. H., Versteeg, C. N., Nelson, V., and Dudnikov, M. The orthopedic aspects of the fetal alcohol syndrome. *Clinical Orthopaedics and Related Research,* 1979, *139,* 58–63.
21. Hermann, J., Pallister, P. D., and Opitz, J. M. Tetraectrodactyly and other skeletal manifestations in the fetal alcohol syndrome. *European Journal of Pediatrics,* 1980, *133,* 221–226.
22. Lesure, J. F. Syndrome d'alcoolisme foetal à l'Ile de la Réunion. *Nouvelle Presse Médicale,* 1980, *9,* 1708, 1710.
23. Iosub, S., Fuchs, M., Bingol, N., and Gromisch, D. S. Fetal alcohol syndrome revisited. *Pediatrics,* 1981, *68,* 475–479.
24. Tanaka, H., Arima, M. and Suzuki, N. The fetal alcohol syndrome in Japan. *Brain Development,* 1981, *3,* 305–311.
25. Finucane, B. T. Difficult intubation associated with the foetal alcohol syndrome. *Canadian Anaesthetists' Society Journal,* 1980, *27,* 576–577.
26. Van Dyke, D., Mackay, L., and Ziaylek, E. N. Management of severe feeding dysfunction in children with fetal alcohol syndrome. *Clinical Pediatrics,* 1982, *21,* 336–339.
27. Rasmussen, B. B., and Christensen, N. Teratogenic effects of maternal alcohol consumption on the mouse fetus: A histopathological study. *Acta Pathologica et Microbiologica Scandinavica, Section A: Pathology,* 1980, *88,* 285–289.
28. Webster, W. S., Walsh, D. A., Lipson, A. H., and McEwen, S. E. Teratogenesis after acute alcohol exposure in inbred and outbred mice. *Neurobehavioral Toxicology,* 1980, *2,* 227–234.
29. Giknis, M. L., Damjanov, I., and Rubin, E. The differential transplacental effects of ethanol in four mouse strains. *Neurobehavioral Toxicology,* 1980, *2,* 235–237.
30. Schwetz, B. A., Smith, F. A., and Staples, R. E. Teratogenic potential of ethanol in mice, rats, and rabbits. *Teratology,* 1978, *18,* 385–391.
31. Sulik, K. K., Johnston, M. C., and Webb, M. A. Fetal alcohol syndrome: Embryogenesis in a mouse model. *Science,* 1981, *214,* 936–938.
32. Schmatolla, E. Retino-tectal course of optic nerves in cyclopic and synopthalmic zebrafish embryos. *Anatomical Record,* 1974, *180,* 377–384.
33. Ellis, F. W., and Pick, J. R. An animal model of the fetal alcohol syndrome in beagles. *Alcoholism: Clinical and Experimental Research,* 1980, *4,* 123–134.
34. Rahwan, R. G., Vecchio, F. R., McGuirk, S. M., and Muir, W. W. Accidental induction of alcohol teratogenesis. *Research Communications in Substances of Abuse,* 1982, *3,* 363–366.
35. Clarren, S. K., and Bowden, D. M. Fetal alcohol syndrome: A new primate model for binge drinking and its relevance to human ethanol teratogenesis. *Journal of Pediatrics,* 1982, *101,* 819–824.

CHAPTER 9

Disorders of Bodily Organs

Cardiac Disorders

Cardiac defects have been detected in about 54% of diagnosed cases of fetal alcohol syndrome. A summary of the frequency of occurrence of cardiac disorders in 305 fetal alcohol syndrome patients is presented in Table 20. The most common anomalies are septal defects, especially ventricular septal defect. In most instances, however, these septal defects are small and are not life-threatening, and they frequently close spontaneously. Interestingly, ventricular septal defect is also the most common anomaly in mice prenatally exposed to alcohol.[7,8]

Tetralogy of Fallot has also been noted in conjunction with fetal alcohol syndrome. This is a fourfold defect that primarily involves a narrowing of the pulmonary valve and a ventricular septal defect. As a result, not enough blood is pumped to the lungs, and unoxygenated blood mixes with oxygenated blood in the left ventricle, causing cyanosis ("blue baby"). Pulmonary valve stenosis is a narrowing of the pulmonary valve that regulates blood flow between the right ventricle and the pulmonary artery. If the condition is mild and there are no other defects, e.g., atrial septal defect, it is not life-threatening.[9] The other main defect is patent ductus arteriosus. This is a failure of the normal closure between the aorta and the pulmonary artery. If uncorrected, this condition often leads to death.[9]

Kidney and Urogenital Tract Anomalies

There is about a 12% incidence of occurrence of urogenital anomalies in connection with fetal alcohol syndrome (see Table 21).

The most commonly occurring abnormalities are hydronephrosis (dilation

123

Table 20. Frequency and Type of Cardiac Disorder Associated with FAE

Source	N cases	N with cardiac disorder	Type and frequency of disorder
Lesure[1]	10	3	Ventricular septal defect (2)
Loser and Majewski[2]	56	16	Atrial septal defect (10), ventricular septal defect (2), pulmonary stenosis (1)
Dehaene et al.[3]	47	14	Systolic murmur or septal defects
Dupuis et al.[4]	62	50	Ventricular septal defect (38), atrial septal defect (13), pulmonary stenosis (1)
Steeg and Woolf[5]	57	26	Ventricular septal defect (7), pulmonary stenosis (2), atrial septal defect (1)
Smith et al.[6]	76	31	Ventricular septal defect (20), Tetralogy of Fallot (4), pulmonary stenosis (2), atrial septal defect 83), patent ductus arteriosus (1)

of the kidney, usually due to obstruction of urine flow), hypoplasia (small kidney), renal agenesis (absence of one or both kidneys), and obstruction of the uteropelvic conjunction.

Although the incidence of kidney and genitourinary tract anomalies appears low, the actual incidence is probably much higher since renal evaluations are not routine. In studies of mice prenatally exposed to alcohol, 86% of the litters tested had at least one pup with a hydronephrotic kidney, and 33% had urogenital tract defects.[25] One such example of hydronephrosis in a mouse fetus exposed to alcohol *in utero* is presented in Figure 12.

Liver Anomalies

Thus far there have been only five reports of liver damage associated with fetal alcohol syndrome,[16,26–29] and there is no consistency in the type of anomalies noted. Prolonged hyperbilirubinemia was noted in several reports,[16,24,30–32] in some cases lasting as long as 11 weeks after birth.[24] Dunigan and Werlin[16] report that a fetal alcohol syndrome patient developed cirrhosis at 3 years of age.

Activity of alcohol dehydrogenase, the enzyme involved in metabolism of alcohol, is increased following chronic alcohol consumption in adult animals.[33,34] In light of this observation, several studies have examined the pos-

Table 21. Frequency and Type of Occurrence of Kidney and Urogenital Tract Anomalies Associated with FAS

Source	N cases	N with kidney/ urogenic anomalies	Type
Tenbrinck and Buchin[10]	1	1	Hydronephrosis
Hanson et al.[11]	41	1	Hydronephrosis
Lemoine et al.[12]	127	1	"Renal anomalies"
Goetzman et al.[13]	1	1	Renal hypoplasia
			Obstruction of uteropelvic junction
Ijaiya et al.[14]	1	1	Renal hypoplasia
			Urogenital sinus
DeBeukelaer et al.[15]	1	1	Renal hypoplasia
Dunigan and Werlin[16]	1	1	Enlarged right kidney, left kidney hypoplasia
Goldstein and Arulanantham[17]	1	1	Agenesis of right kidney
			Obstruction of uteropelvic junction
Manzke and Grosse[18]	1	1	Hydrospadia
Havers et al.[19]	110	9	Agenesis or hypoplastic kidney (2 cases)
			Hydronephrosis
			Urogenital sinus
			Bladder diverticula (2 cases)
			Urethral duplication
			Vesicovaginal fistula
			Coliceal cyst
			Hydroureter
Qazi et al.[20]	32	6	Hypoplastic kidney (2 cases)
			Hydronephrosis
			Obstruction of uteropelvic junction
Cahuana et al.[21]	1	1	Hypoplastic kidney (1 case)
Santolaya et al.[22]	4	1	Hydronephrosis (1 case)
Sokol et al.[23]	14	5	Unspecified
Giaretto et al.[24]	1	1	Renal hypoplasia

sibility that a comparable increase in the activity of this enzyme may occur in offspring prenatally exposed to alcohol. The results of these studies are inconsistent, however. For example, both increases[35,36] and decreases[37] in alcohol dehydrogenase activity have been reported following *in utero* alcohol exposure using the same period and protocol for treatment, the same strain of animals, and

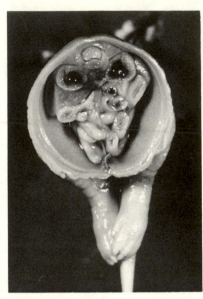

Figure 12. Hydronephrosis in a mouse fetus prenatally exposed to alcohol. Photo courtesy Dr. C. Randall.

the same method of analysis. Two other studies[38,39] reported no changes in activity of this enzyme in rat fetuses or neonates. In contrast to most studies of this question reported thus far, only the study by Sjoblom[39] employed nutritional controls for alcohol-related undernutrition.

Effects on aldehyde dehydrogenase, the enzyme that metabolizes acetaldehyde, are also inconsistent. Activity of this enzyme was noted in day-old rats prenatally exposed to alcohol but not until day 8 in control (not pair-fed) offspring. By day 8, differences between the two groups were no longer significant.[40] Comparable results were not observed in another study in which pair-feeding procedures were used.[39]

In summary, activity of enzymes involved in alcohol metabolism do not appear to be influenced by *in utero* alcohol exposure.

Genital Anomalies

Genital anomalies are not uncommonly associated with prenatal alcohol exposure in both humans and animals. One-half of the patients seen by Majewski[41] exhibited such anomalies. In most instances, these were slight abnormalities such as an undescended testicle or clitoral hypertrophy. A comparable case of undescended testicle in a mouse fetus exposed to alcohol *in utero* is presented in Figure 13.

In some males, however, hypospadia has been noted, and pseudohermaphroditism has been noted in female children with fetal alcohol syndrome. Lindor and co-workers[42] reported a case of absent clitoris in a fetal alcohol syndrome patient.

Several studies indicate that prenatal alcohol exposure may cause a delay in time of menarche in girls[43] and in time of vaginal opening in animals.[44,45] The reason for these effects, however, has not been determined.

Since alcohol has profound effects on sex hormones in adults, it is possible that comparable effects might also occur in the developing fetus. This is an especially important consideration since sex hormones play a crucial role in the organization and development of sexual features *in utero*. Suppression of androgens during fetal development, for instance, will result in feminization of male offspring with underdeveloped or absent male genitalia and absence of male sexual behavior. This possibility was tested. Day-old rats prenatally exposed to alcohol were found to have significantly lower dihydrotestosterone brain levels and smaller ratios of testis weights to body weights than pair-fed controls, but brain and blood testosterone levels were not significantly decreased.[46] Plasma testosterone levels were also unaffected in another study in which rats were

Figure 13. Undescended testicle in a mouse fetus prenatally exposed to alcohol. Photo courtesy Dr. C. Randall.

exposed to alcohol prenatally and for the first 7 days postpartum. There was also no effect on male sex organs or sexual behavior.[47] In this latter study, however, alcohol was administered in drinking water, and blood alcohol levels may have been too low to produce any effects.

In light of the congenital abnormalities and the delays in female sexual maturation that have been reported in conjunction with *in utero* alcohol exposure,[36] it would appear that considerably more information would be of value regarding the issue of prenatal alcohol exposure and sexual maturation and behavior.

Limb and Joint Anomalies and Other Skeletal Disorders

Limb and joint anomalies have frequently been mentioned in connection with fetal alcohol syndrome but have not been systematically studied. Table 22 presents a summary of some of these studies along with a frequency of occurrence.

Microcephaly is among the most serious and most common abnormalities associated with prenatal alcohol exposure but likely reflects decreased brain growth rather than decreased skeletal growth. Cervical fusion has not been frequently noted but occurred in 43% of the cases examined by Smith and his co-workers.[6] Radioulnar fusions (see Figure 14a) were noted in 20% of the fetal alcohol syndrome patients examined by Jaffer nad his co-workers.[48]

Cervical fusion anomalies have also been observed in mice prenatally exposed to alcohol.[47]

Hypoplastic nails, shortened fingers, camptodactyly, and clinodactyly (see Figures 14b–14d) are frequently mentioned in conjunction with *in utero* alcohol exposure in both humans (Table 22) and animals.[7,50–54] An instance of syndactyly in a mouse fetus exposed to alcohol *in utero* is illustrated in Figure 14e.

Van Rensburg[55] reported an unusual case of phocomelia and amelia in an infant born to an alcoholic woman. The child died within 24 hours of birth. She was a full-term infant but weighed only 1600 grams at birth. No observable brain anomalies were evident during autopsy.

Missing bones have also been noted in animals prenatally exposed to alcohol.[7,56] Skeletal maturation was delayed in 27% of the children examined by Smith[6] and has also been reported in rats prenatally exposed to alcohol.[57,58]

Anomalous palmar crease patterns and dermal ridge patterns have also been frequently observed in fetal alcohol syndrome patients.[18,41,61–65] Simian creases (see Figure 14f) are especially commonly found in conjunction with the syndrome.[65] Tillner and Majewski[65] compared palmar creases and dermal ridge patterns in 34 fetal alcohol syndrome patients with those seen in 470 normal individuals. Simian creases occurred in 6% of the fetal alcohol patients compared

Table 22. Skeletal Disorders

Source	N cases	Disorder and frequency (%)	
Spiegel et al.[59]	8	Hip dislocation	(13%)
		Microcephaly	(88%)
		Hypoplastic nails	(100%)
		Shortened fingers	(75%)
		Radioulnar synostosis	(50%)
		Camptodactyly of fingers	(50%)
		Clinodactyly of toes	(50%)
		Flexion contractures	(50%)
Hermann et al.[60]	11	Microcephaly	(45%)
		Hypoplastic nails	(45%)
		Shortened fingers or toes	(73%)
		Ectrodactyly (missing fingers or toes)	(18%)
		Syndactyly	(18%)
		Camptodactyly	(36%)
		Clinodactyly	(18%)
		Tetraectodactyly (four fingers or toes on hand or foot)	(9%)
		Extra digit	(9%)
		Flexion contractures	(9%)
Smith et al.[6]	76	Microcephaly	(54%)
		Cervical spinal fusions	(43%)
		Radioulnar synostosis	(24%)
		Abnormal chest, e.g., funnel chest	(27%)
Sokol et al.[23]		Hip dislocations	(5%)
Majewski[43]	95	Camptodactyly	(18%)
		Clinodactyly	(57%)
		Hypoplastic nails	(14%)
		Hip dislocations	(11%)
Jaffer et al.[48]	15	Clinodactyly	(66%)
		Carpal fusions	(20%)
		Radioulnar synostosis	(13%)
		Pectus excavatum	(6%)

to 1.3% in the normals. There was no relation between the frequency of these creases and severity of symptoms of fetal alcohol exposure.[65] Thenar creases were clearly developed in fetal alcohol patients, and the incidence of abnormalities in such patients did not differ from normals. The proximal transverse crease, especially in the central segment, was frequently reduced in length in fetal alcohol patients.

Digital and palmar crease patterns develop as a result of flexion movements of the skin in the fetal hand occurring between the 7th and 14th weeks of gestation[66] and are suggestive of hand malformation.[66] This suggestion in con-

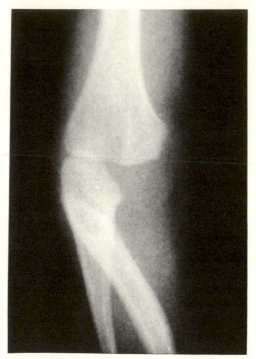

Figure 14a. Radiograph of radioulnar synostosis of elbow in patient with fetal alcohol syndrome. Photo courtesy of Dr. Phillip Spiegel.

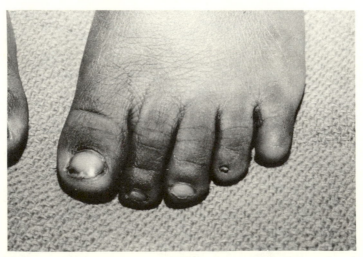

Figure 14b. Hypoplastic toenails in patient with fetal alcohol syndrome. Photo courtesy Dr. Phillip Spiegel.

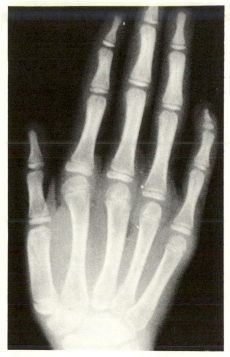

Figure 14c. Radiograph showing absence of terminal phalanges. Photo courtesy Dr. Phillip Spiegel.

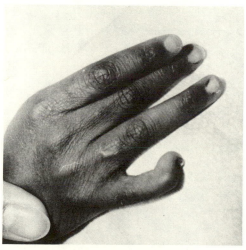

Figure 14d. Clinodactyly of fifth finger in patient with fetal alcohol syndrome. Photo courtesy Dr. Phillip Spiegel.

Figure 14e. Syndactyly in a mouse fetus prenatally exposed to alcohol. Photo courtesy Dr. Carrie Randall.

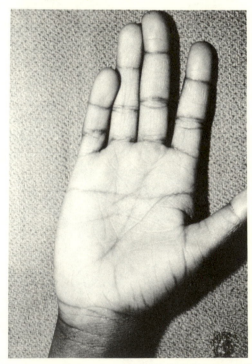

Figure 14f. Abnormal palmar creases in patient with fetal alcohol syndrome. Note especially simian crease (horizontal crease in center of hand). Photo courtesy Dr. Phillip Spiegel.

Table 23. Neural-Tube Defects

Source	N cases	Disorder (frequency)
Collins and Turner[68]	6	Lumbar meningomyelocele (1)
Loiodice et al.[69]	1	Anencephaly (1)
Arulanantham and Goldstein[70]	177[a]	Meningomyelocele (3)[b]
Clarren and Smith[71]	65	Meningomyelocele (2)
		Lumbrosacral Lipomeningocele
		Anencephaly
Fuster et al.[72]	1	Sacral Meningomyelocele (1)
Goldstein and Arulanantham[73]	1	Sacral Meningomyelocele (1)
Majewski[41]	108	Lumbar Meningomyelocele (1)
Smith et al.[6]	76	Meningomyelocele (1)

[a]Total number of cases of myelomeningocele investigated.
[b]Number of cases in which maternal alcoholism suspected.

nection with fetal alcohol syndrome is supported by the many abnormalities in the hand that have been previously described.

Neural-Tube Defects

The frequency of neural-tube defects in conjunction with fetal alcohol syndrome is relatively low but still far exceeds the random expected frequency.[41,67] The most common defect is sacral meningomyelocele. Other neural-tube defects are described in Table 23.

Carcinogenesis

Neoplasms have now been detected in a few patients with fetal alcohol syndrome (see Table 24).

Horstein and his co-workers[74] reported the first such case in 1977. The

Table 24. Reports of Neoplasms in Patients with Fetal Alcohol Syndrome

Neoplasm	Source
Adrenal cortical carcinoma	Hornstein et al.[74]
Hepatoblastoma	Khan et al.[75]
Neuroblastoma	Kinney et al.[76]
Ganglioneuroblastoma	Seeler et al.[77]

patient was a girl who was hospitalized for abdominal pain and was found to have an adrenal cortical carcinoma, from which she died shortly thereafter.

Neuroblastomas have been noted in two patients with fetal alcohol syndrome,[75,76] but in one of these cases, the patient may also have been exposed to diphenylhydantoin *in utero*.

Thus far, only diethylstilbestrol and diphenylhydantoin have been identified as transplacental carcinogens in humans. The reports of carcinogens in patients with fetal alcohol syndrome, though they are few in number, raise the possibility that alcohol may also be a transplacental carcinogen in man.

References

1. Lesure, J. F. Syndrome d'alcoolisme foetal à l'Ile de la Réunion. *Nouvelle Presse Médicale,* 1980, *9,* 1708, 1710.
2. Loser, H., and Majewski, F. Type and frequency of cardiac defects in embryofetal alcohol syndrome: Report of 16 cases. *British Heart Journal,* 1977, *39,* 1374–1379.
3. Dehaene, P. H. Titran, M., Samaille-Villette, C. H., Samaille, P.-P., Crepin, G., Walbaum, R., Deroubais, P., and Blanc-Garin, A. P. Le syndrome d'alcoolisme foetal dans le nord de la France. *Revue de l'Alcoolisme,* 1977, *23,* 145–158.
4. Dupuis, C., Dehaene, P., Deroubaix-Tella, P., Blanc-Garin, A. P., Rey, C., and Carpentier-Courault, C. Les cardiopathies des enfants nés de mère alcoolique. *Archives des Maladies du Coeur et des Vaisseaux,* 1978, *71,* 565–572.
5. Steeg, C. N., and Woolf, P. Cardiovascular malformations in the fetal alcohol syndrome. *American Heart Journal,* 1979, *98,* 635–637.
6. Smith, D. F., Sander, G. G., Macleod, P. M., Tredwell, S., Wood, B., and Newman, D. E. Intrinsic defects in the fetal alcohol syndrome: Studies on 76 cases from British Columbia and the Yukon Territory. *Neurobehavioral Toxicology and Teratology,* 1981, *3,* 145–152.
7. Chernoff, G. F. The fetal alcohol syndrome in mice: An animal model. *Teratology,* 1977, *15,* 223–229.
8. Randall, C. L., Taylor, W. J., and Walker, D. W. Ethanol-induced malformations in mice. *Alcoholism: Clinical and Experimental Research,* 1977, *1,* 219–223.
9. DeBakey, M., and Gotto, A. *The living heart.* New York: David McKay, 1977.
10. Tenbrinck, M. S., and Buchin, S. Y. Fetal alcohol syndrome: Report of a case. *Journal of the American Medical Association,* 1975, *232,* 1144–1147.
11. Hanson, J. W. Streissguth, A. P., and Smith, D. W. The effects of moderate alcohol consumption during pregnancy on fetal growth and morphogenesis. *Journal of Pediatrics,* 1978, *92,* 457–460.
12. Lemoine, P., Harousseau, H., Borteryu, J. P., and Menuet, J. C. Les enfants de parents alcooliques: Anomalies observées, à propros 127 cas. *Ouest Medical,* 1968, *21,* 476–482.
13. Goetzman, B. W., Kagan, J., and Blankenship, W. J. Expansion of the fetal alcohol syndrome. *Clinical Research,* 1975, *23,* 100.
14. Ijaiya, K., Schwenk, A., and Gladtke, E. Fetales Alkoholsyndrom. *Deutsche Medizinische Wochenschrift,* 1976, *101,* 1563–1568.
15. Debeukelaer, M. M., Randall, C. L., and Storud, D. R. Renal anomalies in the fetal alcohol syndrome. *Journal of Pediatrics,* 1977, *91,* 759–760.
16. Dunigan, T. H., and Werlin, S. L. Extrahepatic biliary atresia and renal anomalies in fetal alcohol syndrome. *American Journal of Diseases of Children,* 1981, *135,* 1067–1068.

17. Goldstein, G., and Arulanantham, K. Neural tube defect and renal anomalies in a child with fetal alcohol syndrome. *Journal of Pediatrics*, 1978, *93*, 636–637.
18. Manzke, H., and Grosse, F. R. Inkomplettes und Komplettes des Alkohol-Syndrom: Bei drei Kindern einer Trinkerin. *Medizinische Welt*, 1975, *26*, 709–712.
19. Havers, W., Majewski, F., Olbing, H., and Eickenberg, H. U. Anomalies of the kidneys and genitourinary tract in alcohol embryopathy. *Journal of Urology*, 1980, *124*, 108–110.
20. Qazi, Q. H., Masakaqa, A., Milman, D. H., McGann, B., Chua, A., and Haller, J. Renal anomalies in fetal alcohol syndrome. *Pediatrics*, 1979, *63*, 886–889.
21. Cahuana, A., Krauel, J., Molina, V., Lizarraga, I., and Alfonso, H. Fetopatia alcoholica. *Anales Espanoles de Pediatria*, 1977, *10*, 673–676.
22. Santolaya, J. M., Martinez, G., Gorostiza, E., Aizpiri, J., and Hernandez, M. Alcoholismo fetal. *Drogalcohol*, 1978, *3*, 183–192.
23. Sokol, R. J., Miller, S. I., and Reed, G. Alcohol abuse during pregnancy: An epidemiologic study. *Alcoholism: Clinical and Experimental Research*, 1980, *4*, 135–145.
24. Giaretto, G., Bini, P., Jarre, J., and Basile, F. Malformazioni morfologiche cerebrali e renali in sospetta sindrome alcoolica fetale: Contribùto clinico. *Minerva Pediatrica*, 1979, *31*, 1185–1190.
25. Boggan, W. O., Randall, C. L., DeBeukelaer, M., and Smith, R. Renal anomalies in mice prenatally exposed to ethanol. *Research Communications in Chemical Pathology and Pharmacology*, 1979, *23*, 127–142.
26. Habbick, B. F., Zaleski, W. A., Casey, R., and Murphy, F. Liver abnormalities in three patients with fetal alcohol syndrome. *Lancet*, 1979, *1*, 580–581.
27. Moller, J., Brandt, N. J., and Tygstrup, I. Hepatic dysfunction in patient with fetal alcohol syndrome. *Lancet*, 1979, *1*, 605–606.
28. Newman, S. L., Flannery, D. B., and Caplan, D. B. Simultaneous occurrence of extrahepatic biliary atresia and fetal alcohol syndrome. *American Journal of Diseases of Children*, 1979, *133*, 101.
29. Peiffer, J., Majewski, F., Fischfach, H., Bierich, J. R., and Volk, B. Alcohol embryofetopathy: Neuropathology of three children and three fetuses. *Journal of Neurological Science*, 1979, *41*, 125–137.
30. Christoffel, K. K., and Salfsky, I. Fetal alcohol syndrome in dizygotic twins. *Journal of Pediatrics*, 1975, *87*, 963–967.
31. Jones, K. L., and Smith, D. W. Recognition of the fetal alcohol syndrome in early infancy. *Lancet*, 1973, *2*, 999–1001.
32. Van Dyke, D., Mackay, L., and Ziaylek, E. N. Management of severe feeding dysfunction in children with fetal alcohol syndrome. *Clinical Pediatrics*, 1982, *21*, 336–339.
33. McClearn, G. E., Bennett, E. L., Herbert, M., Kakihana, R., and Schlessinger, K. Alcoholdehydrogenase activity and previous ethanol consumption in mice. *Nature*, 1964, *203*, 793.
34. Hawkins, D., Kalant, H., and Khanna, I. M. Effects of chronic intake of ethanol on rate of ethanol metabolism. *Canadian Journal of Physiology and Pharmacology*, 1966, *44*, 241–247.
35. Sze, P. Y., Yanai, J., and Ginsburg, P. W. Effects of early ethanol input on the activities of ethanol-metabolizing enzymes in mice. *Biochemical Pharmacology*, 1976, *25*, 215–217.
36. Niimi, Y. Studies on effects of alcohol on fetus. *Sanfujinka No Shimpo*, 1973, *25*, 55–78.
37. Duncan, R. J. S., and Woodhouse, B. The lack of effect on liver alcohol dehydrogenase in mice of early exposure to alcohol. *Biochemical Pharmacology*, 1978, *27*, 2755–2756.
38. Raiha, N. C. R., Kiskinen, M., and Pikkarainen, P. Developmental changes in alcohol-dehydrogenase activity in rat and guinea-pig liver. *Biochemical Journal*, 1967, *103*, 623–626.
39. Sjoblom, M., Oisund, J. F., and Morlund, J. Development of alcohol dehydrogenase and aldehyde dehydrogenase in the offspring of female rats chronically treated with ethanol. *Acta Pharmacologica et Toxicologica*, 1979, *44*, 128–131.

40. Burke, J. P., and Fenton, M. R. The effect of maternal ethanol consumption on aldehyde dehydrogenase activity in neonates. *Research Communications in Psychiatry and Behavior,* 1978, *3,* 169–172.

41. Majewski, F. Alcohol embryopathy: Some facts and speculations about pathogenesis. *Neurobehavioral Toxicology and Teratology,* 1981, *3,* 129–144.

42. Lindor, E., McCarthy, A. M., and McRae, M. G. Fetal alcohol syndrome: A review and case presentation. *Journal of Obstetric, Gynecologic, and Neonatal Nursing,* 1980, *9,* 222–223.

43. Robe, L. B., Robe, R. S., and Wilson, P. A. Maternal heavy drinking related to delayed onset of daughters' menstruation. In M. Galanter (Ed.), *Currents in alcoholism* (Vol. 7). New York: Grune and Stratton, 1980. pp. 515–520.

44. Tittmar, H. G. Some effects of ethanol, presented during the prenatal period, on the development of rats. *British Journal on Alcohol and Alcoholism,* 1977, *12,* 71–83.

45. Boggan, W. O., Randall, C. L., and Dodds, H. M. Delayed sexual maturation in female C57B1/6J mice prenatally exposed to alcohol. *Research Communications in Chemical Pathology and Pharmacology,* 1979, *23,* 117–125.

46. Kakihana, R., Butte, J. C., and Moore, J. A. Endocrine effects of maternal alcoholization: Plasma and brain testosterone, dihydrotestosterone, estradiol, and corticosterone. *Alcoholism: Clinical and Experimental Research,* 1980, *4,* 57–61.

47. Chen, J. J., and Smith, E. R. Effects of perinatal alcohol on sexual differentiation and open-field behavior in rats. *Hormones and Behavior,* 1979, *13,* 219–231.

48. Jaffer, Z., Nelson, M., and Beighton, P. Bone fusion in the foetal alcohol syndrome. *Journal of Bone and Joint Surgery,* 1981, *63B,* 569–571.

49. Webster, W. S., Walsh, D. A., Lipson, A. H., and McEwen, S. E. Teratogenesis after acute alcohol exposure in inbred and outbred mice. *Neurobehavioral Toxicology,* 1980, *2,* 227–234.

50. Giknis, M. L., Damjanov, I., and Rubin, E. The differential transplacental effects of ethanol in four mouse strains. *Neurobehavioral Toxicology,* 1980, *2,* 235–237.

51. Czajka, M. R. Daniels, G., Kaye, G. I., and Tucci, S. M. Effects of ethanol on mouse embryos: Teratology and chromosome abnormalities. *Anatomical Record,* 1979, *193,* 515–516.

52. Kronick, J. B. Teratogenic effects of ethyl alcohol administered to pregnant mice. *American Journal of Obstetrics and Gynecology,* 1976, *124,* 676–670.

53. Randall, C. L., and Taylor, W. J. Prenatal ethanol exposure in mice: Teratogenic effects. *Teratology,* 1979, *19,* 305–312.

54. West, J. R., Black, A. C., Reimann, P. C., and Alkana, R. L. Polydactyly and polysyndactyly induced by prenatal exposure to ethanol. *Teratology,* 1981, *24,* 13–18.

55. Van Rensburg, L. J. Major skeletal defects in the fetal alcohol syndrome: A case report. *South African Medical Journal,* 1981, *59,* 687–688.

56. Schwetz, B. A., Smith, F. A., and Staples, R. E. Teratogenic potential of ethanol in mice, rats, and rabbits. *Teratology,* 1978, *18,* 385–391.

57. St. Sandor, S., and Amels, D. The action of aethanol on the praenatal development of albino rats. *Revue Roumaine d'Embryologie et de Cytologie, Série d'Embryologie,* 1968, *8,* 105–118.

58. Hadad, R., Canlon, B., Dumas, R., Lee, M., and Rabe, A. *Maternal ethanol consumption during pregnancy affects fetal skeletal development in the rat.* Paper presented at the Laboratory Animal Science Meeting, Atlanta, Ga., October 1979.

59. Spiegel, P. G., Peckman, W. M., Rich, B. H., Versteeg, C. N., Nelson, V., and Dudnikov, M. The orthopedic aspects of the fetal alcohol syndrome. *Clinical Orthopaedics and Related Research,* 1979, *139,* 58–63.

60. Hermann, J., Pallister, P. D., and Opitz, J. M. Tetraectordactyly and other skeletal manifestations in the fetal alcohol syndrome. *European Journal of Pediatrics,* 1980, *133,* 221–226.

61. Jones, K. L., Smith, D. W., Ulleland, C. N., and Streissguth, A. P. Pattern of malformation in offspring of chronic alcoholic mothers. *Lancet,* 1973, *1,* 1267–1271.

62. Palmer, R. H., and Ouelette, E. M. Congenital malformations in offspring of a chronic alcoholic mother. *Pediatrics,* 1974, *53,* 490–494.

63. Bierich, J. R., Majewski, F., Michaelis, R., and Tillner, I. Über das embryo-fetale Alkohol-syndrom. *European Journal of Pediatrics,* 1976, *121,* 155–177.

64. Iosub, S., Fuchs, M., Bingol, N., and Gromisch, D. S. Fetal alcohol syndrome revisited. *Pediatrics,* 1981, *68,* 475–479.

65. Tillner, I., and Majewski, F. Furrows and dermal ridges of the hand in patients with alcohol embryopathy. *Human Genetics,* 1978, *42,* 307–314.

66. Popich, G. A., and Smith, D. W. The genesis and significance of digital and palmar hand creases: Preliminary report. *Journal of Pediatrics,* 1970, *77,* 1017–1023.

67. Clarren, S. K. Neural tube defects and fetal alcohol syndrome. *Journal of Pediatrics,* 1979, *95,* 328–329.

68. Collins, E., and Turner, G. Six children affected by maternal alcoholism. *Medical Journal of Australia,* 1978, *2,* 606–608.

69. Loiodice, G., Gortuna, G., Guidetti, A., Ria, N., and D'Elia, R. Considerazioni cliniche intorno à due casi di malformazioni congenite in bambine nati da madri affete da alcoolismo cronico (primi casi Italiani). *Minerva Pediatrica,* 1975, *27,* 1891–1893.

70. Arulanantham, K., and Goldstein, G., Neuronal tube defects with fetal alcohol syndrome: Reply. *Journal of Pediatrics,* 1979, *95,* 329.

71. Clarren, S. K., and Smith, D. W. The fetal alcohol syndrome: A review of the world literature. *New England Journal of Medicine,* 1978, *298,* 1063–1067.

72. Fuster, J. S., Guell, S., Cahuana, A. B., and Garciatornel, S. Neuronal tube defects with fetal alcohol syndrome. *Journal of Pediatrics,* 1979, *95,* 328.

73. Goldstein, G., and Arulanantham, K. Neural tube defect and renal anomalies in a child with fetal alcohol syndrome. *Journal of Pediatrics,* 1978, *93,* 636–637.

74. Hornstein, L., Crowe, C., and Gruppo, R. Adrenal carcinoma in child with history of fetal alcohol syndrome. *Lancet,* 1977, *2,* 1292–1293.

75. Khan, A., Bader, J. L., Hoy, G. R., and Sinks, L. F. Hepatoblastoma in child with fetal alcohol syndrome. *Lancet,* 1979, *1,* 1403–1404.

76. Kinney, H., Faix, R., and Brazy, J. The fetal alcohol syndrome and neuroblastoma. *Pediatrics,* 1980, *66,* 130–132.

77. Seeler, R. A., Israel, J. N., Roayl, J. E., Kaye, C. I., Rao, S., and Abulaban, M. Ganglioneuroblastoma and fetal hydantoin alcohol syndromes. *Pediatrics,* 1979, *63,* 524–527.

Disorders of the Central Nervous System

Mental retardation is the most serious behavioral problem associated with fetal alcohol exposure, but other behavioral problems, e.g., "hyperactivity," have also been connected with such exposure.

Patients bearing the most serious physical stigmata of fetal alcohol exposure tend to be the most seriously impaired cognitively,[1,2] but cognitive impairment may also occur in the absence of physical signs caused by fetal alcohol exposure.[1] Structural anomalies have been observed in the brains of humans, and both structural and neurochemical anomalies have been found in brains of animals prenatally exposed to alcohol (see below). Conceivably, some of these structural and neurochemical anomalies may underlie the behavioral problems associated with such exposure.

Behavioral Deficits

Mental Retardation

Most fetal alcohol syndrome patients on whom IQ tests have been performed have scored about 2 standard deviations below the mean (see Table 25). Follow-up studies in which patients were retested for IQ indicate that these deficits remain fairly stable.[11]

Animal studies in which offspring that have been prenatally exposed to alcohol are examined for their learning ability provide an analogue for these IQ studies. In one such study,[12] pregnant rats were intubated with alcohol (3 g/kg/twice daily) or water throughout gestation. Animals in the two groups received the same amount of food and water. After birth, offspring were re-

Table 25. IQ Scores of FAS/FAE Patients

Source	N cases	Average IQ or general comments
Belgium		
Fryns et al.[3]	4	<50
France		
Lemoine et al.[4]	127	70
Dehaene et al.[5]	22	66
		(Range: 33–112)
Germany		
Majewski[6]	18	18
		(Range: 47–130)
		FAE I: 67
		FAE II: 80
		FAE III: 92
Russia		
Shurygin[7]	23	"Varying degrees of mental retardation"
Sweden		
Olegård et al.[8]	48	<70
		(9 children)
		70–85
		(19 children)
United States		
Jones et al.[9]	13	73
		(living in own home)
		84
		(living in foster home)
Streissguth et al.[2]	20	65
		Range: (16–105)
Steinhausen et al.[10]	32	89

moved from their biological mothers and placed with surrogate mothers that had not been treated during pregnancy. This surrogate fostering procedure was conducted to avoid any residual effects of alcohol affecting maternal behavior or lactational performance (see Chapter 12). When offspring were about 3 months old, they were tested for their learning ability in an active avoidance task. In this situation, the animal was required to learn an association between a signal and a forthcoming shock. If the animal learned this association, it could avoid the shock by moving to a safe area in response to the signal rather than having to make an escape response to shock.

Figure 15 shows that the number of avoidances made by male rats prenatally exposed to alcohol is far lower than that of control rats, suggesting poorer learning ability.

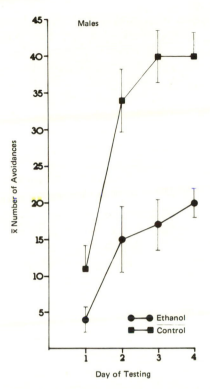

Figure 15. Shock avoidance behavior in male rats prenatally exposed to alcohol compared to their pair-fed controls (see text for details). Data from Abel et al.[12]

Attention Deficit Disorder

"Hyperactivity," also called "minimal brain dysfunction" or "attentional deficit disorder," has also been frequently mentioned in conjunction with fetal alcohol effects (see, e.g., references 2 and 13 through 18). The primary characteristics of this disorder[19] are difficulty in focusing attention and impulsivity. Increased activity may or may not be present.

This disorder is usually apparent by age 3 but often remains undiagnosed or is not referred for professional attention until the child enters school.[19] As a result of this disorder, school failure and conduct disorders are not uncommon. In some cases, all of the symptoms continue on into adolescence or adulthood. In other instances, all symptoms disappear around puberty. The third possibility is that the hyperactivity disappears around puberty but the attentional problems and impulsiveness continue into adulthood.

The estimated prevalence of this disorder in the United States is about 3%, and it is about 10 times more common in boys than in girls.[19]

Hyperactive children often come from homes where alcoholism is a problem, but it appears that it is the biological parents rather than the adoptive parents that are the transmitting agents.[20-22] Since it is likely that the biological parents probably drank prior to, during, and after the birth of these children, it is difficult to separate genetic factors from prenatal factors in the etiology of this disorder as far as alcohol is concerned.

The frequency of this disorder among those with fetal alcohol syndrome is unknown. In Majewski's report,[23] two-thirds of the 95 patients he observed were considered to be "hyperactive," although no systematic measures were taken to substantiate this impression.

Shaywitz and her co-workers[13] reported that in a group of 87 children with learning problems there were 15 children who were born to heavy-drinking mothers. All children exhibited "hyperactivity" despite normal intelligence (IQ range: 82-113). By grade 1, 13 of these 15 children had received recommendations for special education services, and by grade 3, all 15 had received such recommendations.

If substantiated, this report would suggest that the contribution of fetal alcohol exposure to early learning and other behavior problems may be as high as 17%. There are a number of questions associated with this report, however, that warrant attention because of the potential inferences that might otherwise be drawn from it.

The first is that there is no way of knowing whether the difficulty arose as a result of being the offspring of a father or mother with a drinking problem. The second is that the role of postnatal factors was not examined, so that the contribution of a poor home environment cannot be assessed. For example, two of the mothers of the 15 children described had died by the time of the examination, four were in the hospital because of alcohol-related problems, and five were divorced. The authors provide no data from the remaining children to compare with the 15 children they identified. As a result, there is no way to evaluate differences between the two groups. The fact that children were below average in birth weight and in later height, or that they had small palpebral fissures, is therefore without consequence since these are common problems associated with many other factors. Not knowing the incidence in the other children therefore defeats the purpose of stating the incidence in the 15 who are described. Thus, whereas prenatal alcohol exposure may indeed have been a factor in the behavioral problems the investigators were called upon to assess, this report is only suggestive of such as possibility, and the incidence of 17% is suspect.

Studies in animals, on the other hand, offer much less equivocal evidence of "hyperactivity" occurring as a result of *in utero* alcohol exposure. While there are some exceptions (see, e.g., references 24 and 25), most studies have found that activity levels are elevated following prenatal alcohol exposure in rats (see, e.g., references 26 through 31). Many of these "activity" measures are derived from observations of animals in the "open field"—an enclosed area of varying size that is marked off in units.

Although differences in activity generated by the open field do not always correlate with activity measures obtained from other test conditions (e.g., activity wheels, activity cages), increased activity following prenatal alcohol exposure has been noted in other activity monitors as well, thereby lending to the robustness of this observation.

Figure 16 illustrates this increased activity effect in rats tested in the open field beginning at 10 days of age after being prenatally exposed to alcohol. In this study,[29] alcohol was administered to pregnant dams in the form of a liquid alcohol diet in which alcohol contributed to 35%, 17.5%, or 0% of the calories ingested by the mothers. Peak activity occurred at 13 days of age for all offspring, but whereas it decreased considerably after this age for both the 0% and the 17.5% animals, it remained elevated for animals whose mothers consumed the diet with the higher amount of alcohol.

Like the clinical reports describing fetal alcohol syndrome, so too does the experimental literature suggest that animals prenatally exposed to alcohol have difficulty in inhibiting their behavior. Figure 17 illustrates such a deficit when animals are tested in a passive avoidance task. In this situation, the animal is required to inhibit its behavior (exploration of the apparatus) if it is to avoid being shocked. As indicated by Figure 17, alcohol-exposed offspring require more trials to learn to inhibit their behavior compared to control animals. Also

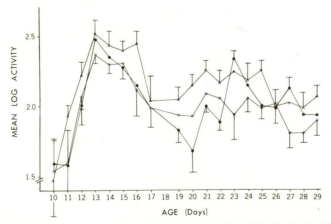

Figure 16. Open-field activity of offspring of rats whose dams ingested a liquid alcohol diet during pregnancy containing 35% (△——△), 17.5% (○——○), or 0% (●——●) of the calories. Different animals were examined at each day of testing (see text for details). Data from Abel.[29]

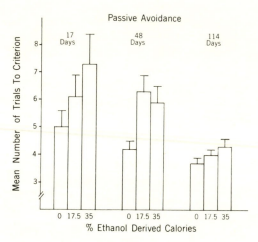

Figure 17. Passive avoidance behavior in rats whose mothers consumed a liquid alcohol diet containing 35%, 17.5%, or 0% ethanol-derived calories. Different animals were tested at each age (see text for details). Data from Abel.[29]

worth noting is that this effect is usually dose-related, and the older the animals, the more readily they learn this inhibition. This age-related improvement may even mask initial differences, suggesting a need to test animals at various ages after birth to demonstrate any such effects as being present at all.

Increased perseverative behavior resulting from *in utero* alcohol exposure has also been observed using the spontaneous alternation paradigm.

In this situation, animals are typically placed in a *T* maze and are allowed to explore the apparatus. After they enter one of the arms of the maze, they are confined for some fixed amount of time (e.g., 30 seconds) and are then put back into the start area. Once a rat has entered one of the arms of the maze, it usually enters the opposite arm on the next trial, spontaneously alternating back and forth with testing. Figure 18 illustrates the results of testing animals in this procedure following prenatal alcohol exposure.[29] As indicated by the figure, prenatal alcohol exposure results in increased perseveration (i.e., less spontaneous alternation), and, as in the case of passive avoidance, this effect diminishes with age.

Another way of testing for perseverative behavior in animals is the reversal learning paradigm. In this situation animals are trained to turn one way in a *T* maze to escape shock, and then after they learn the proper response, the previously safe area becomes the shock area and the previous shock area becomes the safe zone. The animal thus has to reverse his learning set. Rats prenatally exposed to alcohol have considerably more difficulty learning this reversal than do controls (see, e.g., references 31 through 33).

Studies of operant behavior provide yet another instance in which prenatal

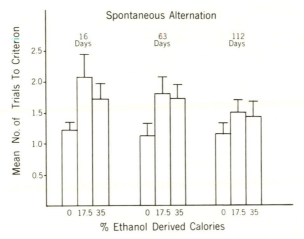

Figure 18. Spontaneous alternation behavior in a *T* maze of rats whose mothers consumed a liquid alcohol diet in which alcohol accounted for 35%, 17.5%, or 0% of the calories. Different animals were tested at each age (see text for details). Data from Abel.[29]

alcohol exposure has been found to affect perseverative behavior. In this situation, an animal is trained to operate a manipulandum for reinforcement, e.g., food or water. If reinforcement is no longer given, the animal will cease to operate the manipulandum. In other words, this behavior will "extinguish." Extinction represents a basic form of learning, namely, that the relationship between a particular kind of behavior and its consequences no longer exists. In this context, Riley and his associates[34] have found that extinction takes much longer to occur in rats that have been exposed to alcohol *in utero* than in control rats. This prolonged responding is thus another example of increased perseverative behavior or a deficit in response inhibition.

In summary, there is considerable similarity between the effects of prenatal alcohol exposure in humans and animals with respect to both learning deficits and the "attention deficit syndrome." This similarity suggests that alcohol is indeed a potent behavioral teratogen in humans, and the reported effects noted in this regard are not likely due to other factors related to alcohol ingestion.

Sleep Disturbances

Sleep disturbances in newborns born to alcoholic women have been noted.[35,36] These children sleep less and are more restless when they sleep compared to other children. EEG activity during sleep is also different in children born to alcoholic women (see below). Thus far, there have been no examinations of any comparable effect in animals.

Miscellaneous Behavioral Effects: Seizure Susceptibility, Aggression

Another issue that has been addressed in animal studies is whether prenatal alcohol exposure affects seizure susceptibility. Some clinical studies report epilepsy or increased incidences of convulsions as a characteristic of fetal alcohol exposure (see, e.g., references 8, 18, and 37). An increase in audiogenic seizure susceptibility in mice prenatally and postnatally exposed to alcohol has also been reported,[38] but this study suffers from inadequate control procedures, e.g., no control for alcohol-related undernutrition. In another study, rats prenatally exposed to alcohol had a lower incidence of deaths induced by pentylenetetrazol.[39]

Until more data are collected concerning seizure susceptibility, no unequivocal conclusions can be made concerning the effects of prenatal alcohol exposure on this parameter.

The effect of perinatal alcohol exposure on aggressive behavior during adulthood has been addressed in a number of studies.[40–43] However, these results have been inconsistent. In some instances increased aggression has been noted, whereas in other instances decreased aggression has been reported. In one study decreased aggression was observed when alcohol-exposed offspring were compared to nontreated controls but not when compared to pair-fed controls. This result suggested that the decreased aggression was due to alcohol-related undernutrition rather than the pharmacological effects of alcohol on the developing fetal/newborn brain.

The possibility that prenatal alcohol exposure may affect adult preference for alcohol has received surprisingly little attention. Bond and DiGiusto[26] and Holloway and Tapp[44] reported increased preference for alcohol on the part of rats exposed to alcohol *in utero*, but methodological problems inherent in these studies (e.g., absence of controls for alcohol-related undernutrition, small sample size) render their results less than conclusive. Miniature swine prenatally exposed to alcohol were also reported to have an increased preference for alcohol, but few details are available from this report.[45] In the only other study of this question, rats whose mothers were intubated with alcohol (1 or 2 g/kg/day) throughout pregnancy did not exhibit any significant preference for an alcohol solution when tested during adulthood.[46] At present, there does not appear to be any unequivocal evidence that prenatal alcohol exposure affects adult preference for alcohol.

Sensitivity to Alcohol

The evidence concerning altered sensitivity to alcohol during adulthood as a result of prenatal alcohol exposure is also equivocal. Prenatal alcohol exposure does not affect "sleep time."[25,47–50] However, preweanling exposure to alcohol did result in decreased alcohol-induced "sleeping." At time of awakening, blood alcohol levels in experimental and control animals were identical.

In another series of studies using the hypothermic response to a challenge dose of alcohol as the test measure, rats prenatally exposed to alcohol experienced less of a decrease in temperature than did control animals.[51-53] This decreased loss in body temperature was also evident when alcohol-exposed offspring were tested with drugs that generally exhibit cross-tolerance to alcohol, e.g., pentobarbital and diazepam, but not with drugs that do not exhibit such cross-tolerance, e.g., chlorpromazine. This decreased hypothermic response to prenatal alcohol exposure has not been corroborated in another study, however.[54]

Developmental Delay of Maturation

Associated with the "failure to thrive" and postnatal growth retardation in children prenatally exposed to alcohol, there are also clinical reports of delayed maturation of various developmental indices, e.g., walking, talking (see, e.g., references 18 and 55 through 57).

In a recent prospective study, Golden and her co-workers[58] matched 12 children with physically identifiable fetal alcohol effects, and whose mothers had a history of alcohol abuse, with 12 children matched for age, sex, and race, but without such effects and whose mothers had no such history. The infants were evaluated "blindly" at an average age of 1 year on the Bayley Mental and Motor scales. Children in the alcohol group scored 20 points below the controls, indicative of significantly delayed mental and motor development. Because most of the alcohol-abusing mothers were also smokers, it is not possible to attribute this difference unequivocally to alcohol, since the interaction between alcohol and smoking may have been an important contributing factor. A comparable result was reported earlier by Streissguth and her co-workers.[59]

Studies in animals have also reported developmental delays in maturation, although there is some inconsistency in these data. Among the more reliable findings associated with *in utero* alcohol exposure in animals are delayed time of earflap uncurling and eye opening (see, e.g., references 28 and 60 through 62). Motor coordination is also delayed in rats prenatally exposed to alcohol. For example, when rats were tested at 17 days of age for their ability to remain on a revolving drum, those exposed to alcohol fell sooner than controls.[62] When testing occurred at 3 months of age, alcohol-exposed animals no longer differed from controls.[53]

Delayed puberty has also been reported in girls born to alcoholic mothers.[7,63] Prenatal alcohol exposure has similarly been reported to cause delayed vaginal opening in rats[64,65] and mice.[66]

Psychopathology

Thus far, there are few studies in which behavioral testing has also involved assessment of psychiatric functioning. Slavney and Grace[67] reported a case of schizophrenia in a 15-year-old patient with fetal alcohol syndrome, but thus far this has been an isolated report.

Steinhausen and his co-workers[10] reported some data, on the other hand, suggesting that psychopathology among fetal alcohol patients may not be uncommon. In this study, children with fetal alcohol syndrome were compared with a control group matched for age, sex, and socioeconomic status. A third control groups consisted of children similarly matched who lived in foster homes. Average age of the children at time of testing was about 6 years. Testing consisted of administration of a structured interview related to development and psychopathology.

Compared to control children, children with fetal alcohol syndrome had greater frequencies of head and body rocking and stereotyped habits such as facial tics, hair plucking, and nail biting, were more dependent, had more problems with peer relationships, and had more problems with management of phobias.

Structural and Biochemical Changes in the Brain

The kinds of behavioral anomalies observed thus far are suggestive of structural or biochemical anomalies occurring in various parts of the brain. Thus far, there have been several examinations of brain tissue from abortuses and newborns who died shortly after birth whose mothers were chronic alcoholics. These autopsy studies are indicative of the kinds of gross neuropathological damage that can occur in the human as a result of prenatal alcohol exposure. There are also several studies in animals suggestive of more subtle neurological and biochemical anomalies arising from such exposure.

Neuropathological Anomalies

The frequency of neuropathological anomalies among fetal alcohol syndrome patients is unknown. The most commonly identified anomalies of this type that have been observed in autopsy studies of abortuses or newborns of chronic alcoholic women are described in Table 26. Similar neuropathological anomalies have also been reported in animals exposed to alcohol in utero, e.g., dilated ventricles,[72] absence of corpus callosum.[72] An instance of hydrocephalus in a mouse fetus prenatally exposed to alcohol is shown in Figure 19.

Whereas these kinds of anomalies are undoubtedly more serious than those occurring in surviving fetal alcohol syndrome patients, they are suggestive of the kinds of central nervous system defects that might be responsible for the more serious kinds of behavioral problems encountered in conjunction with fetal alcohol syndrome, e.g., profound mental retardation (see below).

Table 26. Neuropathological Anomalies

Type of defect	Source
Incomplete cortical development	Clarren et al.[68]
	Peiffer et al.[69]
Enlarged lateral ventricles	Clarren et al.[68]
	Jones and Smith[70]
Fusion of ventricles	Peiffer et al.[69]
Aberrant neuronal and glial migration	Clarren et al.[68]
	Peiffer et al.[69]
Absence or underdevelopment of corpus callosum	Clarren et al.[68]
	Peiffer et al.[69]
	Jones and Smith[80]
	Kinney et al.[71]
Absence of anterior commissure	Clarren et al.[68]
	Peiffer et al.[69]
Rudimentary cerebellum	Clarren et al.[68]
	Peiffer et al.[69]
Absence of olfactor bulbs	Peiffer et al.[69]
Underdevelopment of caudate nucleus	Peiffer et al.[69]

Microcephaly is one of the most common physical features associated with fetal alcohol syndrome (see Table 13) and probably reflects decreased brain growth. Herrmann and co-workers[73] have also called attention to the presence of abnormal scalp hair patterns, such as scalp-hair whorls, which he suggests may also reflect impaired brain development.

Studies in animals have revealed more subtle kinds of neuropathological anomalies that can occur following *in utero* alcohol exposure. For example,

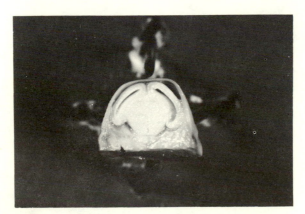

Figure 19. Hydrocephaly in a mouse prenatally exposed to alcohol. Photo courtesy Dr. C. Randall.

aberrations in the organization of neural fibers have been observed in the hippo-campus in rats prenatally exposed to alcohol.[74–77] West and his co-workers[74] noted that rats exposed to alcohol throughout gestation had abnormally dis-tributed nerve fibers in the hippocampus when these animals were examined long after birth (see Figure 20). Fewer nerve cells and decreased dendritic size in the hippocampus of rats and mice prenatally exposed to alcohol were also reported by Barnes and Walker[75] and by Davies and Smith.[76] Abel and his co-workers[12] found that alcohol-exposed rats had fewer dendritic spines than controls, and there was also a difference in the number of particular spines. Alcohol-treated offspring had fewer long, thin-necked spines with small end bulbs and more short, thick-necked spines with large end bulbs (see Table 27).

These reported structural changes in the hippocampus are of special interest

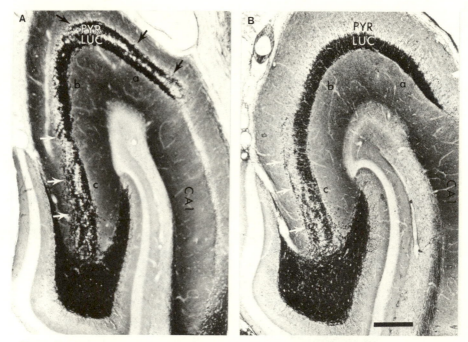

Figure 20. Effects of prenatal alcohol exposure on rat hippocampus. Section A is from an adult rat exposed to a liquid alcohol diet during gestation days 1–21. Black arrows indicate darkly stained aberrant "distal" infrapyramidal mossy fiber terminal field. White arrows indicate normally occur-ring "proximal" infrapyramid mossy fiber staining. Suprapyramidal mossy fiber staining with characteristic "fishhook" shape can also be seen. Section B is from a control rat. Note absence of distal infrapyramidal mossy fiber staining. PYR + pyramid cell layer; LUC = stratum lucidum; CA1 = hippocampal field CA1; a, b, c = subfields of hippocampal field CA3. Magnification bar = 250 M. Photo courtesy Dr. James West.

**Table 27. Percentage of Various Types of Spines on
Dendrites from the Hippocampal Area of Rats Prenatally
Exposed to Alcohol Compared to Controls ($\bar{X} \pm SE$)[a]**

Type	Alcohol	Pair-fed control
Type 1 (long, thin neck; small end bulb)	58 ± 4	74 ± 1
Type 2 (short, thin neck; large end bulb)	36 ± 4	20 ± 1
Type 3 (thick, short neck; large end bulb)	5 ± .3	5 ± .3

[a]Data from Abel et al.[77]

because this area of the brain is involved in learning/memory function and in inhibitory control of behavior.[77] As such, they suggest a structural basis for some of the behavioral problems that have been noted in conjunction with fetal alcohol exposure (see above). Also of interest is the fact that peak concentrations of alcohol have been found in this part of the fetal brain following maternal exposure to alcohol (see Chapter 2). The developing hippocampus may thus be particularly sensitive to alcohol or it may be more affected because of a relatively high concentration of alcohol in this part of the brain during development, or both.

Several studies also suggest that the cerebellum is also affected by prenatal alcohol exposure.[78–80] However, damage to this part of the brain does not appear to be irreversible. Kornguth and his co-workers[80] reported a slowing down in the normal thinning of the external granule cell layer in the cerebellum in rats, which they interpreted as evidence in a delay in the inward migration of granule cells. This interpretation is supported by Volk and his co-workers,[81] who likewise reported a delay in the reduction of the external granular cell layer in neonatal rats prenatally exposed to alcohol. By 25 days of age, however, the external granular layer was no longer visible. In addition, these investigators noted that while alcohol-exposed animals had less apical cytoplasm in Purkinje cells at 4 days of age compared to pair-fed controls, at 7 days of age this difference, while still present, was less apparent. And by 12 days of age, differences between alcohol-exposed and control animals were no longer evident.

Smith and Davies[82] reported that apical dendrites were not observable in Purkinje cells of rats at 7 days of age following prenatal alcohol exposure. At 21 days of age, however, differences between alcohol-exposed and control animals were less discernible. Similarly, dendritic aborization in neurons from hippo-campal pyramidal cells was reduced at 7 days of age, but differences between alcohol-exposed and control animals were less evident at 21 days of age.[82]

Decreased dendritic branching has also been observed in pyramidal neurons in the somatic sensory-motor cortex of rats prenatally exposed to alcohol by Hammer and Sheibel.[83] As in the Abel et al.[12] study, alcohol exposure reduced apical and basilar dendritic branching.

In addition to the growing evidence that the hippocampus and cerebellum are particularly vulnerable to insult from in utero alcohol exposure, there is thus also evidence that prenatal alcohol exposure inhibits dendritic branching in various areas of the brain. Such underdevelopment of dendritic systems could ultimately result in altered neuronal interconnectivity due to decreased synaptic contact.[83] The fact that some of the anomalies that have been observed in connection with alcohol's effects on the developing brain do not seem to be permanent is also of interest because it corroborates many behavioral studies that also suggest that alcohol causes a developmental delay rather than a permanent interruption in behavioral organization (see above).

Although they are subject to criticism on methodological grounds, there are also reports of delayed myelination of neurons in animals prenatally exposed to alcohol, which are also consistent with the behavioral deficits that have been noted and with the reversibility of these deficits.[84–89]

Havlicek and his co-workers[36] have reported that infants with fetal alcohol syndrome have prominent hypersynchrony during sleeping, particularly in the delta and theta frequencies of rapid-eye-movement sleep. The authors claim that they were able to identify 20 out of 22 infants born to alcoholic mothers on the basis of EEG activity alone. Abnormal EEGs were also noted in 38% of a group of fetal alcohol patients seen by Majewski.[23] (Cf. also reference 91.) Hypersynchrony and dysrhythmia were especially noticeable. Eight percent experienced convulsions. These EEG effects may be indicative of neural damage and could be another potentially valuable aid in diagnosing infants at risk for later problems associated with prenatal alcohol exposure.

Computer Tomography

Two studies have reported cranial computer tomography examinations in patients with fetal alcohol syndrome. Tanaka and co-workers[17] did not observe anomalies in the brains of three patients, but in a fourth patient slight cortical atrophy was evident along with enlargement of the right lateral ventricle. Goldstein and Arulanantham[91] reported dilated third and lateral ventricles in another patient with fetal alcohol syndrome. No comparable anomalies were observed by DeBeukelaer and co-workers[92] in their patient.

Abnormal Brain Electrical Activity

Olegard et al.[8] reported that a number of children born to alcoholic mothers had abnormal evoked potentials at birth. Six had abnormal visual evoked responses, 16 had abnormal somatosensory evoked responses, and 8 had abnormal laterality differences. However, no control data were presented in this report against which these responses could be compared. If children with fetal alcohol effects do indeed have abnormal evoked responses, this might be a useful screening technique for discovering neural damage in such patients (cf. also reference 94).

Neurochemical Effects

One possibility by which alcohol may affect the developing fetus and result in long-term behavioral effects is by interfering with maturation of neurotransmitter systems. Such systems are affected by alcohol in adult animals,[94] and many kinds of behavior are directly affected by changes in neurotransmitter status,[95] In addition, CNS disorders such as Parkinson's disease and Huntington's chorea[96,97] are associated with brain neurotransmitter function, e.g., dopamine and gamma-aminobutyric acid, respectively, and conceivably other CNS disorders may also be related to neurotransmitter function. Because of the role of neurotransmitters in these and basic neuronal communication, studies of alcohol's effects on these systems are of considerable interest and importance.

Interference of developing neurotransmitter systems by alcohol could arise as a result of the direct actions of alcohol on these systems or indirectly through effects on transmission of amino acids across the placenta. Amino acids such as tyrosine and tryptophan, for example, are precursors for neurotransmitters.[98] Unavailability of precursors at critical periods during development could unalterably affect development and functioning of these systems.

Although several studies have been reported concerning the effects of prenatal alcohol exposure on neurochemicals in animals, there are no unequivocal patterns discernible in this literature. These studies have recently been reviewed by Boggan,[99] Druse,[100] and Abel *et al.*[102] and are summarized in Table 28.

The reported changes in serotonin (5-hydroxytryptophan) levels in animals prenatally exposed to alcohol are typical of the inconsistency in these data. However, some studies are methodologically less rigorous than others and less weight should therefore be attached to their results (see below).

The report of Elis and co-workers[102–104] that mice prenatally exposed to alcohol had significantly lower brain serotonin levels can be criticized on several grounds. The most obvious shortcoming was the absence of pair-feeding procedures for control animals. Druse[100] also points out that the serotonin levels reported in these studies for both alcohol and control animals were considerably lower than those reported for mice in other laboratories, and the pH used in these assays was capable of oxidizing serotonin.

Iwase's[105] report of increased serotonin levels in mice prenatally exposed to alcohol is difficult to evaluate since it was reported in Japanese. According to the information available from the English abstract, pregnant mice consumed alco-

Table 28. Effects of Prenatal Alcohol Exposure on Levels of Neurochemicals in Brain and Other Tissues

Neurochemical	Species	Method and time of administration		Tissue	Pair-fed	Effect	Source
Serotonin	Mouse	pregnancy	1–21	Brain	No	→	Elis et al.[103,104]
			1–7			→	Krsiak et al.[105]
		(1 g/kg, p.o.)	8–14			→	
			15–21			→	
	Mouse	pregnancy (liquid diet)	5–11	Brain	Yes	—	Boggan et al.[107]
	Mouse	pregnancy (10% v/v in water)	1–21	Brain	?	←	Iwase et al.[106]
Dopamine	Rat	pregnancy (liquid diet)	1–10	Brain	Yes	—	Rawat[108]
	Mouse	pregnancy	1–21	Brain	?	—	Iwase et al.[106]
	Mouse	pregnancy	1–21	Brain	No	—	Elis et al.[104]
			1–7			—	
		(1 g/kg, p.o.)	8–14			—	Krsiak et al.[105]
			15–21			—	
	Rat	pregnancy (liquid diet)	14–21	Brain	?	—	Detering et al.[109]

Compound	Species	Treatment	Age	Tissue	Change	Direction	Reference
Norepinephrine	Rat	pregnancy (liquid diet)	7–21	Telencephalon	Yes	—	Shoemaker et al.[110]
	Rat	pregnancy (liquid diet)	1–21	Liver	Yes	→	Rawat and Kumar[111]
	Mouse	pregnancy	1–21	Brain	No	—	Elis et al.[104]
		(1 g/kg, p.o.)	1–7			—	Krsiak et al.[105]
			8–14				
			15–21				
	Mouse	pregnancy	1–21	Brain		—	Iwase et al.[106]
	Rat	pregnancy (liquid diet)	13–17	Adrenal[a]	?	→	Lau et al.[112]
			13–21		Yes		
	Rat	pregnancy (liquid diet)	14–21	Brain	?	→	Detering et al.[109]
	Rat	pregnancy (liquid diet)	7–21	Telencephalon	Yes	←	Shoemaker et al.[110]
Acetylcholine	Rat	pregnancy	14 days	Brain	Yes	←	Rawat[108]
Gamma-aminobutyric acid	Rat	pregnancy	1–21	Brain	Yes	→	Rawat[108]
	Mouse	pregnancy (10% v/v in water)	1–21	Brain	?	—	Iwase et al.[106]
Histamine	Rat	pregnancy (liquid diet)	1–21	Brain	Yes	←	Rawat[108]
	Rat	pregnancy	1–21	Brain	Yes	←	Rawat[113]

[a] All catecholamines.

hol (10% v/v) in their drinking water during gestation. Peak blood alcohol was as much as 126 mg%. It is not clear whether or not control animals were pair-fed or watered. Offspring were sacrificed at 1, 2, 5, 8, or 30 days after birth. Brain serotonin levels were significantly higher in alcohol-exposed animals on all test days except day 2.

Boggan and co-workers[106] placed pregnant mice on a liquid alcohol diet on gestation days 5–11. Control animals were pair-fed. Assays were performed on gestation day 19 and on postnatal days 7, 14, 21, 28, and 60. Prenatal alcohol exposure did not affect whole brain levels of serotonin, tryptophan (the precursor for serotonin), or 5-hydroxyindoleacetic acid (metabolite of serotonin) and did not affect the rate of synthesis of serotonin from tryptophan or rate of serotonin uptake into crude synaptosomal preparations. There was, however, a significant reduction in potassium-stimulated release of serotonin from crude synaptosomal preparations in 19-day-old fetuses and 7- and 14-day-old mice.

Chan and Abel[114] did not find any significant effects of prenatal alcohol exposure on serotonin binding in the rat brain at 4 to 5 months of age. Control animals in this study were pair-fed, and at birth all offspring were surrogate-fostered to non-drug-treated dams (for further details see below). These data are presented in Table 29.

At present there does not appear to be any significant effect of prenatal alcohol exposure on brain serotonin levels. Studies showing such an effect can be criticized because of poor methodological procedures.

Most studies have reported that prenatal alcohol exposure does not affect dopamine levels in brain tissue (see Table 28). The one study showing a decrease in dopamine lebels was performed on liver tissue.

Two studies have reported decreased dopamine-β-hydroxylase activity in the adrenals as a result of *in utero* alcohol exposure.[108,111] This enzyme is involved in conversion of dopamine to norepinephrine in the adrenals. Effects

Table 29. Effects of Prenatal Exposure to Alcohol on Serotonin Receptor Binding (fmoles/mg protein) at 4–5 Months of Age in the Rat ($\bar{X} \pm SE$)[a]

Tissue	Alcohol treatment		
	35% EDC[b]	17.5% EDC	0% EDC
Cortex	39 ± 4	33 ± 4	33 ± 9
Caudate/putamen	76 ± 14	47 ± 11	52 ± 15
Thalamus/hypothalamus	71 ± 15	78 ± 18	75 ± 14

[a]Data from Chan and Abel.[114]
[b]EDC = ethanol-derived calories.

were transitory, however, in one study, since enzyme activity returned to normal 2 days after last alcohol exposure.[111]

Norepinephrine levels were reported increased in two studies,[107,109] not affected in three studies,[103–105] and decreased in one study.[108] Methodological problems inherent in some of the studies,[103,104] brief descriptions of procedures in others,[93] and publication in Japanese[105] preclude adequate evaluation of these data.

Branchey and Friedhoff[114] reported that activity of tyrosine hydroxylase, the enzyme that converts dopamine to norepinephrine in the brain, was increased in the caudate nucleus of animals prenatally exposed to alcohol. However, Boggan[99] points out that this result may have been due to maternal withdrawal from alcohol. Offspring in this study were not cross-fostered, and withdrawal from alcohol has previously been shown to increase tyrosine hydroxylase activity. When offspring of alcohol-consuming dams were cross-fostered after birth, tyrosine hydroxylase activity was not affected.[115]

Thadani and her co-workers[115] reported increased uptake of tyramine (a metabolite of tyrosine) into fetal and neonatal rat brain synaptosomes. Conversion of tyramine to octopamine by dopamine-β-hydroxylase within noradrenergic synapses was also increased relative to pair-fed controls. Differences were no longer significant at 24 days of age. These results were interpreted as evidence for an acceleration of noradrenergic development resulting from prenatal alcohol exposure.

Further evidence for accelerated development of noradrenergic neurons in animals prenatally exposed to alcohol was reported by Bartolome and co-workers.[116] These investigators examined hypoglycemia-induced (by insulin) reflex cardiac sympathetic neurotransmission as indicated by increases in cardiac ornithine decarboxylase (ODC). Offspring prenatally exposed to alcohol exhibited a mature cardiac ODC response at 4 days of age, compared to 7 days for pair-fed controls. Cardiac ODC response was higher for alcohol-exposed animals at 4 and 10 days of age, was lower at 7 days of age, and did not differ at 12 days of age. Offspring were surrogate-fostered after birth.

Thus far, cholinergic function in animals prenatally exposed to alcohol has not been studied to any great extent. Rawat[107] reported that prenatal exposure to alcohol resulted in decreases in fetal brain acetylcholine(ACh) levels, had no effect on brain choline levels (precursor for ACh), and increased acetylcholinesterase (enzyme that metabolizes ACh) levels.

Using responsiveness to scopolamine (a cholinergic receptor blocking agent) as a measure of cholinergic receptor status, Abel[117] observed increased activity on the part of both alcohol-exposed and pair-fed control animals but no differences in responsiveness to scopolamine at 13–21 days of age between these two groups. These data are presented in Figure 21.

Chan and Abel[113] did not observe any differences in cholinergic receptor

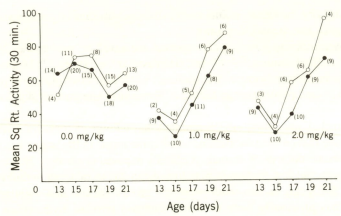

Figure 21. Responsiveness of rats, prenatally exposed to alcohol, to scopolamine (0, 1, or 2 mg/kg) at 13–21 days of age. Different animals were used at each age and for each dose of scopolamine. Alcohol-exposed (O——O); pair-fed control (●——●).

binding between animals prenatally exposed to alcohol and pair-fed controls. In this study, pregnant rats were placed on a liquid alcohol diet containing 35%, 17.5%, or 0% ethanol-derived calories from gestation day 5 to parturition. All diets were isocaloric. At birth, offspring were placed with non-drug-treated surrogate dams. At 4–5 months of age, offspring were sacrificed and receptor binding in cortex, caudate/putamen, and thalamus/hypothalamus was determined using ^{3}H-quinuclidinyl benzilate (QNB). Binding was defined as that bound in the absence of scopolamine minus that bound in its presence. The data are presented in Table 30.

Data pertaining to gamma-aminobutyric acid and histamine are presented in Table 28. Too little information is also available with respect to these neurochemicals from which to derive any meaningful conclusions.

Table 30. Binding to Cholinergic Receptors in Rats Prenatally Exposed to Alcohol ($\bar{X} \pm SE$) (fmoles/mg protein) at 4–5 Months of Age

Tissue	35% EDC	17.5% EDC	0% EDC
Cortex	1322 ± 126	1507 ± 49	1412 ± 70
Caudate/putamen	1740 ± 88	1829 ± 81	1726 ± 117
Thalamus/hypothalamus	526 ± 30	550 ± 32	551 ± 28

[a]Data from Chan and Abel.[114]

In summary, thus far there is a general absence of any patterns of changes in neurochemical systems associated with prenatal exposure to alcohol. In his review of this literature, Boggan[99] cites several additional conclusions and observations that are pertinent in considering these data, among which are absence of systematic time and dose studies, minimal attention to correlation between biochemical changes and behavior, reliance exclusively on mice and rats, and possible role of nonspecific factors in affecting outcomes of analyses such as ethanol-induced decreases in body temperature.

References

1. Majewski, F., Bierich, J. R., Loser, H., Michaelis, R., Leiber, B., and Bettecken, F. Zur Klinik und Pathogenese der Alkohol Embryopathie; Bericht über 68 Fälle. *Münchener Medizinische Wochenschrift*, 1976, *118*, 1635–1642.
2. Streissguth, A. P., Herman, C. S., and Smith, D. W. Intelligence, behavior, and dysmorphogenesis in the fetal alcohol syndrome: A report on 20 clinical cases. *Journal of Pediatrics*, 1978, *92*, 363–367.
3. Fryns, J. P., Deroover, J., Parloir, C., Goffaux, P., Lebas, E., and Van Den Berghe, H. The foetal alcohol syndrome. *Acta Paediatrica Belgica*, 1977, *30*, 117–121.
4. Lemoine, P., Harousseau, H., Borteryu, J. P. and Menuet, J. C. Les enfants de parents alcooliques; anomalies observées, à propos 127 cas. *Ouest Medical*, 1968, *21*, 476–482.
5. Dehaene, P. H., Samaille-Villette, C. H., Samaille, P. P., Crepin, G., Walbaum, R., Deroubaix, P., and Blanc-Garin, A. P. Le syndrome d'alcoolisme foetal dans le nord de la France. *Revue de l'Alcoolisme*, 1977, *23*, 145–158.
6. Majewski, F. Alcohol embryopathy: Some facts and speculations about pathogenesis. *Neurobehavioral Toxicology and Teratology*, 1981, *3*, 129–144.
7. Shurygin, G. I. Characteristics of the mental development of children of alcoholic mothers. *Pediatriya*, 1974, *11*, 71–73.
8. Olegård, R., Sabel, K. G., Aronsson, M., Sandin, B., Johansson, P. R., Carlsson, C., Kyllerman, M., Iversen, K., and Hrbek, A. Effects on the child of alcohol abuse during pregnancy: Retrospective and prospective studies. *Acta Paediatrica Scandinavica, Supplement* 1979, *275*, 112–121.
9. Jones, K. L., Smith, D. W., Ulleland, C. N., and Streissguth, A. P. Pattern of malformation in offspring of chronic alcoholic mothers. *Lancet*, 1973, *1*, 1267–1271.
10. Steinhausen, H., Nestler, V., and Spohr, H. Development and psychopathology of children with the fetal alcohol syndrome. *Developmental and Behavioral Pediatrics*, 1982, *3*, 49–54.
11. Streissguth, A. P., Herman, C. S., and Smith, D. W. Stability of intelligence in the fetal alcohol syndrome: A preliminary report. *Alcoholism: Clinical and Experimental Research*, 1978, *2*, 165–170.
12. Abel, E. L., Jacobsen, S., and Sherwin, B. T. In utero alcohol exposure: Functional and structural brain damage. *Neurobehavioral Toxicology and Teratology*, 1983, *5*, 363–366.
13. Shaywitz, S. E., Cohen, D. J., and Shaywitz, B. A. Behavior and learning deficits in children of normal intelligence born to alcoholic mothers. *Journal of Pediatrics*, 1980, *96*, 978–982.
14. Seidenberg, J., and Majewski, F. Zur Häufigkeit der Alkoholembryopathie in den verschiedenen Phasen der mütterlichen Alkoholkrankheit. *Suchtgefahren*, 1978, *24*, 63–65.
15. Wood, R. E. Fetal alcohol syndrome: Its implications for dentistry. *Journal of the American Dental Association*, 1977, *95*, 596–599.

16. Iosub, S., Fuchs, M., Bingol, N., and Gromisch, D. S. Fetal alcohol syndrome revisited. *Pediatrics*, 1981, *68*, 475–479.
17. Tanaka, H., Arima, M., and Suzuki, N. The fetal alcohol syndrome in Japan. *Brain and Development*, 1981, *3*, 305–311.
18. Bierich, J. R., Majewski, F., Michaelis, R., and Tillner, I. Über das embryo-fetale Alkohol-syndrom. *European Journal of Pediatrics*, 1976, *121*, 155–177.
19. American Psychiatric Association, *Diagnostic and statistical manual of mental disorders*. Washington, D.C.: Author, 1980.
20. Morrison, J. R., and Stewart, M. A. The psychiatric status of the legal families of adopted hyperactive children. *Archives of General Psychiatry*, 1973, *28*, 888–891.
21. Goodwin, D. W., Schulsinger, F., Hermansen, L., Guze, S. B., and Winokur, G. Alcoholism and hyperactive child syndrome. *Journal of Nervous and Mental Disease*, 1975, *160*, 349–353.
22. Cantwell, D. P. Psychiatric illness in the families of hyperactive children. *Archives of General Psychiatry*, 1972, *27*, 414–417.
23. Majewski, F. Über schädigende Einflüsse des Alkohols auf die Nachkommen. *Nervenarzt*, 1978, *49*, 410–416.
24. Abel, E. L. Effects of ethanol on pregnant rats and their offspring. *Psychopharmacology*, 1978, *57*, 5–11.
25. Da Silva, V. A., Ribeiro, M. J., and Masur, J. Developmental, behavioral, and pharmacological characteristics of rat offspring from mothers receiving ethanol during gestation and lactation. *Developmental Psychobiology*, 1980, *13*, 653–660.
26. Bond, N. W., and DiGiusto, E. L. Effects of prenatal alcohol consumption on open-field behavior and alcohol preference in rats. *Psychopharmacology*, 1976, *46*, 163–168.
27. Branchey, L., and Friedhoff, A. J. Biochemical and behavioral changes in rats exposed to ethanol *in utero*. *Annals of the New York Academy of Sciences*, 1976, *273*, 328–330.
28. Martin, J. C., Martin, D. C., Sigman, G., and Radow, B. Maternal ethanol consumption and hyperactivity in cross-fostered offspring. *Physiological Psychology*, 1978, *6*, 362–365.
29. Abel, E. L. *In utero* alcohol exposure and developmental delay of response inhibition. *Alcoholism: Clinical and Experimental Research*, 1982, *6*, 369–376.
30. Osborne, G. L., Caul, W. F., and Fernandez, K. Behavioral effects of prenatal ethanol exposure and differential early experience in rats. *Pharmacology, Biochemistry and Behavior*, 1980, *12*, 393–401.
31. Riley, E. P., Lochry, E. A., Shapiro, N. R., and Baldwin, J. Response perseveration in rats exposed to alcohol prenatally. *Pharmacology, Biochemistry and Behavior*, 1979, *11*, 513–519.
32. Lochry, E. A., and Riley, E. P. Retention of passive avoidance and T-maze escape in rats exposed to alcohol prenatally. *Neurobehavioral Toxicology*, 1980, *2*, 107–115.
33. Lee, M. H., Haddad, R., and Rabe, A. Developmental impairments in the progeny of rats consuming ethanol during pregnancy. *Neurobehavioral Toxicology*, 1980, *2*, 189–198.
34. Riley, E. P., Shapiro, N. R., Lochry, E. A., and Broide, J. P. Fixed-ratio performance and subsequent extinction in rats prenatally exposed to ethanol. *Physiological Psychology*, 1980, *8*, 47–50.
35. Rosett, H. L., Snyder, P., Sander, L. W., Lee, A., Cook, P., Weiner, L., and Gould, J. Effects of maternal drinking on neonate state regulation. *Developmental Medicine and Child Neurology*, 1979, *21*, 464–473.
36. Havlicek, V., Childiaeva, R., and Chernick, V. EEG frequency spectrum characteristics of sleep rates in infants of alcoholic mothers. *Neuropaediatrie*, 1977, *8*, 360–373.
37. Vidwan, K. S., and Mangurten, H. H. Fetal alcohol syndrome. *Quarterly Pediatric Bulletin*, 1977, *3*, 17–21.

38. Yanai, J., and Ginsburg, B. E. Audiogenic seizures in mice whose parents drank alcohol. *Journal of Studies on Alcohol,* 1976, *37,* 1564–1571.
39. Da Silva, V. A., Ribeiro, M. J., and Masur, J. Developmental, behavioral and pharmacological characteristics of rat offspring from mothers receiving ethanol during gestation or lactation. *Developmental Psychobiology,* 1980, *13,* 653–660.
40. Yanai, J., and Ginsburg, B. E. Long-term effects of early ethanol on predatory behavior in inbred mice. *Physiological Psychology,* 1976, *4,* 409–411.
41. Elis, J., and Krsiak, M. Effect of alcohol administration during pregnancy on social behavior of offspring in mice. *Activitas Nervosa Superior,* 1975, *17,* 281–282.
42. Krsiak, M., Elis, J., Poschlova, N., and Masek, K. Increased aggressiveness and lower brain serotonin levels in offspring of mice given alcohol during gestation. *Journal of Studies on Alcohol,* 1977, *38,* 1696–1704.
43. Abel, E. L. Procedural considerations in evaluating prenatal effects of alcohol in animals. *Neurobehavioral Toxicology,* 1980, *2,* 167–174.
44. Holloway, J. A., and Tapp, W. N. Effects of prenatal and/or early postnatal exposure to ethanol on offspring of rats. *Alcohol Technical Reports,* 1978, *7,* 108–115.
45. Tumbleson, M. E., and Dexter, J. D. Ethanol consumption of gilts farrowed by alcoholic and control miniature swine. *Alcoholism: Clinical and Experimental Research,* 1980, *4,* 231.
46. Abel, E. L., and York, J. L. Absence of effect of prenatal ethanol on adult emotionality and ethanol consumption in rats. *Journal of Studies on Alcohol,* 1979, *40,* 547–553.
47. Anandam, N., Felegi, W., and Stern, J. M. *In utero* alcohol heightens juvenile reactivity. *Pharmacology, Biochemistry and Behavior,* 1980, *13,* 531–535.
48. Randall, C. L., and Boggan, W. D. Effect of low-dose prenatal alcohol exposure on behavior and the response to alcohol. *Alcoholism: Clinical and Experimental Research,* 1980, *4,* 226.
49. Harris, R. A., and Case, J. Maternal consumption of ethanol, barbital, or chloridazepoxide: Effects on behavior of the offspring. *Behavioral and Neural Biology,* 1979, *8,* 360–373.
50. Abel, E. L. Prenatal effects of alcohol on open-field behavior, step-down latencies, and "sleep time." *Behavioral and Neural Biology,* 1979, *25,* 411–413.
51. Anandam, N., Strait, T., and Stern, J. M. *In utero* ethanol retards early discrimination learning and decreases adult responsiveness to ethanol. *Teratology,* 1980, *21,* 25A.
52. Abel, E. L., Bush, R., and Dintcheff, B. A. Exposure of rats to alcohol in utero alters drug sensitivity in adulthood. *Science,* 1981, *212,* 1531–1533.
53. Abel, E. L., Dintcheff, B. A., and Bush, R. Behavioral teratology of alcoholic beverages compared to ethanol. *Neurobehavioral Toxicology and Teratology,* 1981, *3,* 339–342.
54. Taylor, A. N., Branch, B. J., Liu, S. H., Weichmann, A. F., Hill, M. A., and Kokka, N. Fetal exposure to ethanol enhances pituitary-adrenal and temperature responses to ethanol in adult rats. *Alcoholism: Clinical and Experimental Research,* 1981, *5,* 237–246.
55. Jones, K. L., and Smith, D. W. Offspring of chronic alcoholic women. *Lancet,* 1974, *2,* 349–353.
56. Mulvihill, J. J., Klimas, J. T., Stokes, D. C., and Riseberg, H. M. Fetal alcohol syndrome: Seven new cases. *American Journal of Obstetrics and Gynecology,* 1976, *125,* 937–941.
57. Hermier, M., Leclercq, F., Duc, H., David, L., and Francois, R. Le nanisme intra-utérin avec débilité mentale et malformations dans le cadre de l'embryofoetopathie alcoólique. *Pédiatrie,* 1976, *31,* 749–762.
58. Golden, N. L., Sokol, R. J., Kuhnert, B. R., and Bottoms, S. F. Maternal alcohol use and infant development. *Pediatrics,* 1982, *70,* 931–934.
59. Streissguth, A. P., Barr, H. M., Martin, D. C., and Herman, C. S. Effects of maternal alcohol, nicotine and caffeine use during pregnancy on infant mental and motor development at 8 months. *Alcoholism: Clinical and Experimental Research,* 1980, *4,* 152–164.

60. Lee, M., and Leichter, J. Effect of litter size on the physical growth and motivation of the offspring of rats given alcohol during gestation. *Growth*, 1980, *44*, 327–335.

61. Shaywitz, B. A., Griffieth, G. G., and Warshaw, J. B. Hyperactivity and cognitive deficits in developing rat pups born to alcoholic mothers: An experimental model of the expanded fetal alcohol syndrome. *Neurobehavioral Toxicology*, 1979, *1*, 113–122.

62. Abel, E. L., and Dintcheff, B. A. Effects of prenatal alcohol exposure on growth and development in rats. *Journal of Pharmacology and Experimental Therapeutics*, 1978, *207*, 916–921.

63. Robe, L. B., Robe, R. S., and Wilson, P. A. Maternal heavy drinking related to delayed onset of daughter's menstruation. In M. Galanter (Ed.), *Currents in alcoholism* (Vol. 7). New York: Grune and Stratton, 1980. pp. 515–520.

64. Fueyo-Silva, A., Menendez-Patterson, A., and Marin, B. Effectos del consumo prenatal del alcohol sobre la fecundidad, natalidad, crecimiento, apertura vaginal y ciclo sexual en la rata. *Reproducción*, 1980, *4*, 265–270.

65. Tittmar, H. G. Some effects of ethanol, presented during the prenatal period, on the development of rats. *British Journal on Alcohol and Alcoholism*, 1977, *12*, 71–83.

66. Boggan, W. O., Randall, C. L., and Dodds, H. M. Delayed sexual maturation in female $C_{57}BL/6J$ mice prenatally exposed to alcohol. *Research Communications in Chemical Pathology and Pharmacology*, 1979, *23*, 117–125.

67. Slavney, P. R., and Grau, J. G. Fetal alcohol damage and schizophrenia. *Journal of Clinical Psychiatry*, 1978, *39*, 782–783.

68. Clarren, S. K., Alvord, E. C., Sumi, S. M., and Streissguth, A. P. Brain malformations related to prenatal exposure to ethanol. *Journal of Pediatrics*, 1978, *92*, 64–67.

69. Peiffer, J., Majewski, F., Fischbach, H., Bierich, J. R., and Bolk, B. Alcohol Embryo- and fetopathy: Neuropathology of three children and three fetuses. *Journal of Neurological Science*, 1979, *41*, 125–137.

70. Jones, K. L., and Smith, D. W. Recognition of the fetal alcohol syndrome in early infancy. *Lancet*, 1973, *2*, 999–1001.

71. Kinney, H., Faix, R., and Brazy, J. The fetal alcohol syndrome and neuroblastoma. *Pediatrics*, 1980, *66*, 130–132.

72. Chernoff, G. F. The fetal alcohol syndrome in mice: An animal model. *Teratology*, 1977, *15*, 223–229.

73. Herrmann, J., Pallister, P. D., and Opitz, J. M. Tetraectrodactyly and other skeletal manifestations in the fetal alcohol syndrome. *European Journal of Pediatrics*, 1980, *133*, 221–226.

74. West, J. R., Hodges, C. C., and Black, A. C. Prenatal exposure to ethanol alters the organization of hippocampal mossy fibers in rats. *Science*, 1981, *211*, 957–959.

75. Barnes, D. E., and Walker, D. W. Prenatal ethanol exposure permanently reduces the number of pyramidal neurons in rat hippocampus. *Developmental Brain Research*, 1981, *1*, 3–14.

76. Davies, D. L., and Smith, D. E. Effects of perinatally administered ethanol on hippocampal development. *Alcoholism: Clinical and Experimental Research*, 1981, *5*, 147.

77. Abel, E. L., Jacobson, S., and Sherwin, B. T. In utero alcohol exposure: Functional and structural brain damage. *Neurobehavioral Toxicology and Teratology*, in press.

78. Douglas, R. J. The hippocampus and behavior. *Psychological Bulletin*, 1967, *67*, 416–442.

79. Bauer-Moffett, C., and Altman, J. Ethanol-induced reductions in cerebellar growth of infant rats. *Experimental Neurology*, 1975, *48*, 378–382.

80. Smith, D. E., and Davies, D. L. The effect of perinatally administered ethanol on the postnatal development of the Purkinje cell in the mouse cerebellum. *Society for Neuroscience Abstracts*, 1981, *7*.

81. Kornguth, S. E., Rutledge, J. J., Sunderland, E., Siegel, F., Carlson, I., Smollens, J., Juhl, U., and Young, B. Impeded cerebellar development and reduced serum thyroxine levels associated with fetal alcohol intoxication. *Brain Research*, 1979, *177*, 347–360.

82. Volk, B., Maletz, J., Tiedemann, M., Mall, G., Klein, C., and Berlet, H. H. Impaired maturation of Purkinje cells in the fetal alcohol syndrome of the rat. Light and electron microscopic investigations. *Acta Neuropathologica,* 1981, *54,* 19–29.

83. Davies, D. L., and Smith, D. E. Morphologic alteration in hippocampal CA1 pyramidal cells following perinatal ethanol administration. *Society for Neuroscience Abstracts,* 1981, *7.*

84. Hammer, R. P., and Scheibel, A. B. Morphologic evidence for a delay of neuronal maturation in fetal alcohol exposure. *Experimental Neurology,* 1981, *74,* 582–596.

85. Jacobson, S., Rich, J. A., and Tovsky, N. J. Retardation of cerebral cortical development as a consequence of the fetal alcohol syndrome. *Alcoholism: Clinical and Experimental Research,* 1978, *2,* 193.

86. Majdecki, T., Beskid, M., Skladzinski, J., and Marciniak, M. Effect of ethanol application during pregnancy on the electron microscopic image of a newborn brain. *Materia Medica Polona,* 1976, *8,* 365–370.

87. Volk, B. Verzögerte Kleinhirnentwicklung im Rahmen des embryofetalen Alkoholsyndromes. Lichtoptische Untersuchungen am Kleinhirn der Ratte. *Acta Neuropathologica,* 1977, *39,* 157–163.

88. Ullrich, K. H., and Dietzmann, K. A contribution to the postnatal enzymatic state of maturity of gyrus hippocampi in the embryofetal syndrome of the rat. *Experimental Pathology,* 1980, *18,* 170–174.

89. Druse, M. J., and Hofteig, J. H. The effect of chronic maternal alcohol consumption on the development of central nervous system myelin subfractions in rat offspring, *Drug and Alcohol Dependence,* 1977, *2,* 421–429.

90. Hofteig, J. H., and Druse, M. J. Central nervous system myelination in rats exposed to ethanol *in utero. Drug and Alcohol Dependence,* 1978, *3,* 429–434.

91. Hill, R. M.,and Tennyson, L. M. An historical review and longitudinal study of an infant with the fetal alcohol syndrome. In F. S. Messiha and G. S. Tyner (Eds.), *Alcoholism: A perspective.* Westbury, N.Y.: PJD Publications, 1980. pp. 177–201.

92. Goldstein, G., and Arulanantham, K. Neural tube defect and renal anomalies in a child with fetal alcohol syndrome. *Journal of Pediatrics,* 1978, *93,* 636–637.

93. DeBeukelaer M. M., Randall, C. L., and Stroud, D. R. Renal anomalies in the fetal alcohol syndrome. *Journal of Pediatrics,* 1977, *91,* 759–760.

94. Buffington, V., Martin, D. C., Streissguth, A. P., and Smith, D. W. Contingent negative variation in the fetal alcohol syndrome: A preliminary report. *Neurobehavioral Toxicology and Teratology,* 1981, *3,* 183–185.

95. Smith, C. M. The pharmacology of sedative/hypnotics, alcohol and anesthetics: Sites and mechanisms of action. In W. R. Martin (Ed.), *Handbook of experimental pharmacology.* New York: Springer-Verlag, 1977. pp. 413–538.

96. Myers, R. D. *Handbook of drug and chemical stimulation of the brain.* New York: Van Nostrand Reinhold, 1974.

97. Perry, T. L., Handsen, S., and Kloster, M. Huntington's chorea. Deficiency of gamma-aminobutyric acid in brain. *New England Journal of Medicine,* 1973, *288,* 337–342.

98. Sourkes, T. L. Parkinson's disease and other disorders of the basal ganglia. In G. J. Siegel, R. W. Albers, R. Katzman, and B. W. Agranoff (Eds.), *Basic neurochemistry.* Boston: Little, Brown, 1976. pp. 705–736.

99. Wurtzman, R. J. Effects of physiologic variations in brain amino acid concentrations on the synthesis of brain monoamines. In P. Seeman and G. M. Brown (Eds.), *Frontiers in neurobiology and neuroscience research.* Toronto: University of Toronto First International Symposium of Neurosciences Institute, 1974. pp. 16–34.

100. Boggan, W. O. Effect of prenatal ethanol exposure on neurochemical systems. In E. L. Abel (Ed.), *Fetal alcohol syndrome* (Vol. 3). Boca Raton, Fla: CRC Press, 1982, pp. 1–14.

101. Druse, M. J. Effects of maternal ethanol consumption on neurotransmitters and lipids in offspring. *Neurobehavioral Toxicology and Teratology*, 1981, *3*, 81–87.
102. Abel, E. L., Randall C. L., and Riley, E. P. Alcohol consumption and prenatal development. In B. Tabikoff, P. B. Sutker, and C. L. Randall (Eds.), *Medical and social aspects of alcohol abuse*. New York: Plenum Press, 1983.
103. Elis, J., Krsiak, M., and Poschlova, N. Effect of alcohol given at different periods of gestation on brain serotonin in offspring. *Activitas Nervosa Superior*, 1978, *20*, 287–288.
104. Elis, J., Krsiak, M., Poschlova, N., and Masek, K. The effect of alcohol administration during pregnancy on concentration of noradrenaline, dopamine and 5-hydroxytryptamine in the brain of offspring of mice. *Activitas Nervosa Superior*, 1976, *18*, 220–221.
105. Krsiak, M., Elis, J., Poschlova, N., and Masek, K. Increased aggressiveness and lower brain serotonin levels in offspring of mice given alcohol during gestation. *Journal of Studies on Alcohol*, 1977, *38*, 1696–1704.
106. Iwase, N. T., Tsuji, M., Takahashi, S., and Komura, S. An experimental study of the fetal alcohol syndrome using an animal model with mice: Neurochemical determination of monamines, polyamines, and nucleic acids in neonatal brain. *Nippon Arukoru Igakkai*, 1980, *15*, 9–18. (In Japanese)
107. Boggan, W. O., Randall, C. L., Wilson-Burrows, C., and Parker, L. S. Effect of prenatal ethanol on brain serotonergic systems. *Transactions of the American Society of Neurochemistry*, 1979, *10*, 186.
108. Rawat, A. K. Developmental changes in the brain levels of neurotransmitters as influenced by maternal ethanol consumption in the rat. *Journal of Neurochemistry*, 1977, *28*, 1175–1182.
109. Detering, N., Collins, R., Ozand, P. T., and Karahasan, A. M. The effects of ethanol (E) on developing catecholamine neurons. *Third International Symposium on Alcohol and Aldehyde Metabolizing Systems*, 1979, p. 24.
110. Shoemaker, W., Baetge, G., Azad, R., Sapin, V., and Bloom, F. Intrauterine exposure to ethanol: Effect on brain neuropeptides and catecholamines. *Teratology*, 1981, *24*, 57A–58A.
111. Rawat, A. K., and Kumar, S. Effects of maternal ethanol consumption on the metabolism of dopamine in rat fetus and neonate. *Research Communications in Psychology, Psychiatry and Behavior*, 1977, *2*, 117–129.
112. Lau, C., Thadani, P. V., Schanberg, S. M., and Slotkin, T. A. Effect of maternal ethanol ingestion on development of adrenal catecholamines and dopamine-beta-hydroxylase in the offspring. *Neuropharmacology*, 1976, *15*, 505–507.
113. Rawat, A. K. Development of histaminergic pathways in brain as influenced by maternal alcoholism. *Research Communications in Chemical Pathology and Pharmacology*, 1980, *27*, 91–103.
114. Chan, A. W. K., and Abel, E. L. Absence of long-lasting effects on brain receptors for neurotransmitters in rats prenatally exposed to alcohol. *Research Communications on Substances of Abuse*, 1982, *3*, 219–224.
115. Branchey, L., and Friedhoff, A. J. The influence of ethanol administered to pregnant rats on tyrosine hydroxylast activity of their offspring. *Psychopharmacology*, 1973, *32*, 151–156.
116. Thadani, P. V., Lau, C., Slotkin, T. A., and Schanberg, S. M. Effects of maternal ethanol ingestion on amine uptake into synaptosomes of fetal and neonatal rat brain. *Journal of Pharmacology and Experimental Therapeutics*, 1977, *200*, 292–297.
117. Bertolome, J. V., Schanberg, S. M., and Slotkin, T. A. Premature development of cardiac sympathetic neurotransmission in the fetal alcohol syndrome. *Life Sciences*, 1981, *28*, 571–576.
118. Abel, E. L. Prenatal alcohol exposure and activity: Effects not due to delayed maturation of cholinergically mediated inhibitory mechanisms. *Journal of Environmental Pathology, Toxicology, and Oncology*, in press.

CHAPTER 11

Risk Factors for Fetal Alcohol Syndrome/Fetal Alcohol Effects

Why some women give birth to fetal alcohol syndrome children whereas others do not, despite equal amounts of alcohol intake, is an enigma. For example, in the Cleveland prospective study of over 12,000 women, Sokol *et al.*[1] identified 204 "alcoholics." Of these 204 women, only 5 gave birth to FAS children.

Conceivably, mothers of FAS children differ from other alcoholic women in one or more important characteristics. However, no single characteristic has as yet been identified that places a particular alcoholic at greater risk than another for FAS. It is possible, on the other hand, that various risk factors may constitute a greater overall risk when taken in conjunction with one another than might otherwise be the case when they are considered individually.

Abel[2] tabulated information from over 300 clinical case studies of fetal alcohol syndrome. In many instances, information concerning the mothers was not recorded or was not available, so that assessment of risk factors vis-à-vis fetal alcohol effects must remain tentative until more conclusive evidence is available. Some of the information gathered from these case studies is presented below.

Maternal Age

Average maternal age of the mothers of fetal alcohol children is about 30 years, with a range of 15 to 53. Mothers of FAS children are thus well within the optimal reproductive age. The fact that women as young as 15 give birth to FAS children means that maternal age is not a critical factor for FAS.

Nutritional Status

Maternal prepregnancy weight was reported for only 10 out of the 358 case studies noted by Abel.[2] Average weight for these 10 women was 109 pounds. Average height was 5 feet, 5 inches.

According to the *Metropolital Life Insurance Tables,*[2] the average weight for a woman 5 feet 5 inches, with a medium frame, is 113–126 pounds. The mothers of fetal alcohol syndrome babies for whom such information is available are thus somewhat underweight for their size.

Weight gain during pregnancy is also far below the optimal 20–24 pound (9–11 kg) increase.[4] Although weight gain was found for only 18 out of the 311 mothers of fetal alcohol syndrome children by Abel,[2] these data also suggest that mothers of FAS children are undernourished: For 14 of these 18 women, average weight gain was 14 pounds, whereas the other 4 women actually lost weight during pregnancy!

Although inadequate maternal nutrition alone cannot account for the physical anomalies observed in FAS children (cf. reference 5), it does represent an important risk factor for many fetal alcohol effects. For example, Edwards *et al.*[6] recently evaluated pregnancy outcome and newborn growth patterns for women whose body weights were also 10% below standard for height. Comparisons were made with normal weight controls matched for age, race, parity, socioeconomic status, and smoking habits. Weight gain during pregnancy was not lower than normal for either group.

Premature delivery occurred in 23% of the infants of underweight women compared to 14% of the controls. Low Apgar scores (<7 at 5 min) also occurred more often in infants born to underweight women. Average birth weight of infants of underweight women was 2977 grams compared to 3208 grams for controls. Underweight women also delivered twice as many "low birth weight" (LBW) infants (16% vs. 8%) compared to controls. At 12 months of age, 31% of the children born to underweight women weighed below standard for length, compared to 19% for controls.

Thus, women who weigh 10% or more below standard for height, such as those identified in the clinical literature (and there is no reason to believe these women to be different from other mothers of FAS children), are at increased risk for premature delivery, low birth weight, low Apgar scores, and postnatal growth retardation, regardless of their alcohol consumption.

Women who are undernourished are also at risk for fetal alcohol syndrome, however, because they may attain higher blood alcohol levels and metabolize alcohol more slowly than women who drink the same but are more adequately nourished. The higher blood alcohol levels of these women would result from lower volumes of distribution (less body water) and slower rates of alcohol metabolism and elimination due to protein deficiency.

**Table 31. Effects of Liquid Ethanol Diets Containing
Different Protein Content on Blood Alcohol Levels and Pup
Weight at Birth[a]**

	BioMix 711-PR (41.4 g/l protein)	Revised diet 1226 (90.0 g/l protein)
Caloric intake	71.9 kcal/day	97.4 kcal/day
Protein intake	2.8 g/day	6.7 g/day
Ethanol intake	12.7 g/kg/day	13.2 g/kg/day
Blood alcohol level	147 mg%	66 mg%
Pup weight at birth	5.1 g/pup	6.7 g/pup

[a]Adapted from Wiener et al.[7]

An example of the effects of diet on risk for fetal alcohol effects is an experiment reported by Wiener and her associates.[7] In this study, pregnant rats were presented with two similar diets that differed primarily in their protein content. Both diets contained alcohol. The results of this study are shown in Table 31. As indicated by the table, the animals in each group consumed about the same amount of alcohol each day, but the animals on the higher protein diet had considerably lower blood alcohol levels, and as a result, the average weight of their offspring was significantly greater than that of the group with the lower protein diet.

Although animal experiments using pair-feeding techniques (see Chapter 12) have been cited as evidence that maternal undernutrition is not a likely explanation for FAS, this argument is valid only insofar as undernutrition *per se* is concerned. As suggested by the Wiener study,[7] undernutrition may be an important cofactor, along with alcohol, in the fetal alcohol syndrome.

Parity

Parity (see also "*Birth Interval,*" below) was found for only 190 women by Abel.[2] In most instances the FAS patient was not a firstborn (only 32 firstborns out of 190). In 66 cases, the women have given birth to 5 or more children. Several women had given birth to 10 or more children (see Table 32).

The FAS mother is thus multiparous. Since the average age for these women is 30, this suggests a very short interval between births for many women. Short intervals in general accelerate the rate of biological aging,[8] which in turn is associated with decreased nutritional support to the conceptus due to increased collagen deposition in the uterus[9] and increased risks of congenital malformations.[10]

Table 32. Birth Order of Children with Fetal Alcohol Syndrome[a]

Birth order	N cases
1st	32
2nd	44
3rd	33
4th	15
5th	14
6th	15
7th	14
8th	9
9th	4
10th	1
11th	4
12th	2
13th	0
14th	1
15th	1
16th	0
17th	0
18th	1

[a]Data drived from retrospective study by Abel.[2]

Later-born children of alcoholics are usually more seriously affected by FAE than their older siblings. Manzke and Grosse,[11] for example, reported a case study of seven children born to an alcoholic woman who drank regularly from age 17. Her first two children were normal. The third had delayed psychomotor development. The fourth and fifth had cardiac disorders. The fifth was also mentally retarded. The sixth child died 10 hours after birth due to a brain hemorrhage. The seventh was born with the "full-blown" FAS.

Fitze and his co-workers[12] reported a case study of five siblings born to an alcoholic mother. Again, anomalies in these children were progressively more serious with parity. The first child, born before the onset of alcoholism, was normal. The second child had low birth weight and postnatal growth retardation. The third child had pre- and postnatal growth retardation, microcephaly, and many of the structural anomalies seen in connection with the FAS. The fourth child had the full-blown FAS. The fifth child died at birth.

Other studies, some of which date back to the turn of the century (see, e.g., reference 13), have consistently noted an increased severity of symptoms with increasing age/parity among children born to alcoholic women. The most frequent effect in this regard has been a decrease in birth weight.

A major difficulty in assessing the impact of parity, birth interval, maternal age, etc., in conjunction with FAS/FAE is the confounding of these factors with drinking history *per se*. Thus far it has not been possible to determine if it is the duration of drinking or the interaction of drinking with parity, birth interval, or maternal age that is the critical factor accounting for the increased severity of symptoms in later-born children of alcoholic women.

Length of Gestation

Although gestational length appears to be a few days shorter for FAS infants, this shortened period cannot account for the markedly lower birth weights of these children. Furthermore, even when gestational age is taken into account, birth weight is still considerably below normal for gestational age. For example, in the retrospective study by Abel,[2] there were 100 term births for which birth weight was reported. In 79 of these cases, birth weight was still below 2500 grams.

Birth Interval

Short intervals between births (6–11 months) are often related to LBW.[14] Births that occur within 2 years of one another often lead to LBW for the following child. Short-term intervals between births also accelerate biological aging,[8] which decreases nutritional support to the conceptus.[9] Black women are particularly more likely than whites to give birth to an LBW child if birth interval is short (14.5% vs. 6.4%).

Since some mothers of FAS children are multiparous, shortened birth interval could contribute somewhat to the LBW of the FAS child. However, the fact that many of these children are firstborn suggests that shortened birth interval is not a major contribution to the LBW of the FAS child.

Sex Differences

Male children tend to weigh about 100–140 g less at birth than females. Although an initial sex bias in favor of girls with FAS was reported,[15] analysis of a larger number of cases did not find any support for this conclusion.[16] In the retrospective study carried out by Abel,[2] there were 148 male and 143 female cases of fetal alcohol syndrome. In any case, the weight difference between males and females at birth is too small to account for the much lower body weights of fetal alcohol syndrome children.

Marital Status

Unmarried women generally give birth to children that weigh less than those born to married women. Among whites, the percentage of low birth weight babies born out of wedlock is 9%, compared to 5% for "legitimate" babies; for blacks, comparable figures are 14% versus 10%.[14]

Examination of the clinical literature[2] leaves the distinct impression that mothers of fetal alcohol syndrome children often do not know who sired their children. In only 38 cases out of over 300 reported in the clinical literature was there any mention of the fathers. Since alcohol may affect sperm morphology (see below), paternal factors are an important question regarding risk factors in fetal alcohol syndrome.

Paternal Factors

The impact of paternal alcoholism on offspring is virtually unknown. Since many mothers of fetal alcohol syndrome children tend to be married to alcoholic men (out of 36 cases in the clinical literature in which fathers were mentioned, 29 fathers were described as "alcoholic"[2]), it is sometimes difficult to determine the role of maternal versus paternal contributions in the development of the fetal alcohol syndrome child.

Alcohol is capable of inhibiting spermatogenesis.[17] In male alcoholics who are able to produce an ejaculate, abnormalities in sperm morphology have been observed, including double-headed spermatozoa, irregularly arranged mitochondria, absence of acrosomes, anomalies in the acrosome, malformations of the nucleus, broken-off heads, curled tails, and distended midsections.[17,18]

While not all sperm produced by male alcoholics are damaged, the possibility exists that damaged sperm could fertilize an ovum. There is also some evidence that alcohol can produce mutagenic effects in humans. Obe and Herha,[19] for example, reported increased chromatid and chromosomal exchange aberrations in male alcoholics compared to nonalcoholics. An increase in the incidence of sister chromatid exchanges has also been noted in connection with alcohol exposure.[20,21] Obe and Ristow[22] reported that acetaldehyde, the primary metabolite of alcohol, can induce chromatid exchanges and cross-linking of DNA strands. Such effects on gametes could theoretically account for some of the adverse effects of being sired by an alcohol-consuming father.

Although there is no evidence of an increase in the frequency of abnormalities among children born to male alcoholics or offspring sired by male animals that consumed alcohol, some studies in animals are suggestive of other kinds of damage to the developing embryo or fetus.

A reduction in litter size, for instance, has been noted in conjunction with male alcohol consumption, suggesting that alcohol causes an increase in domi-

Table 33. Effects of Male Alcohol Consumption on Dominant Lethal Mutation Rates in Rats and Mice ($\bar{X} \pm SE$)

Species	Alcohol		Method of alcohol exposure	Control		Pair-feeding	Source
Mouse	4.4	.8	Intubation	7.2	.5	No	Badr and Badr[23]
Mouse	4	1	Liquid alcohol diet	8	2	No	Anderson et al.[24]
Mouse	10	5	Liquid alcohol diet	10	4	Yes	Anderson et al.[25]
Mouse	8.3	.6[a]	Liquid alcohol diet	8.7	.4[a]	Yes	Randall et al.[26]
	15.8	7.0[b]		14.5	3.0[b]		
Rat	7.0	2.5	Liquid alcohol diet	12.1	.5	No	Klassen and Persaud[27]
Rat	10.7	6.5	30% v/v in drinking water	14.0	1.7	No	Tanaka et al.[28]
Rat	11.2	.5[a]	15–30% v/v in drinking water	11.4	.5[a]	No	Chauhan et al.[29]
	10.3	.6		10.4	.6[b]		
Rat	No differences in resorptions or live fetuses[c]		Liquid alcohol diet			Yes	Bennett et al.[30]
Rat	Smaller litter size		8% v/v in drinking water			No	Pfeifer[31]

[a]Number of implantation.
[b]Percent prenatal mortality per litter.
[c]Abstract report, no data.

nant lethal mutations. These studies are summarized in Table 33. As indicated by the table, most studies reporting such an effect have not incorporated pair-fed control procedures. When such procedures were incorporated, differences in dominant lethal mutations between alcohol-exposed and control animals were no longer significant.

Table 34. Fetal or Newborn Body Weights (in Grams) of Animals Sired by Males Consuming Alcohol ($\bar{X} \pm SE$)

Species	Alcohol			Control		Pair-fed	Source
Mouse		.96	.16	.99	.07	Yes	Anderson et al.[25]
Mouse	(M)	1.09	.02	1.09	.02	Yes	Randall et al.[26]
	(F)	1.05	.02	1.04	.02		
Rat		2.84	.10	2.29	.07	No	Klassen and Persaud[27]
Rat		4.39	.77	4.73	.30	No	Tanaka et al.[28]
Rat		Not significant[a]				Yes	Bennett et al.[30]

[a]Brief abstract report, no data.

Table 34 summarizes a number of studies in which fetal or newborn body weights of animals sired by alcohol-exposed males are compared with those sired by controls. As indicated by the table, only when controls are not pair-fed is there a marked difference between alcohol-exposed and control offspring.

Placenta Size and Function

Placenta size is positively correlated with birth weight.[32] Alcohol-induced decreases in placental growth could thus be expected to affect fetal growth adversely. Although such decreases have been reported,[33] these appear to be isolated instances and have not been corroborated by other epidemiological data[1] or animal studies.[34,35]

Although Sokol and co-workers[1] did not observe placental pathology associated with maternal alcohol usage, some recent studies in animals have found such damage. Padmanabhan and his co-workers[36] reported that intraperitoneal injection of pregnant rats during organogenesis reduced placental weight and resulted in placental necrosis. The decidua basilis of the placentas of rats injected with alcohol also contained inflammatory cells.

In pregnant monkeys, intravenous administration of alcohol (35% v/v), resulting in a peak blood alcohol level of 250 mg%, produced a collapse of umbilical vasculature within 10 to 15 minutes after administration. This collapse resulted in severe fetal acidosis and hypoxia. Restoration of umbilical circulation occurred between 30 and 60 minutes after injection.[37]

Premature placental separation has also been reported to occur more frequently among alcoholics,[1,33] but the frequency of occurrence is too low to account for most fetal alcohol effects.

Maternal Infections and Complications of Pregnancy

Maternal infections and complications of pregnancy have been noted in several mothers of fetal alcohol syndrome children. Absence of such information does not necessarily indicate a good maternal health but may rather be due to omission of information. Among the most frequently encountered problems in the survey conducted by Abel[2] were cirrhosis (26 cases) and other liver problems (26 cases), anemia (3 cases), gastritis (9 cases), gastrointestinal bleeding (5 cases), delirium tremens (24 cases), kidney disorders (4 cases), diabetes (4 cases), goiter (2 cases), pancreatitis (4 cases), venereal disease (3 cases), and diptheria, tuberculosis, and ovarian tumors.

In their large-scale prospective study, Sokol and co-workers[1] reported that alcohol abusers had a higher incidence of uterine tetany, precipitous delivery, amnionitis, abruptio placentae, and meconium in the amniotic fluid. Streissguth and her co-workers[38] have also noted a higher incidence of preeclampsia, amnionitis, leakage of amniotic fluid, and meconium in the amniotic fluid in heavy drinkers compared to other women.

Maternal infections, e.g., rubella, venereal disease, are commonly associated with low birth weight, as are maternal hypertension, amnionitis, toxemia, renal disease, etc.[39] It is thus quite conceivable that poor maternal health and various complications of pregnancy may be important risk factors associated with alcohol consumption during pregnancy. These secondary factors may be responsible for some, if not much, of the intrauterine growth retardation and poor developmental status in fetal alcohol syndrome.

Hormonal Imbalances and Endocrinopathy

Although there are several cases in which mothers of fetal alcohol syndrome children were diabetic, there is little evidence that fetal alcohol effects are due to hormonal imbalance (See Chapter 7).

Genetic Factors

FAS is represented among the major racial groups, including Orientals (see Table 35). There does not appear to be a genetic-racial factor predisposing some women of their offspring to FAS. This does not exclude the possibility, however, that other genetic factors are involved in FAS. Three twin studies, in fact, suggest that genetic factors may affect the susceptibility to FAS (see Table 36).

Christoffel and Salafsky's report[42] of FAS in fraternal twin males is illustra-

Table 35. Racial Background of Mothers of Children with Fetal Alcohol Syndrome[a]

Racial background	N cases
Caucasian	194
Negro	48
Mulatto	1
American Indian	13
Indian/Caucasian	2
Oriental	6
Australian Aborigine	2

[a]Data derived from retrospective survey by Abel.[2]

Table 36. Fetal Alcohol Effects in Twins

	Dizygotic twins				Monozygotic twins	
	Christoffel and Salafsky[25]		Santolaya et al.[26]		Palmer et al.[27]	
	Twin A	Twin B	Twin A	Twin B	Twin A	Twin B
Birth weight (g)	1048	1540	2070	2090	1500	1600
Birth length (cm)	36.5	38.5	—	—	40.5	41.0
Head circumference (cm)	27.5	30.5	—	—	28.8	29.0
Apgar series (1 min/5 min)	7/8	5/7	9	8	8/9	8/9
Weight at 11 months	—	—	8200	6600	—	—
Length at 11 months	—	—	74	69	—	—

tive. The mother was a 30-year-old alcoholic who consumed at least 1 quart of red wine and an unspecified amount of hard liquor daily throughout pregnancy. The twins were born at 32 weeks' gestation. Birth statistics are presented in Table 36. Twin A was not only the more seriously affected in terms of birth weight and length, he also had several morphological abnormalities not observable in Twin B, such as simian creases and pronounced low-set and posteriorly rotated ears. Twin A was also more jittery. The authors state that had it not been for Twin A's more serious anomalies, they would not have detected FAS in Twin B.

A second case of dizygotic twin boys with FAS was reported by Santolaya and co-workers.[43] The mother was a 27-year-old alcoholic who drank 3 liters of beer and wine per day. The boys were born at 38 weeks' gestation. The difference between the twins in weight at birth was not as marked. No information was given regarding length or head circumference at birth. At 11 months of age one twin was measurably heavier and longer than the other (see Table 36). Twin B exhibited more pronounced physical features of FAS but was less retarded in terms of psychomotor development.

These two studies indicate that genetic factors may account for differential susceptibility to teratogens such as alcohol. It is also possible, however, that the differential severity of signs arose as a result of differences in placental and fetal blood supply, which affect the rate of embryonic development. In other words, due to differential blood supply, the twins may be chronologically the same age, but developmentally one twin might be slightly younger or older than the other. As a result, each twin could have been exposed to alcohol at a different stage of embryonic development, thus accounting for the differences in severity of symptoms.

The third twin study[44] involved monozygotic females born to a 22-year-old alcoholic woman who consumed at least 14 drinks of hard liquor a week. The twins were born after 36 weeks' gestation, and there was a single placenta and umbilical artery. Birth characteristics were very similar (see Table 36), but there were some differences. Whereas both exhibited small palpebral fissures, abnormal palmar creases, and various minor anomalies, Twin A had a partial ptosis and a shortened fifth finger digit not seen in Twin B. Twin B had a rudimentary accessory dimple and poor hip joint movement not seen in Twin A. The fact that these genetically similar twins had some slightly different anomalies indicates that genotype is not the sole reason for differential susceptibility to alcohol's teratogenic effects; nevertheless, genotype is certainly an important factor.

One way in which maternal genotype could contribute to FAS/FAE apart from tissue sensitivity is metabolic. Véghelyi and co-workers[45] have argued that the acetaldehyde levels achieved by the mother are critical in determining whether or not a child develops FAS. On the basis of their studies, they predict that FAS could occur in women who drink "lightly" or "moderately" if their blood acetaldehyde levels rise to 40 μM (normally, levels do not rise above 21–30 μM). One of their patients reached a level of 140 μM after drinking only .5 ml/kg alcohol. Thus, because of some genetically determined or acquired liver functional problem, acetaldehyde levels could rise to abnormally high levels, and the embryo/fetus would then be exposed to equally high levels of acetaldehyde, which is considerably more toxic than alcohol.

A number of studies have, in fact, suggested that some individuals may achieve higher blood acetaldehyde levels than others due to genetic factors. In one such study, for example, facial flushing (which has been associated with acetaldehyde[46]) occurred in 83% of Orientals who drank alcohol, compared to only 5% of a similarly tested group of non-Orientals.[47] In another study, native American Indians also responded to alcohol with facial flushing.[48] As suggested by these and related studies, some individuals may be more prone to fetal alcohol syndrome because of genetic factors that result in higher acetaldehyde levels in their mothers after drinking alcohol.

Although *in vitro* studies have demonstrated that alcohol is capable of exerting some of its actions on the developing fetus even when conversion to acetaldehyde is minimal,[49] this does not preclude acetaldehyde from acting *in vivo*.

Multiple Drug Use

Women who drink heavily are also likely to smoke heavily (1 or more packs of cigarettes per day) and to use other drugs. Cahalan and co-workers[50] reported that 36% of the women they categorized as heavy drinkers smoked more than one pack of cigarettes each day. Since that study was reported, an even greater association between drinking and smoking has been reported.

In their prospective study of pregnant women attending a maternity clinic in Boston, Ouellette and her associates[51] reported that 60% of the heavy drinkers smoked one or more packs of cigarettes a day. In a second study based at this center, 50% of the heavy drinkers smoked one pack a day, compared to 13.5% for those women who drank less.[52] Pregnant heavy drinkers were also more likely than other women to use marihuana (42.9% versus 14%), sedatives, barbiturates, and tranquilizers (13.9% versus 2%), and heroin (1.3% versus .4%).

In the prospective study of pregnant women conducted in Cleveland, 40% of the alcoholic women smoked one or more packs of cigarettes per day.[1] Pregnant alcoholics were 2.3 times more likely to be smokers and were 3.3. times more likely to be heavy smokers than pregnant nonalcoholics. Alcoholics were also 4 times more likely to be narcotics users, although the percentage of use among alcoholics was relatively low (5%). The link between heavy drinking and smoking and other drug use has also been noted in a prospective study from California.[53]

In this latter study, use of illicit drugs was 21 times higher among heavy drinkers compared to nondrinkers.

In the Boston and Cleveland studies, the patient populations were primarily low socioeconomic minority women. However, the women in the California study were mainly white middle class.

Smoking during pregnancy has been consistently shown to result in lowered birth weight, increased neonatal mortality and morbidity, and behavioral anomalies (see review by Abel[54]). The possibility that the combination of smoking and drinking during pregnancy may have a greater effect on fetal development than either smoking or drinking alone is suggested by several recent studies. For instance, Kaminski and her co-workers[33] noted a higher incidence of stillbirths and lower birth weights for women who both drank and smoked during pregnancy, compared to those who either drink or smoke but did not do both. Sokol and co-workers[1] reported that the combination of drinking and smoking increased the risk of intrauterine growth retardation 3.9-fold, compared to a 2.4-fold increase for drinking and a 1.8-fold increase for smoking. Similarly, Little and her co-workers[55] noted in their studies that women who drank relatively little during pregnancy but who also smoked gave birth to infants that weighed less than those born to women alcoholics who did not smoke.

There are also reports indicating that the behavior of newborns is affected more when mothers drink and smoke. Newborns exposed to both alcohol and smoking during gestation spent more time resting in an atypical sleep position than those exposed to the same amount of alcohol but not to smoking.[56]

Two-day-old infants born to mothers who both drank and smoked heavily during pregnancy performed significantly worse on two simple operant learning tasks (head turning and sucking) compared to infants born to mothers who either drank or smoked the same amount but did not do both.[57] Infants exposed to this combination have also been found not to suck as hard as those exposed to either alcohol or smoking alone.[58]

Poverty and Physical Stress

Mothers of FAS children are often from the lower socioeconomic classes of society. Numerous studies have shown that the risk of low birth weight and other birth defects is significantly increased among women who live in substandard housing and work at physically tiring jobs during pregnancy.[59,60]

Stressful life situations during pregnancy (e.g., marital discord) can also result in an increased risk of birth anomalies, including behavioral problems.[60]

Stressful life situations during pregnancy (e.g., marital discord) can also result in an increased risk of birth anomalies, including behavioral problems.[60] Since chronic drinking is often associated with stressful life conditions, it is conceivable that the combination of drinking and adverse psychosocial factors could also increase the risk of fetal anomalies to a greater extent than either drinking or stress alone.

Obstetric Factors

Yet another possibility accounting for some of the behavioral anomalies associated with fetal alcohol effects is that these problems arise during the intrapartum period. For example, out of the 86 FAS cases described in Abel[2] in which reference was made to type of birth, 14 infants were breech births (16%), 14 were born by Cesarean section, 1 was born by vacuum extraction, 1 was born by heavy traction, and in 1 instance birth had to be induced. In a sample of 68 FAS cases described by Majewski *et al.*,[61] there was also a 15% incidence of breech births. Breech birth generally occurs in only about 3% of births[62] and is associated with neonatal asphyxia, which may result in brain damage.[63] Children born by breech birth are at significantly higher risk for mental retardation[63] and "hyperactivity."[64] While breech presentation could be a secondary effect of maternal alcohol consumption, breech presentations do occur in the absence of chronic maternal alcohol abuse.[63] There is thus the possibility that alcohol is associated with, but not necessarily a causal factor in, breech presentation and therefore is secondarily rather than directly related to mental retardation.

Obstetric Medication

The use of anesthetics and analgesics in childbirth is another important consideration since alcohol exhibits cross-tolerance to many anesthetics and analgesics.[65,66] As a result of this cross-tolerance, more anesthetic/analgesic will be required to produce maternal narcosis/analgesia. Such medication can result in newborn behavioral depression and altered EEG activity lasting several days after birth,[67,68] inferior tracking and orientation to novel stimuli,[69] and decreased motor maturity, as well as increased newborn irritability.[70] In some instances, these disturbances have been observed as long as 4 months after obstetric medication.[71] Thus, all of the behavioral effects reported in conjunction with maternal alcohol consumption (see, e.g., references 72–74) could be due to intrapartum exposure to obstetric medication (cf. reference 75), especially since in many cases these studies were conducted during the first 3 days of life, a possibility acknowledged in some of these reports.[73]

Assuming that the alcoholic woman is not likely to deliver her child by the Lamaze method without obstetric medication, and the possibility that she may require more anesthetic than the nonalcoholic because of cross-tolerance between anesthetics and alcohol, there is a likely possibility that many of the behavioral anomalies seen in FAS children shortly after birth may not be directly related to maternal alcohol abuse during pregnancy but to intrapartum exposure to obstetric medication.

References

1. Sokol, R. J., Miller, S. I., and Reed, G. Alcohol abuse during pregnancy: An epidemiological study. *Alcoholism: Clinical and Experimental Research*, 1980, *4*, 135–145.
2. Abel, E. L. *Marihuana, tobacco, alcohol, and reproduction*. Boca Raton, Fla.: CRC Press, 1983.
3. Metropolitan Life Insurance Company Tables. *Statistical Bulletin*, 1977, *58*, 3–6.
4. Guyton, A. C. *Textbook of medical physiology*. Philadelphia: Saunders, 1976.
5. Smith, C. A. Effects of maternal undernutrition upon the newborn infant in Holland. *Journal of Pediatrics*, 1949, *30*, 229–243.
6. Edwards, L. E., Alton, I. R., and Barrada, M. I. Pregnancy in the underweight woman. *American Journal of Obstetrics and Gynecology*, 1979, *135*, 297–302.
7. Wiener, S. G., Shoemaker, W. J., Koda, L. Y., and Bloom, F. E. Interaction of ethanol and nutrition during gestation: Influence on maternal and offspring development in the rat. *Journal of Pharmacology and Experimental Therapeutics*, 1981, *216*, 572–579.
8. Arvay, A. Reproduction and aging. In A. V. Everitt and J. A. Burgess (Eds.), *Hypothalamus, pituitary and aging*. Springfield, Ill.: Charles C Thomas, 1976.
9. Finn, C. A., Fitch, S. M., and Harkness, R. D. Collagen content of barren and previously pregnant uterine horns in old mice. *Journal of Reproduction and Fertility*, 1963, *6*, 405–407.
10. Maibenco, H. C., and Krehbiel, R. H. Reproductive decline in aged female rats. *Journal of Reproduction and Fertility*, 1973, *32*, 121–123.

11. Manzke, H., and Grosse, F. R. Inkomplettes und Komplettes des Alkohol-Syndrom: Bei Drei Kindern einer Trinkerin. *Medizinische Welt,* 1975, *26,* 709–712.

12. Fitze, F., Spahr, A., and Pescia, G. Familienstudie zum Problem des embryo-foetalen Alkohol-syndroms. *Schweizerische Rundschau Medizin,* 1978, *67,* 1338–1354.

13. Sullivan, W. C. A note on the influence of maternal inebriety on the offspring. *Journal of Mental Science,* 1899, *45,* 489–503.

14. Eisner, V., Brazie, J., Pratt, M., and Hexter, A. The risk of low birthweight. *American Journal of Public Health,* 1979, *69,* 887–893.

15. Qazi, Q. H., and Masakawa, A. Altered sex ratio in fetal alcohol syndrome. *Lancet,* 1976, *1,* 42.

16. Abel, E. L. Sex ratio in fetal alcohol syndrome. *Lancet,* 1979, *2,* 105.

17. Lester, R., and Van Thiel, D. H. Gonadal function in chronic alcoholism. *Advances in Experimental Medicine and Biology,* 1977, *85A,* 399–414.

18. Semczuk, M. Further investigations on the ultrastructure of spermatozoa in chronic alcoholics. *Zeitschrift für Mikroskopisch-Anatomische Forschung,* 1978, *92,* 494–508.

19. Obe, G., and Herha, J. Chromosomal damage in chronic alcohol users. *Humangenetik,* 1975, *29,* 191–200.

20. Czajka, M. R., Tucci, S. M., and Kaye, G. I. Sister chromatid exchange frequency in mouse embryo chromosomes after in utero ethanol exposure. *Toxicology Letters,* 1980, *6,* 257–261.

21. Alvarez, M. R., Cimino, L. E., and Pusateri, T. J. Induction of sister chromatid exchanges in mouse fetuses resulting from maternal alcohol consumption during pregnancy. *Cytogenetics and Cell Genetics,* 1980, *28,* 173–180.

22. Obe, G., and Ristow, H. Acetaldehyde, but not ethanol, induces sister chromatid exchanges in Chinese hamster cells *in vitro. Mutation Research,* 1977, *56,* 211–213.

23. Badr, F. M., and Badr, R. S. Induction of dominant lethal mutation in male mice by ethyl alcohol. *Nature,* 1975, *253,* 134–136.

24. Anderson, R. A., Beyler, S. A., and Zaneveld, L. J. D. Alterations of male reproduction induced by chronic ingestion of ethanol: Development of an animal model. *Fertility and Sterility,* 1978, *30,* 103–105.

25. Anderson, R. A., Furby, J. E., Oswald, C., and Zaneveld, L. J. D. Teratological evaluation of mouse fetuses after paternal alcohol ingestion. *Neurobehavioral Toxicology and Teratology,* 1981, *3,* 117–120.

26. Randall, C. L., Burling, T. A., Lochry, E. A., and Sutker, P. B. The effect of paternal alcohol consumption on fetal development in mice. *Drug and Alcohol Dependence,* 1982, *9,* 89–95.

27. Klassen, R. W., and Persaud, T. V. N. Experimental studies on the influence of male alcoholism on pregnancy and progeny. *Experimental Pathology,* 1976, *12,* 38–45.

28. Tanaka, H., Suzuki, N., and Arima, M. Experimental studies on the influence of male alcoholism on fetal development. *Brain and Development,* 1982, *4,* 1–6.

29. Chauhan, P. S., Aravinkakshan, M., Kumar, N. S., and Sundaram, K. Failure of ethanol to induce dominant lethal mutations in Wistar male rats. *Mutation Research,* 1980, *79,* 263–275.

30. Bennett, A. L., Sorette, M. P., and Greenwood, M. R. C. Effect of chronic paternal ethanol consumption on 19-day rat fetuses. *Federation Proceedings,* 1982, *41,* 710.

31. Pfeifer, W. D. Adverse effects of paternal alcohol consumption on offspring in the rat. *Bulletin of the Psychonomic Science Society,* 1977, *10,* 246.

32. McLaren, A. Genetic and environmental effects of foetal and placental growth in mice. *Journal of Reproduction and Fertility,* 1965, *9,* 79–98.

33. Kaminski, M., Rumeau-Ruoquette, C., and Schwartz, D. Consumation d'alcool chez les femmes enceintes et issue de la grossesse. *Revue d'Epidémiologie Médecine Sociale et Santé Publique,* 1976, *24,* 27–40.

34. Wunderlich, S. M., Baliga, B. S., and Munro, H. N. Rat placental protein synthesis and peptide

hormone secretion in relation to malnutrition from protein deficiency or alcohol administration. *Journal of Nutrition*, 1979, *109*, 1534–1541.

35. Abel, E. L., and Greizerstein, H. B. Ethanol-induced prenatal growth deficiency: Changes in fetal body composition. *Journal of Pharmacology and Experimental Therapeutics*, 1979, *211*, 668–671.

36. Padmanabhan, R., Sreenathan, R. N., and Singh, S. Histopathological changes of the placenta following treatment with ethanol and acetaldehyde. *Teratology*, 1982, *26*, 13A.

37. Mukherjee, A. B., and Hodgen, G. D. Maternal ethanol exposure induces transient impairment of umbilical circulation and fetal hypoxia in monkeys. *Science*, 1982, *218*, 700–702.

38. Streissguth, A. P., Barr, H. M., and Martin, D. C. Offspring effects and pregnancy complications related to self-reported maternal alcohol use. *Developmental Pharmacology and Therapeutics*, 1982, *5*, 21–32.

39. Lechtig, A., Delgado, H., Irwin, M., Klein, R., Martorell, R., and Yarbrough, C. Intrauterine infection, fetal growth and mental development. *Tropical Pediatrics and Environmental Child Health*, 1979, *25*, 127–138.

40. Majewski, F. Über schadigende Einflusse des Alkohols auf die Nachkommen. *D Nervenarzt*, 1978, *49*, 410–416.

41. Root, A. W., Reiter, E. O., Andriola, M., and Duckett, G. Hypothalamic-pituitary function in the fetal alcohol syndrome. *Journal of Pediatrics*, 1975, *87*, 585–588.

42. Christoffel, K. K., and Salafsky, I. Fetal alcohol syndrome in dizygotic twins. *Journal of Pediatrics*, 1975, *87*, 963–967.

43. Santolaya, J. M., Martinez, G., Gorostiza, E., Aizpiri, J., and Hernandez, M. Alcoholismo fetal. *Drogalcohol*, 1978, *3*, 183–188.

44. Palmer, R. H., Ouellette, E. M., Warner, L., and Leichtman, S. R. Congenital malformations in offspring of a chronic alcoholic mother. *Pediatrics*, 1974, *53*, 490–494.

45. Véghelyi, P. V., Osztovics, M., and Szaszovsky, E. Maternal alcohol consumption and birth weight. *British Medical Journal*, 1978, *2*, 1365–1366.

46. Seto, A., Tricomi, S., Goodwin, D. W., Kolodney, R., and Sullivan, T. Biochemical correlates of ethanol-induced flushing in Orientals. *Journal of Studies on Alcohol*, 1978, *39*, 1–11.

47. Wolff, P. H. Ethnic differences in alcohol sensitivity. *Science*, 1972, *175*, 449–450.

48. Wolff, P. H. Vasomotor sensitivity to alcohol in diverse Mongoloid populations. *American Journal of Human Genetics*, 1973, *25*, 193–199.

49. Brown, N. A. Goulding, E. H., and Fabro, S. Ethanol embryotoxicity: Direct effects on mammalian embryos *in vitro*. *Science*, 1979, *206*, 573–575.

50. Cahalan, D., Cissin, I. H., and Crossley, H. M. *American drinking practices*. New Brunswick, N.J.: Rutgers Center for Alcohol Studies, 1968.

51. Ouellette, E. M., Rosett, H. L., Rosman, N. P., and Weiner, L. Adverse effects on offspring of maternal alcohol abuse during pregnancy. *New England Journal of Medicine*, 1977, *297*, 528–530.

52. Alpert, J. J., Day, N., Dooling, E., Hingson, R., Oppenheimer, E., Rosett, H. L., Weiner, L., and Zuckerman, B. Maternal alcohol consumption and newborn assessment: Methodology of the Boston City Hospital Prospective study. *Neurobehavioral Toxicology and Teratology*, 1981, *3*, 195–201.

53. Kuzma, J. W., and Kissinger, D. G. Patterns of alcohol and cigarette use in pregnancy. *Neurobehavioral Toxicology and Teratology*, 1981, *3*, 211–221.

54. Abel, E. L. Smoking during pregnancy: Effects on growth and development of offspring. *Human Biology*, 1980, *52*, 593–625.

55. Little, R. E., Schultz, F. A., and Mandell, W. Drinking during pregnancy. *Journal of Studies on Alcohol*, 1976, *37*, 375–380.

56. Landesman-Dwyer, S., Keller, L. S., and Streissguth, A. P. Naturalistic observations of new-

borns: Effects of maternal alcohol intake. *Alcoholism: Clinical and Experimental Research,* 1978, *2,* 171–177.

57. Martin, J. C., Martin, D. C., Lund, C. A., and Streissguth, A. P. Maternal alcohol ingestion and cigarette smoking and their effects on newborn conditioning. *Alcoholism: Clinical and Experimental oesearch,* 1977, *1,* 243–247.

58. Martin, D. C., Martin, J. C., Streissguth, A. P., and Lund, C. A. Sucking frequency and amplitude in newborns as a function of maternal drinking and smoking. In M. Galanter (Ed.), *Biomedical issues and clinical effects of alcoholism.* Grune and Stratton: New York, 1979. pp. 359–364.

59. Stewart, A. M. A note on the obstetric effects of work during pregnancy. *British Journal of Preventative and Social Medicine,* 1955, *9,* 57–61.

60. Stott, D. H., and Latchford, S. A. Prenatal antecedents of child health, development, and behavior. *Journal of the American Academy of Child Psychiatry,* 1976, *15,* 161–191.

61. Majewski, F., Bierich, J. R., Loser, H., Michaelis, R., Leiber, B., and Bettecken, F. Clinical aspects and pathogenesis of alcohol embryopathy: A report of 68 cases. *Münchener Medizinische Wochenschrift,* 1976, *118,* 1635–1642.

62. Barden, T. P. Perinatal care. In S. Romney, M. J. Gray, A. B. Little, J. A. Merrill, E. J. Quilligan, and R. Stander (Eds.), *Gynecology and obstetrics,* New York: McGraw-Hill, 1975.

63. Manzke, H. Morbidity among infants born in breech position. *Journal of Perinatal Medicine,* 1978, *6,* 127–140.

64. Fianu, S., and Joelsson, I. Minimal brain dysfunction in children born in breech presentation. *Acta Obstetrica et Gynecologica Scandinavica,* 1979, *58,* 295–299.

65. Han, Y. H. Why do chronic alcoholics require more anesthesia? *Anesthesiology,* 1969, *30,* 341–342.

66. Adriani, J., and Morton, R. C. Drug dependence: Important considerations from the anesthesiologist's viewpoint. *Analgesia Current Research,* 1968, *47,* 472.

67. Brazelton, T. B. Psychophysiologic reactions in the neonate. II. Effect of maternal medication on the neonate and his behavior. *Journal of Pediatrics,* 1961, *58,* 513–517.

68. Borgstedt, A. D., and Rosen, M. G. Medication during labor correlated with behavior and EEG of the newborn. *American Journal of Diseases of Children,* 1968, *115,* 21–24.

69. Conway, E., and Brackbill, Y. Delivery medication and infant outcome: An empirical study. *Monograph of the Society for Research in Child Development,* 1970, *35,* 24–34.

70. Standley, K., Soule, A. B., Copans, S. A., and Duchowny, M. I. Local regional anesthesia during childbirth: Effects on newborn behavior. *Science,* 1974, *186,* 634–636.

71. Friedman, S. L., Brackbill, Y., Caron, A. J., and Caron, R. F. Obstetric medication and visual processing in 4- and 5-month old infants. *Merill-Palmer Quarterly,* 1978, *24,* 111–128.

72. Landesman-Dwyer, S., Keller, L. S., and Streissguth, A. P. Naturalistic observations of newborns: Effects of maternal alcohol intake. *Alcoholism: Clinical and Experimental Research,* 1978, *2,* 171–177.

73. Martin, J. C., Martin, D. C., Sigman, P., and Radow, B. Maternal alcohol ingestion and cigarette smoking and their effects on newborn conditioning. *Alcoholism: Clinical and Experimental Research,* 1977, *1,* 243–247.

74. Streissguth, A. P., Martin, D. C., and Barr, H. M. *Neonatal Brazelton assessment and relationship to maternal alcohol use.* Paper presented at the 5th International Congress on Birth Defects, International Congress Series, No. *426,* 62.

75. Myers, R. E., and Myers, S. E. Use of sedative analgesic and anesthetic drugs during delivery: Bane or boon? *American Journal of Obstetrics and Gynecology,* 1979, *133,* 83–104.

CHAPTER 12

"Animal Models" for Fetal Alcohol Effects

Difficulties in separating cause and effect, in identifying mechanisms of action, and in assessing the contribution of various risk factors described in the previous chapter in conjunction with alcohol's effects have been difficult to resolve from the available clinical or epidemiological data. For example, speaking of the higher rates of mental retardation associated with maternal alcohol abuse at the turn of the century, Elderton and Pearson[1] contended that such retardation was not due to alcohol "but to certain physical and possibly mental characteristics which appear to be associated with the tendency to alcohol." Likewise, Rosenau[2] commented that "it is necessary to recognize that what may be inherited is not the result of alcoholism, but rather the predisposition which led the parents to become alcoholic." Writing in 1942, Haggard and Jellinek[3] espoused a similar viewpoint: "While alcohol does not made bad stock, many alcoholics come from bad stock. The offspring inherit the defects of the parents. . . ."

This nature–nurture issue has once again reasserted itself. For instance, Streissguth and her co-workers[4] have reported that children born to recovered alcoholics have significantly lower IQ scores than those born to nondrinking women. Likewise, Little and her associates[5] noted lower birth weights among children born to recovered alcoholics compared to offspring of nonalcoholics. Although prior chronic alcohol consumption by these recovered alcoholics could in some way have adversely affected their reproductive function, resulting in these fetal effects, it is also conceivable that preexisting differences between these women and nonalcoholics may have been responsible for these observations. Conceivably, there may be maternal "constitutional" factors that contribute to some of the effects associated with fetal alcohol exposure, e.g., low birth weight, lower IQ, which would occur even if the mother had not consumed alcohol.

Table 37. Effect of *in utero* Alcohol Exposure on % Anomalies in Mice

Source	Strain	Duration of exposure	Route exposure	Amount administered	% Anomalies
Chernoff[10]	CBA/J	Prior to and during preg-nancy	p.o. (liquid diet)	0 (EDC)[a] 15 20 25	0 36 100 100
	$C_3H/1g$	Prior to and during preg-nancy	p.o. (liquid diet)	0 (EDC) 20 25 30	2 78 100 100
Chernoff[11]	CBA	Prior to and during preg-nancy	p.o. (liquid diet)	0 (EDC) 20	~2[b] 100
	C_3H	Prior to and during preg-nancy	p.o. (liquid diet)	0 (EDC) 20	~2 ~80
	$C_{57}BL/6J$	Prior to and during preg-nancy	p.o. (liquid diet)	0 (EDC) 20	1 40
Giknis *et al.*[12]	Swiss Webster	Days 8, 10, 12, and 14 of pregnancy	i.p.	0 g/kg 4 6	1 4 11
	CD_1	Days 8, 10, 12, and 14 of pregnancy	i.p.	0 4 6	1 5 10
	$C_{57}BL/6J$	Days 8, 10, 12, and 14 of pregnancy	i.p.	0 4	7 13
	DBA/6J	Days 8, 10, 12, and 14 of pregnancy	i.p.	0 4	6 34

(continued)

Studies in Animals

Throughout this book frequent references have been made and will continue to be made to animal studies. Such studies in the area of fetal alcohol effects have been receiving increased attention (see, e.g., references 6–9) because of the numerous striking similarities between the results of these animal studies and the related clinical and epidemiological literature.

For example, Table 16 summarized studies of the effects of prenatal alcohol exposure on birth weight in animals. As in the clinical and epidemiological literature, a decrease in intrauterine growth is the most common effect of *in utero* exposure in animals.

Table 37. (*Continued*)

Source	Strain	Duration of exposure	Route exposure	Amount administered	% Anomalies
Kronick[13]	$C_{57}BL/6J$ x DBA/2J	(See below)	i.p.	(See below)	(See below)
Randall and Taylor[15]	$C_{57}BL/6J$	Days 5–10 of pregnancy	p.o. (liquid diet)	0 (EDC)	8
				17	7
				25	30
				35	39
Rasmussen and Christensen[16]	C_3H	Days 1–18 of pregnancy	p.o. (water)	0% v/v	3
				10	15
				20	73
Webster *et al.*[17]	$C_{57}BL/6J$	(See below)	i.p.	(See below)	(See below)

			Duration of exposure					
	Dose	Days	7	8	9	10	11	12
Kronick[13]	g/kg	%						
	6	Anomalies	17	34	60	51	3	14
			7	8	9	10	11	
Webster *et al.*[17]	g/kg	%						
	0	Anomalies	0	0	0	0	0	
	2.9		7	2	10	16	0	
	4.3		6	9	26	46	0	
	5.8		15	36	21	50	25	

[a]EDC = ethanol-derived calories.
[b]~ = approximately.

Table 10 summarized a number of studies in mice demonstrating that *in utero* alcohol exposure increases the incidence of resorptions (the equivalent of spontaneous abortions in humans).

Table 37 summarizes studies in mice demonstrating that prenatal alcohol exposure causes birth defects and shows that the incidence of these defects increases as the amount of exposure increases.

In Table 38 a summary of the kinds of anomalies that have been observed in conjunction with *in utero* alcohol exposure is presented. Virtually all of the anomalies noted in the clinical literature with respect to fetal alcohol exposure are represented in these studies.

The various animal "models" for fetal alcohol effects thus have clear face

Table 38. Teratogenic Effects of Alcohol in Animals

Effect	Source
Skeletal anomalies	
Syndactyly, adactyly, ectrodac-tyly, polydactyly	Czajka *et al.*[18]
	Giknis *et al.*[12]
	Kronick[13]
	Randall and Taylor[15]
	Randall *et al.*[21]
	Webster *et al.*[17]
	West *et al.*[19]
Missing bones (vertebrae, ster-num, supraoccipital)	Chernoff[10]
	Schwetz *et al.*[20]
Fusion and misalignment anomalies	Chernoff[10]
C.N.S. anomalies	
Exencephaly	Chernoff[10]
	Czajka *et al.*[18]
	Kronick[13]
	Randall and Taylor[15]
	Randall *et al.*[21]
	Schwetz *et al.*[20]
	Sulik *et al.*[22]
	Webster *et al.*[17]
Dilated ventricles	Chernoff[10]
	Rasmussen and Christensen[16]
Absent corpus callosum	Chernoff[10]
Hydrocephalus	Randall and Taylor[15]
	Randall *et al.*[21]

(continued)

validity. As such, these animal models provide an opportunity for more systematic studies of the relationships between prenatal alcohol exposure and subsequent anomalies that would otherwise be possible in human studies.

Thus, animal studies allow for the control of variables that are difficult to manage in human studies. As a result, the effects of alcohol can be assessed independently of, or in conjunction with, specific risk factors (e.g., maternal age, other drug use). Systematic studies in which alcohol is administered to women are also unethical and unconscionable. Consequently, one of the main remaining alternatives for delving further into the relationship between *in utero* alcohol exposure and embryo/fetal development is through experiments in animals. Studies in animals are also of importance because they permit evaluation of

Table 38. (*Continued*)

Effect	Source
Microcephaly	Rasmussen and Christensen[16]
	West *et al.*[19]
Anophthalmia, microphthalmia	Randall and Taylor[15]
	Randall *et al.*[21]
	Sulik *et al.*[22]
	Webster *et al.*[17]
Cardiac anomalies	
Ventricular septal defect	Chernoff[10]
	Giknis *et al.*[12]
	Randall and Taylor[15]
	Randall *et al.*[21]
Facial anomalies	
Low-set, absent ears, posterior rotation	Clarren and Bowden[23]
	Rasmusen and Christensen[16]
	Webster *et al.*[17]
Cleft lip or palate	Giknis *et al.*[12]
	Schwetz *et al.*[20]
	Webster *et al.*[17]
Shortening of nose	Rasmussen and Christensen[16]
Maxillary, mandibular hypoplasia	Webster *et al.*[17]
	Clarren and Bowden[23]
Deficient philtrum	Sulik *et al.*[22]
	Clarren and Bowden[23]
Urogenital anomalies	
Hydronephrosis, hydroureter	Kronick[13]
	Randall *et al.*[21]

treatments in a much shorter time frame than would be possible in human studies. For instance, assessment of prenatal exposure to alcohol on learning behavior might not be possible for several years in humans but could be assessed in a matter of weeks or months in animals. Moreover, these effects can be examined in a context in which postnatal histories can be rigidly monitored, a situation that is not possible in human studies. Animal studies also permit a more extensive examination of outcomes in terms of both malformations and behavioral aberrations. In recent years, numerous advances have been achieved in fetal alcohol research that were in no small measure due to the development of various animal analogues of fetal alcohol effects.

Although questions are often raised about the relevance of animal studies to the human situation, the fact that these animal models are able to duplicate virtually all reported clinical and epidemiological effects of *in utero* alcohol exposure should mollify even the most ardent critics who feel that the only proper study of man is man.

A related issue involves the many attempts to define criteria for animal models of "alcoholism"[10] and for fetal alcohol syndrome.[11] These attempts are unrealistic. For one thing, there is no unified concept of alcoholism. Just as there are many different kinds of cancer, there are also many "alcoholisms." Although cancer and alcoholism are both talked about as unitary disorders, this is hardly so for either. Definitions of *alcoholism* and *alcoholic* are vague, and the criteria outlined by paradigms for alcoholism or fetal alcohol syndrome are rarely met in all individuals. It is therefore unrealistic to ask that animals fulfill all these criteria. Duplication in animals of all the components associated with excessive drinking in humans is simply not a worthwhile preoccupation.

It is possible and worthwhile, on the other hand, to identify certain components associated with excessive alcohol consumption and to devise animal analogues for these particular components. For instance, if the question of human exposure to alcohol during pregnancy is of concern, a simple experimental analogue can be developed in animals as a representation of this human situation without being overly concerned about those social and psychological factors that maintain excessive drinking. The value of animal models rests on the identification and standardization of all factors that could influence the action of those factors that are of direct interest. Simulation by animal models of every known human concomitant of a particular behavior is not necessary for that model to be of value in understanding and learning more about a particular set of variables that may then be extrapolated to humans. Thus, if the biochemical, metabolic, neural, or behavioral consequences of exposure to alcohol are of interest, whether or not the animal voluntarily ingests alcohol is of minor importance. The model need only be concerned with the consequences of such exposure, not the factors that might precipitate excessive drinking. Methodologically, the means of exposure may be of importance in terms of their relevance to the way humans consume alcohol. But this is a different issue from that of the resemblance between "animal alcoholism" and "human alcoholism."

Methodological Issues

The value of any animal study for shedding light on a particular issue depends upon numerous issues, such as the species of animal being studied, the procedures incorporated in the design to control for various factors, or the methods of analysis. The following discussion will address in detail some of the more important factors that affect the outcome of fetal alcohol studies in animals.

Species

The choice of which animal species to use as an experimental model for studying fetal alcohol effects is an important consideration since different species exhibit different sensitivies to alcohol, have different gestation lengths, and have different behavioral repertoires, among other differences.

Chernoff's[10,11] studies demonstrating different blood alcohol levels in CBA and CH_3 mouse strains despite equivalent caloric intake emphasize the value of looking at different species and strains of animals for fetal alcohol effects. If Chernoff's data are extrapolated to the human condition, it could be argued that one reason some women give birth to fetal alcohol syndrome children while others do not, despite equivalent amounts of drinking, is that women differ markedly in pharmacokinetic variables such as absorption, metabolism, and elimination of alcohol.

Thus far, chicks,[26] rats,[27] mice,[21] cats,[28] dogs,[29] miniature swine,[30] sheep,[31] and monkeys[23,32] have all been used to study fetal alcohol effects. Some of the major advantages and disadvantages of these various species is this type of research, including the practical issue of cost, are reviewed by Boggan.[33] Since the rat and the mouse have been the most widely used species in fetal alcohol research, most of the comments dealing with animals will involve these two species, except where noted.

Method of Administration

The method of alcohol administration to animals is another important consideration. Human consumption, of course, occurs by mouth. Unlike humans, however, few animal species studied thus far will voluntarily consume alcohol to the point of intoxication or will maintain sufficient high blood alcohol levels for tolerance and dependence to occur. Currently, there are several different methods for administering alcohol and other drugs to animals. These methods are summarized in Table 39, along with advantages and disadvantages associated with each.

Neither the inhalation method (see, e.g., reference 34) nor the polydipsia method (see, e.g., reference 35) is used very frequently in fetal alcohol research. The intraperitoneal route of administration has been used to some extent (see, e.g., references 12, 13, and 17), but it is frequently criticized in pregnancy research because of the many disadvantages listed in Table 39.

The three main methods of alcohol administration to pregnant animals are intubation, placement of alcohol in drinking water, and placement of alcohol in a liquid diet. Of these, the second is the least satisfactory since it does not result in consumption of enough alcohol to maintain blood alcohol levels above 100 mg%—a level that on empirical evidence seems minimally necessary to reliably observe teratogenic effects.

Table 39. Advantages and Disadvantages of Methods of Alcohol Administration in Fetal Alcohol Research

Method	Advantages	Disadvantages
Intubation	1. Each animal receives same dose at same time 2. Dose-response relations can be studied 3. High blood alcohol levels can be sustained at high doses 4. Same dosage levels can be maintained all through pregnancy 5. Similar to human route of consumption 6. Relative ease of administration 7. Relatively inexpensive	1. Stressful 2. Unlike human usage 3. Possible gastric irritation 4. High rate of pregnancy loss with high doses 5. Can cause marked reductions in food and water intake 6. Death due to injection into lung 7. Labor-intensive
EtOH as sole fluid	1. Nonstressful 2. Ease of administration 3. Inexpensive	1. Animals do not voluntarily drink very concentrated solutions because of aversive taste so blood alcohol levels are relatively low 2. Wide variability in consumption 3. Decreased fluid and food consumption at higher ethanol intakes 4. Decreased consumption just before parturition 5. Bottles may leak
Liquid EtOH diet	1. Nonstressful 2. Steady blood alcohol levels 3. Balanced diet associated with alcohol intake 4. Similar to human route of consumption 5. Ease of administration	1. Wide variability in intersubject rates of consumption 2. Variability in intrasubject consumption from day to day 3. Decreased consumption just prior to parturition 4. Dietary components may separate 5. Nutritional adequacy of various diets is questionable

(*continued*)

Table 39. (*Continued*)

Method	Advantages	Disadvantages
		6. Excessive consumption of water for *ad lib* controls
		7. Costly
		8. Bottles may clog
Inhalation	1. Stable, high blood alcohol levels	1. Unlike human route of exposure
	2. Ease of administration	2. Irritation of respiratory passages
	3. Can generate dose–response effects	3. Marked reductions in food and water consumption
		4. Local irritation of eyes, nose, skin, etc.
		5. Can treat only a few animals per day
Intraperitoneal	1. Rapid absorption and high blood alcohol levels	1. Possible rupture of amniotic sac
	2. Dosage easily controlled	2. Possible injection of fetus
	3. Can generate dose–response relations	3. Local irritation
	4. Ease of administration	4. Peritonitis
	5. Inexpensive	5. Stressful
Polydipsia	1. High levels of consumption	1. Initial decrease in body weight required
	2. Similar to human route	2. Unsuitable for large numbers of animals
		3. Relatively expensive equipment needed
		4. Large volumes of fluid ingested
"Pup in the cup"	1. Control over dosage received by pups	1. Time-consuming
	2. Control over time of exposure	2. Unsuitable for large numbers of animals
	3. Control over pair-feeding of neonates	3. Composition of milk is unlike maternal milk
	4. Avoidance of maternally mediated effects	4. Deprivation of tactual olfactory, and other sensory cues from mother.

The intubation method consists of delivery of solutions of alcohol via a tube directly into the stomach. Control animals are intubated with either water or an isocaloric sucrose solution. This method has the advantage of delivering specific amounts of alcohol at specific times. As a result, within-subject variability in terms of alcohol exposure is considerably reduced in comparison to situations in which animals self-administer alcohol. Dosages can be administered all at once or at different times of the day. The former procedure will result in a larger dose of drug, which will render animals more comatose and produce higher blood alcohol levels than will the latter. The latter procedure will produce lower blood alcohol levels, but this will be sustained for a longer time.

The main disadvantages of the intubation method are that it can be stressful to animals and can be time-consuming. It should be pointed out with respect to the stress component, however, that alcohol-treated animals will be less stressed than controls by this procedure since alcohol-treated animals are often sedated at the time of treatment.

The other widely used method of administration is via liquid diet. In this procedure, alcohol is added to commercially available diets (e.g., Sustacal, BioServ) or to specifically prepared diets, along with vitamin and mineral supplements. For control animals, isocaloric carbohydrate is substituted for alcohol-derived calories. Although sucrose is the most frequently used carbohydrate substitute, dextrose has also been used. The diets are usually described in terms of ethanol-derived calories (EDC). A representative composition of the amount of diet, ethanol, and sucrose presented to animals given a 35%, 17.5%, and 0% ethanol-derived caloric diet is illustrated in Table 40.

Some of the advantages of this method are that it does not require handling of animals and is less time-consuming than other methods such as intubation.

Animals will ingest fairly large amounts of alcohol (e.g., 13 g/kg/day), and blood alcohol levels of over 200 mg% have been reported. On the negative side, there is a great deal of variability in patterns of ingestion. Rats and mice do not eat all their food over a short time but rather space their meals over the 24-hour

Table 40. Composition of Liquid Alcohol Diet for Rats

| | | Amount (per 1000 ml) | |
Ingredient	Control diet (0% EDC)	17.5% EDC	35% EDC
Sustacal	641 ml	641 ml	641 ml
Ethanol (99.9%)	0 ml	32 ml	63 ml
Sucrose	87.5 g	43.8 g	0 g
Vitamins	2.4 g	2.4 g	2.4 g
Tap water	359 ml	327 ml	296 ml

feeding period. This means that in the alcohol-treated group blood alcohol levels will be high at different times for different animals. In other words, animals in the alcohol-exposed group are not homogeneously exposed to alcohol. If critical events occur in the development of fetuses during alcohol exposure, some fetuses could be more affected than others, resulting in greater within-group variability in outcome. Daily consumption of diet also tends to vary, making it difficult to generate reliable dose–response relations.

There is also disagreement about the nutritional adequacy of the diets being used. This point has been argued most cogently by Wiener and her associates.[36] The type of diet animals are fed has implications both for the control procedures (discussed in more detail below) incorporated in fetal alcohol studies and for blood alcohol levels.

With lab chow (e.g., Teklad, American Institute on Nutrition) animals can choose when to drink and eat. With a liquid diet, food and fluid are consumed at the same time, and animals may consume more fluid when ingesting a liquid diet than with lab chow. This is especially so for animals given *ad lib* access to the control diet (see below). In Figure 22 the fluid intake of pregnant animals on a liquid diet (BioServe) is compared with fluid consumption for pregnant rats on two solid diets—A.I.N. and Taklad. As indicated by the figure, fluid intake is considerably greater with the liquid diet, although total food consumption is not very different. Total maternal weight gain during pregnancy is also slightly greater on the liquid diet, but pup weight at birth is almost identical in all groups. The latter, of course, is the most important consideration in assessing the nutritional adequacy of a diet and in devising control procedures for fetal alcohol effects.

In addition to composition, the nutritional adequacy of a particular diet is a very important factor in fetal alcohol research since diet composition will affect blood alcohol levels. Wiener and her associates[36] compared maternal blood alcohol levels in two diets—BioMix 711-PR, which contained 41.4 grams per liter of protein, and a revised diet (#1226), which contained 90.0 grams per liter of protein. Although fluid consumption was similar, maternal blood alcohol levels (and hence fetal blood alcohol levels) were considerably lower in those ingesting the diet that contained more protein.

The important points about the nutritional adequacy of diets for animal studies in fetal alcohol research is that (1) these diets should best be evaluated in terms of fetal outcome, and (2) nutritional factors may interact with alcohol exposure to place the fetus more at risk for fetal alcohol effects.

Control Procedures

As noted previously, one of the advantages of experimenting with animals is the potential for matching animals on many variables so that only those

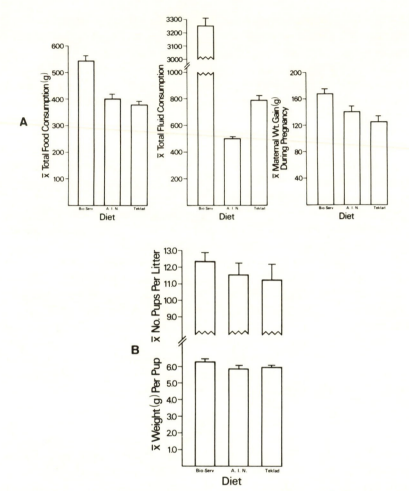

Figure 22. (A) Food and fluid consumption and maternal weight gain, and (B) litter size and weight per pup at birth as a function of maternal diet during pregnancy. Data from Abel.[6]

variables that are of interest distinguish experimental from control subjects. Thus, animals can be matched for species, strain, age, weight, breeding history, prior drug exposure, and other factors.

Perhaps the most important control procedure that can be brought to bear on fetal alcohol research with animals is that associated with alcohol's secondary effects on food and water consumption. While alcohol's pharmacological actions on the fetus are generally the issue of interest, alcohol is also a source of energy, producing 7.1 calories per gram. These are "empty" calories since they provide no nutrients. They have the effect, however, of reducing maternal caloric intake from sources that do provide nutrients. The resultant decrease in food consumption means that alcohol consumption is confounded with maternal undernutrition.

The effects of alcohol exposure on food and water consumption by pregnant rats is illustrated in Figure 23. As indicated by the figure, as the dosage of alcohol the animal receives increases, food *and* water consumption decreases. This basic association between alcohol exposure and food and water consumption must be considered before any unequivocal conclusions can be made regarding alcohol's pharmacological effects on the developing fetus.

The most commonly used method to control for this source of confounding is the pair-feeding or yoked-feeding technique. By this technique, the control group is given the same amount of calories as that consumed on the previous day by the alcohol-treated group. This can be done by matching each animal in the control group with one animal in the alcohol group (individual pair-feeding) or by averaging the food consumption per day for the alcohol group and giving this average amount to the control group (average pair-feeding). The individual method allows more careful matching of animals but is more time-consuming and more subject to loss of animals from the experiment since, if either the alcohol-exposed or the pair-fed animal is removed from the study, both animals will be lost.

With the intubation method (see above), pair-feeding should be done by giving the control group the same amount of food *and* water as that consumed on the previous day by alcohol-consuming animals. (Frequently, animals are only pair-fed and not also pair-watered.) With the liquid diet procedure, control animals also receive the same amount of food as alcohol-treated animals, but sucrose or some other carbohydrate is substituted for the alcohol calories.

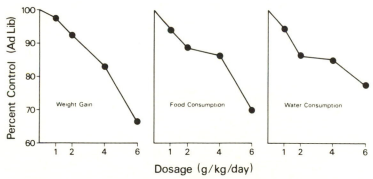

Figure 23. Weight gain and food and water consumption during pregnancy in rats treated throughout pregnancy with alcohol, relative to non-drug-treated animals given *ad lib* food and water. Data from Abel.[6]

A second level of control is often included in fetal alcohol studies, consisting of a group of animals allowed *ad lib* access to food and water. By comparing alcohol-exposed animals with pair-fed and *ad lib* control animals, pharmacological effects can be assessed in the context of nutritional effects. For example, if alcohol-treated animals differed from *ad lib*-fed animals but not pair-fed animals, this difference would reflect secondary effects of alcohol on nutritional status rather than alcohol's direct pharmacological effects on the fetus. However, if alcohol-treated animals differed from pair-fed animals as well, then this difference could be more readily attributed to alcohol's pharmacological effects on the fetus.

The importance of the *ad lib* control group for assessing alcohol's effects is illustrated in Table 41. The data presented in this table are from a study of the prenatal effects of alcohol in rats on muricide. Pregnant rats in this study were intubated with either 4 or 6 g/kg/day of alcohol throughout gestation. A second group was pair-fed and pair-watered with these animals, whereas a third control group was given *ad lib* access to food and water. Offspring were removed at birth and were placed with non-drug-treated dams. During adulthood, these offspring were food-deprived and a mouse was introduced into their cages. The data in Table 41 show that while muricide was significantly decreased in alcohol-exposed females compared to *ad lib*-fed females, alcohol-exposed animals did not differ from pair-fed controls. This observation indicates that the decrease in muricidal behavior on the part of alcohol-exposed females was due to alcohol's secondary effects on nutritional status rather than to its direct pharmacological effects on the developing fetus.

Although seemingly an easily performed technique, pair-feeding is not without its problems and subtleties. For instance, even if animals are matched for body weight, age, etc., differences in metabolic rate may mean that one animal may require considerably more food to maintain its body weight than another. In other words, pair-feeding does not equate animals for caloric "need." Differences in metabolic rate may explain why in some cases control animals do not consume all the food allotted to them although such allotments are generally well below what most animals consume per day.

Table 41. Prenatal Effects of Ethanol on Muricide

	Males					Females				
Group[a]	C	4	4P	6	6P	C	4	4P	6	6P
N	10	11	23	13	12	12	10	10	12	11
Percent muricide	40	27	36	36	42	50	50	36	8	9

[a]C = nontreated, *ad lib*-fed controls; 4 = intubated with 4/g/kg/day; 4P = pair-fed with group 4 animals; 6 = intubated with 6 g/kg/day; 6P = pair-fed with group 6 animals.

There is also a difference in the pattern by which food is consumed. Experimental animals given alcohol are permitted *ad lib* access to food and tend to space their meals over 24 hours. Pair-fed animals, on the other hand, are food-deprived and tend to gobble their allotted food as soon as it is given them. As a result, they may be without food for most of the 24-hour feeding period.

Another important consideration with respect to pair-feeding is that alcohol affects absorption of nutrients across the intestine and the placenta.[37,38] As a result, alcohol-treated animals could still be undernourished relative to pair-fed animals. If the diet eaten by animals is only marginal in meeting nutritional needs, alcohol's effects on absorption of nutrients could result in significant undernutrition.

Alcohol also interferes with utilization of nutrients. For example, even though some alcoholics have a caloric intake above that needed to maintain normal body weight, they are still underweight.[39] This alcohol-related "energy wastage" has been demonstrated experimentally by comparing body weight changes in men given the same daily amount of calories in the form of alcohol or chocolate. When alcohol was the caloric source, body weight did not change over the 44-day test period. When chocolate was the caloric source, body weight increased by about 3 grams.[40] In the present context, a noteworthy observation is that, despite pair-feeding, pregnant rats given alcohol often weigh less than their pair-fed controls.[13,14,17,41]

In addition to these effects on absorption and utilization of nutrients, excessive alcohol consumption produces vomiting and diarrhea and impairs absorption of water (up to 4 times) in humans.[39] These effects on bodily fluids could be expected to affect electrolyte balance and could account for studies showing electrolyte imbalances in rat fetuses following chronic alcohol exposure.[42]

Despite all these problems associated with controlling for nutritional differences between alcohol-treated and pair-fed animals, pair-feeding still represents the most important control procedure for assessing secondary effects of alcohol intake on nutritional status.

Drug Dosage

Determination of dose–response relations should be an essential component of any study of drug action. By varying the amount of drug exposure, it is possible to determine threshold levels for particular effects as well as the relationship between drug levels and magnitude of effect. In some instances the test measure may be too insensitive to reveal differences between animals. Unless a number of doses are studied, however, it is not possible to determine if the test is insensitive or if there is indeed no effect of drug exposure. Figure 24 illustrates the importance of evaluating more than one dose in behavioral teratology. These data were taken from a study by Riley and co-workers[44] investigating the effects

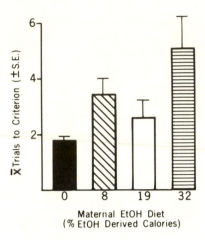

Figure 24. Passive avoidance learning in 18-day-old rats prenatally exposed to alcohol. Data from Riley *et al.*[43]

of prenatal alcohol exposure on reversal learning. Pregnant animals consumed 0%, 8%, 19%, or 32% ethanol-derived calories. As indicated by the figure, offspring of mothers consuming the 8% or the 19% diet did not differ from controls, whereas those born to mothers consuming the 32% diet were significantly worse in learning the reversal problem. Had only the 19% diet been studied, one might have concluded that alcohol exposure was not behaviorally teratogenic or that the test was not sensitive enough to differentiate between alcohol-exposed and control animals.

Postnatal Factors

In teratological studies examining morphological changes, animals are sacrificed prior to birth so that postnatal considerations are irrelevant. In behavioral teratological studies, however, offspring must be kept alive and, where possible, variables intervening between prenatal drug exposure and testing must be assessed and controlled for. In rats and mice, considerable development occurs postnatally, so events occurring after birth can have marked influences on later behavior. One such event that is of major importance is the interaction between the mother and her offspring. If drug exposure during pregnancy does not have any residual effects on maternal behavior or lactation, then potential confounding of prenatal drug exposure and impairment of postnatal maternal behavior or lactation would not be a consideration. Residual effects may occur, however, and therefore the most conservative approach to avoiding this problem is to use a fostering procedure after birth.

There are several methods by which fostering may be accomplished. The most straightforward is to place all offspring with a nontreated mother that has given birth at the same time as the biological mother. This procedure necessitates removal of the mother's own litter, which could introduce some stress to the mother and thus in turn affect her behavior. A second method is to cross-foster all offspring among all mothers. This will result in either four or nine groups, depending on whether an *ad lib*-fed group (see above) is included in the design. Usually, only the experimental and pair-fed groups are cross-fostered, resulting in the formation of four groups: alcohol mothers with alcohol-exposed offspring, alcohol mothers with pair-fed offspring, pair-fed mothers with alcohol-exposed offspring, and pair-fed mothers with pair-fed offspring. This cross-fostering paradigm is used, for example, in the studies by Martin and co-workers[45] and Shaywitz and his associates.[46] This paradigm, including provision for *ad lib*-fed mothers, is incorporated into the study described by Osborne and his co-workers.[41]

The cross-fostering design has the advantage over the more straightforward surrogate-fostering approach of allowing more information to be obtained about the contribution of maternal and offspring effects. Leaving alcohol mothers to raise alcohol-exposed offspring also more closely resembles the situation in which children born to alcoholic women remain with their biological mothers. The disadvantage of this method, of course, is that considerably greater numbers of animals are needed to balance all groups, and if more than one dose of drug is being evaluated, it becomes considerably more difficult to cross-foster.

One of the residual effects the surrogate-fostering procedure may circumvent is depressed postnatal maternal body weight. For example, Fernandez and Vorhees[47] noted that maternal body weight reductions were observable postnatally in rats even though mothers were intubated with alcohol only on gestation days 10–14.

Figure 25 illustrates possible residual effects on maternal–offspring interactions when alcohol-treated mothers are left in the cage with their newborn offspring. In this study, pregnant animals were intubated with 2 g/kg/day and pup retrieving behavior was evaluated within 24 hours of birth. As evident from the figure, mothers exposed to alcohol took significantly longer to retrieve pups compared to control dams.

Figure 26 illustrates the effects of daily maternal treatment with 6 g/kg/day of alcohol on cannibalism on postnatal days 1 and 2. As indicated by the figure, dams exposed to alcohol engaged in significantly more cannibalism than pair-fed mothers. Also worth noting is that pair-fed mothers also engaged in more cannibalism than *ad lib*-treated mothers.

In this second study of maternal behavior, offspring were born to non-drug-treated dams and were placed in the cages with alcohol-treated, pair-fed, and *ad lib*-fed dams. The fact that differences in maternal behavior occurred in response

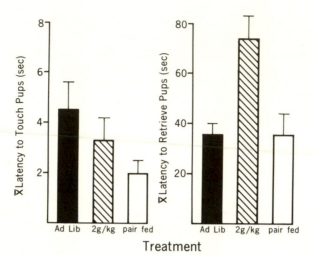

Figure 25. Latency of mother rats intubated with alcohol during pregnancy to touch and retrieve pups. Data from Abel.[49]

to these ''normal'' neonates indicates that alcohol exposure during pregnancy can have residual effects postnatally. In large measure, however, this effect was due to the decreased food intake associated with alcohol administration.

In a third study using the liquid diet method of alcohol administration rather than intubation, alcohol-exposed dams did not differ in responsiveness to ''nor-

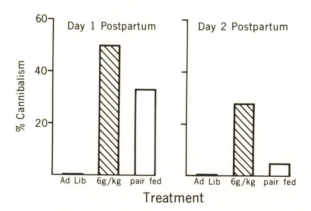

Figure 26. Effects of intubation during pregnancy with 6g/kg of alcohol on postnatal cannibalism in mother rats. Data from Abel and Dintcheff.[27]

mal'' pups compared to to pair-fed controls, but nontreated mothers spent significantly less time in the vicinity of alcohol-exposed pups compared to pair-fed pups. These data are shown in Figure 27 and suggest that alcohol exposure during gestation can also have residual effects on pup behavior such that mothers are less attentative postnatally. As far as residual effects on mothers is concerned, it appears that the intubation procedure can have a significant residual effect on maternal behavior, whereas the liquid diet method is less likely to do so. There is, in fact, little evidence to indicate that the reported effects of prenatal alcohol exposure in animals is modified in any way by postnatal maternal factors when animals are fed by liquid diet.[7] One reason that residual effects on maternal behavior are observed with the intubation method is that alcohol was administered up to the day of birth, whereas with the liquid diet method, alcohol administration ceased 1 or 2 days before birth.

Testing Considerations

In evaluating the behavior of alcohol-exposed animals compared to controls, it is important to keep in mind the possibility that differences may arise from impaired sensory or motor abilities rather than from impaired cognitive function. Physical size is another important consideration since one of the most common effects of prenatal alcohol exposure is reduced body weight during adulthood (see above), and this reduction can affect behavior.

Reduced body size may affect motivation, for example. Smaller rats have

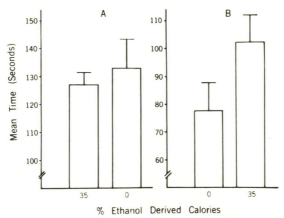

Figure 27. (A) Responsiveness of alcohol-consuming and pair-fed dams to newborn pups. (B) Responsiveness of nontreated dams to alcohol-exposed and pair-fed newborn pups. Data from Abel.[50]

lower shock thresholds than larger rats.[51] These lower shock thresholds may make animals more emotionally responsive. Depending on the complexity of the task, this increased responsiveness could facilitate or interfere with performance.[52]

Tasks that are appetitively motivated may also be affected by pretest differences in body weight. If food is used to reward animals, the food reward will be proportionately larger for the smaller animals. If food deprivation is used to motivate animals to respond for food, depriving animals for a fixed period of time or reducing body weight by a given percentage could have a greater impact on the smaller animal. Smaller animals would therefore be more deprived than larger animals. These differences in motivation could mask cognitive abilities.

Unit of Analysis

A perennial issue in teratological studies of animals that give birth to more than one offspring is the appropriate unit of analysis. Should this be the individual pup or the litter? Since littermates share a common genetic inheritance as well as a common intrauterine and postnatal environment, measures of individual pups within litters are likely to be correlated. Using the individual pup as the unit of analysis would unduly inflate the sample size and would violate the principle of independence of sampling. The most conservative approach is therefore to use the litter mean rather than the pup as the datum, thereby preserving statistical independence of samples.

An alternative and more involved method of analysis is to include litters as a random variable "nested" within experimental treatments. If the litter variable were found to be a statistically significant factor, it would be used as the error term; if not, individual subjects could then be used to assess the main treatments variable. These considerations and methods of analyses are discussed at greater length by Abbey and Howard[53] and Denenberg.[54]

Yet another alternative in behavioral studies is to test only one subject of each sex from each litter. Whatever the option that is chosen, relatively large numbers of litters must be sampled, especially in studies evaluating the effects of prenatal alcohol exposure, since intralitter variability is markedly increased by such treatment (see, e.g., references 42, 43, and 55). Studies incorporating 2 or 3 litters per treatment are unlikely to result in statistically significant differences due to small sample size if only one offspring per litter or the litter mean is used. (Basing the analysis on all offspring is, as previously noted, not good procedure.) Because of the increased variability among alcohol-exposed offspring, a minimum of 10 to 15 litters per group is often necessary for statistical significance to occur (provided there is some difference between alcohol-exposed and control offspring).

References

1. Elderton, E., and Pearson, K. A. A first study of the influence of prenatal alcoholism on the physique and ability of the offspring. *Eugenic Laboratory Memoirs,* 1910, *10,* 46–57.
2. Rosenau, M. J. *Preventative medicine and hygiene.* New York: Appleton, 1916.
3. Haggard, H. W., and Jellinek, E. M. *Alcohol explored.* Garden City, N.Y.: 1942.
4. Streissguth, A. P., Little, R. E., Herman, C. S., and Woodell, B. S. I.Q. in children of recovered alcoholic mothers compared with maternal controls. *Alcoholism: Clinical and Experimental Research,* 1979, *3,* 197.
5. Little, R. E., Streissguth, A. P., Woodell, S., and Norden, R. Birth weights of infants born to recovered alcoholic women. *Alcoholism: Clinical and Experimental Research,* 1979, *3,* 184.
6. Abel, E. L. Procedural considerations in evaluating prenatal effects of alcohol in animals. *Neurobehavioral Toxicology,* 1980, *2,* 167–174.
7. Abel, E. L. Behavioral teratology of alcohol. *Psychological Bulletin,* 1981, *90,* 564–581.
8. Randall, C. L., and Nobel, E. P. Alcohol abuse and fetal growth and development. In N. K. Mello (Ed.), *Advances in substance abuse, behavioral and biological research.* Greenwich, Conn.: JAI Press, 1980. pp. 327–367.
9. Riley, E. P., and Lochry, E. A. Genetic influences in the etiology of fetal alcohol syndrome. In E. L. Abel (Ed.), *Fetal alcohol syndrome* (Vol. 3). Boca Raton, Fla. CRC Press, 1983 (pp. 113–130).
10. Chernoff, G. F. The fetal alcohol syndrome in mice: An animal model. *Teratology,* 1977, *15,* 223–229.
11. Chernoff, G. F. The fetal alcohol syndrome in mice: Maternal variables. *Teratology,* 1980, *22,* 71–75.
12. Giknis, M. L., Damjanov, I., and Rubin, E. The differential transplacental effects of ethanol in four mouse strains. *Neurobehavioral Toxicology,* 1980, *2,* 235–237.
13. Kronick, J. B. Teratogenic effects of ethyl alcohol administered to pregnant mice. *American Journal of Obstetrics and Gynecology,* 1976, *124,* 676–680.
14. Henderson, G. I., and Schenker, S. The effects of maternal alcohol consumption on the viability and visceral development of the newborn rat. *Research Communications in Chemical Pathology and Pharmacology,* 1977, *16,* 15–32.
15. Randall, C. L., and Taylor, W. J., Prenatal ethanol exposure in mice: Teratogenic effects. *Teratology,* 1979, *19,* 305–312.
16. Rasmussen, B. B., and Christensen, N. Teratogenic effect of maternal alcohol consumption on the mouse fetus: A histopathological study. *Acta Pathologica Microbiologica Scandinavica, Section A, Pathology,* 1980, *88,* 285–289.
17. Webster, W. S., Walsh, D. A., Lipson, A. H., and McEwen, S. E. Teratogenesis after acute alcohol exposure in inbred and outbred mice. *Neurobehavioral Toxicology,* 1980, *2,* 227–234.
18. Czajka, M. R., Daniels, G., Kaye, G. I., and Tucci, S. M. Effects of ethanol on mouse embryos: Teratology and chromosome abnormalities. *Anatomical Record,* 1979, *193,* 515–516.
19. West, J. R., Black, A. C., Reimann, P. C., and Alkana, R. L. Polydactyly and polysyndactyly induced by prenatal exposure to ethanol. *Teratology,* 1981, *24,* 13–18.
20. Schwetz, B. A., Smith, F. A., and Staples, R. E. Teratogenic potential of ethanol in mice, rats and rabbits. *Teratology,* 1978, *18,* 385–392.
21. Randall, C. L., Taylor, W. J., and Walker, D. W. Ethanol-induced malformations in mice. *Alcoholism: Clinical and Experimental Research,* 1977, *1,* 219–223.
22. Sulik, K. K., Johnston, M. C., and Webb, M. A. Fetal alcohol syndrome: Embryogenesis in a mouse model. *Science,* 1981, *214,* 936–938.
23. Clarren, S. K., and Bowden, D. M. Fetal alcohol syndrome: A new primate model for binge

drinking and its relevance to human ethanol teratogenesis. *Journal of Pediatrics*, 1982, *101*, 819–824.

24. Lester, D., and Freed, E. X. Criteria for an animal model of alcoholism. *Pharmacology, Biochemistry, and Behavior*, 1973, *1*, 103–107.

25. Altshuler, H. L., and Shippenberg, T. S. A. subhuman primate model for fetal alcohol syndrome research. *Neurobehavioral Toxicology and Teratology*, 1981, *3*, 121–126.

26. Shoemaker, W. J., Doda, L. Y., Shoemaker, C. A., and Bloom, F. E. Ethanol effects in chick embryos: Cerebellar Purkinje neurons. *Neurobehavioral Toxicology*, 1980, *2*, 239–242.

27. Abel, E. L., and Dintcheff, B. A. Effects of prenatal alcohol exposure on growth and development in rats. *Journal of Pharmacology and Experimental Therapeutics*, 1978, *207*, 916–921.

28. Himwich, W. A., Hall, J. S., and Macarthur, W. F. Maternal alcohol and neonatal health. *Biological Psychiatry*, 1977, *12*, 495–505.

29. Ellis, F. W., and Pick, J. R. An animal model of the fetal alcohol syndrome in beagles. *Alcoholism: Clinical and Experimental Research*, 1980, *4*, 123–134.

30. Dexter, J. D., Tumbleson, M. E., Decker, J. D., and Middleton, C. C. Fetal alcohol syndrome in Sinclair (S-1) miniature swine. *Alcoholism: Clinical and Experimental Research*, 1980, *4*, 146–151.

31. Potter, B. J., Belling, G. B., Mano, M. T., and Hetzel, B. S. Experimental production of growth retardation in the sheep fetus after exposure to alcohol. *Medical Journal of Australia*, 1980, *2*, 191–193.

32. Jacobson, S., Sehgal, P, Bronson, R., Door, B., and Burnap, J. Comparison between an oral and an intravenous method to demonstrate the *in utero* effects of ethanol in the monkey. *Neurobehavioral Toxicology*, 1980, *2*, 253–258.

33. Boggan, W. O. Animal models of the fetal alcohol syndrome. In E. L. Abel (Ed.), *Fetal alcohol syndrome*. Boca Raton, Fla.: 1981.

34. Bauer-Moffett, C., and Altman, J. Ethanol-induced reductions in cerebellar growth of infant rats. *Experimental Neurology*, 1975, *48*, 378–382.

35. Samson, H. H. Maternal ethanol consumption and fetal development in the rat: A comparison of ethanol exposure techniques. *Alcoholism: Clinical and Experimental Research*, 1981, *5*, 67–74.

36. Wiener, S. G., Shoemaker, W. J., Doda, L. Y., and Bloom, F. E. Interaction of ethanol and nutrition during gestation: Influence on maternal and offspring development in the rat. *Journal of Pharmacology and Experimental Therapeutics*, 1981, *216*, 572–579.

37. Barone, E. R., Pirola, R. C., and Lieber, C. S. Small intestinal damage and changes in cell population produced by ethanol ingestion in the rat. *Gastroenterology*, 1974, *66*, 226–234.

38. Wunderlich, S. M., Baliga, B. S., and Munro, H. N. Rat placental protein synthesis and peptide hormone secretion in relation to malnutrition from protein deficiency or alcohol administration. *Journal of Nutrition*, 1979, *109*, 1534–1541.

39. Smith, J. C. Marginal nutritional states and conditioned deficiencies. In T. K. Li, S. Schenker, and L. Lumeng (Eds.). *Alcohol and nutrition*. Rockville, Md.: U.S. Department of Health, Education and Welfare, 1979. pp. 23–46.

40. Lieber, C. S. Alcohol–nutrition interactions. In T. K. Li, S. Schenker, and L. Lumeng (Eds.), *Alcohol and nutrition*. Rockville, Md.: U.S. Department of Health, Education and Welfare, 1979. pp. 47–63.

41. Osborne, G. L., Caul, W. F., and Fernandez, K. Behavioral effects of prenatal ethanol exposure and differential early experience in rats. *Neurobehavioral Toxicology*, 1980, *12*, 393–401.

42. Abel, E. L., and Greizerstein, H. B. Ethanol-induced prenatal growth deficiency: Changes in fetal body composition. *Journal of Pharmacology and Experimental Therapeutics*, 1979, *211*, 668–671.

43. Riley, E. P., Lochry, E. A., and Shapiro, N. R. Lack of response inhibition in rats prenatally exposed to alcohol. *Psychopharmacology*, 1979, *62*, 47–52.

44. Riley, E. P., Lochry, E. A., Shapiro, N. R., and Baldwin, J. Response perseveration in rats exposed to alcohol prenatally. *Pharmacology, Biochemistry, and Behavior,* 1979, *10,* 255–259.

45. Martin, J. C., Martin, D. C., Sigman, G., and Radow, B. Maternal ethanol consumption and hyperactivity in cross-fostered offspring. *Physiological Psychology,* 1978, *6,* 362–366.

46. Shaywitz, B. A., Griffieth, G. G., and Warshaw, J. B. Hyperactivity and cognitive deficits in developing rat pups born to alcoholic mothers: An experimental model of the expanded fetal alcohol syndrome (EFAS). *Neurobehavioral Toxicology,* 1979, *1,* 113–119.

47. Fernandez, K., and Vorhees, C. V. Persistent body weight deficits in lactating rats treated with alcohol during pregnancy. *Neurobehavioral Toxicology and Teratology,* 1982, *4,* 495–496.

48. Abel, E. L. Behavioral teratology of alcohol. *Psychological Bulletin,* 1981, *90,* 564–581.

49. Abel, E. L. Effects of ethanol on pregnant rats and their offspring. *Psychopharmacology,* 1978, *57,* 5–11.

50. Abel, E. L. In utero alcohol exposure and developmental delay of response inhibition. *Alcoholism: Clinical and Experimental Research,* 1982, *6,* 369–376.

51. Pare, W. P. Age, sex and strain differences in the aversive threshold to grid shock in the rat. *Journal of Comparative and Physiological Psychology,* 1969, *69,* 214–218.

52. Crnic, L. S. Effects of infantile undernutrition on adult learning in rats: Methodological and design problems. *Psychological Bulletin,* 1976, *83,* 715–728.

53. Abbey, H., and Howard, E. Statistical procedures in developmental studies on species with multiple offspring. *Developmental Psychobiology,* 1973, *6,* 329–335.

54. Denenberg, V. H. Assessing the effects of early experience. In R. D. Myers (Ed.), *Methods in psychobiology.* New York: Academic Press, 1977.

55. Leichter, J., and Lee, M. Effect of maternal ethanol administration on physical growth of the offspring in rats. *Growth,* 1979, *43,* 288–297.

CHAPTER 13

Mechanisms of Action

Alcohol produces many different kinds of effects in the body, and it is unlikely that all these effects are mediated by the same mechanism(s) of action. For instance, the growth-retarding effects of alcohol on the fetus may derive from mechanisms that are different from those by which alcohol produces congenital disorders. The severity and type of effect will also depend upon amount and time of exposure to alcohol in association with various risk factors, such as those discussed in Chapter 11.

While undernutrition itself is not responsible for any of the effects of fetal alcohol exposure, there is still the possibility that alcohol-related deficiencies in certain nutrients may contribute to various fetal alcohol effects. Deficiencies in zinc and magnesium, for example, could affect fetal development by altering DNA and RNA synthesis, since these two metals are involved in such synthesis. The evidence for this mechanism, however, is still equivocal.

There have also been some attempts[1,2] to attribute various fetal alcohol effects to the actions of acetaldehyde, the metabolite of alcohol. Acetaldehyde is more toxic than alcohol and it also more lipid-soluble.[3] Levels of acetaldehyde in blood are generally proportional to alcohol intake but are significantly higher in alcoholics than in nonalcoholics.[3] O'Shea and Kaufman[4] have reported that direct administration of acetaldehyde to pregnant rats will result in increased resorption rates and decreased fetal growth. *In vitro* studies have also shown that acetaldehyde is capable of arresting development.[5]

On the other hand, alcohol has been found to decrease embryonic growth *in vitro*,[6] where acetaldehyde production does not occur. Another series of studies[7,8] has shown that tertiary butanol produces many of the same effects in the developing fetus as alcohol. Tertiary butanol is a short chain alcohol that is not metabolized to acetaldehyde but, like ethyl alcohol, causes disruption of membranes and is cross-tolerant to alcohol.[9] Thus, whereas acetaldehyde may be responsible for some of the reported fetal alcohol effects, the most parsimonious explanation for these effects at this time is that they are due to the direct effects of alcohol rather than its metabolite.

Alcohol-Induced Hypoxia

Although very little effort has as yet been devoted to the mechanism(s) by which alcohol adversely affects embryonic or fetal development, there is considerable indirect evidence suggesting that one of the more plausible means by which such adverse effects occur is via hypoxia. By decreasing oxygen to cells during their development, alcohol may produce the structural, physiological, and biological aberrations associated with fetal alcohol exposure. The evidence for alcohol-related hypoxia came from two main sources—acute studies of alcohol's effects on human fetuses, and studies of alcohol's actions on blood flow and tissue respiration.

Acute Studies on Human Fetuses

Much of the evidence for alcohol-related hypoxia in the human fetus derives from acute studies of alcohol administration to pregnant women or animals. While somewhat removed from the kind of exposure that occurs in conjunction with chronic drinking, these studies provide insights into comparable changes that probably occur with greater intensity in fetal alcohol syndrome.

Fetal apnea has been noted following consumption of about 1 ounce of vodka by pregnant women. Apnea in such cases lasted 50 minutes or longer. No apnea was noted in fetuses of control subjects.[10] In another study,[11] fetal apnea was noted when mothers drank alcohol in orange juice but not after consumption of orange juice alone.

Fetal apnea has also been noted in some instances when alcohol was used as an anesthetic during pregnancy[12] or to arrest premature labor.[13] Two reports of death in newborns from unknown causes were associated with mothers receiving alcohol prior to giving birth,[14,15] and descriptions of the cases were consistent with fetal hypoxia.

Zervoudakis and co-workers[16] reported that premature infants born within 12 hours of *in utero* alcohol exposure had significantly higher incidence of respiratory depression than expected.

Streissguth and her co-workers[17] noted that women rated as "risk-level" drinkers gave birth to more children with low Apgar scores compared to other women. This effect was independent of maternal smoking, coffee consumption, parity, and socioeconomic status.

Blood oxygen content was considerably reduced and acidosis was noted in fetal sheep 30 minutes after maternal alcohol infusion.[18] Horiguchi and his co-workers[19] likewise noted acidosis in fetal monkeys, along with a decrease in arterial blood pressure and an increase in heart rate, following administration of alcohol to pregnant monkeys. These physiological changes are each suggestive of fetal hypoxia.

Complications of Pregnancy

Aspiration pneumonia and severe lactic acidosis in pregnant women following consumption of alcohol have been reported.[20,21] Alcoholic ketoacidosis has also been reported in pregnant women.[22,23] While these complications do not prevent oxygen exchange from mother to fetus, they reduce it considerably. Infants born to alcoholics have higher incidences of meconium in amniotic fluid,[17,24] a generally accepted indication of fetal hypoxia.[25,26]

Women who drink heavily also have higher incidences of premature placental separation, antepartum bleeding, amniotic fluid bacterial infections, tetanic uterine contractions, and anemia.[17,24,27,28] Such complications can also result in fetal hypoxia. Two cases of neonatal deaths in children born to alcoholic women were attributed to premature separation of the placenta and subsequent hypoxia by Olegård and his associates.[28]

In pregnant monkeys, alcohol produced a marked collapse of umbilical vasculature for about 15 minutes, which resulted in fetal acidosis and a decrease in fetal blood oxygenation.[29]

Women who drink and smoke are especially at risk for fetal hypoxia since smoking can also produce hypoxia due to increased carbon monoxide and carbon dioxide levels in the blood, decreased blood flow, and inhibition of respiratory enzymes.[30]

Effects on Tissue Oxidation

Following chronic alcohol consumption, the rate of oxygen usage by the liver is increased up to 100%.[31] This increased demand for oxygen by the liver may deprive other tissues of needed oxygen. If this deprivation cannot be compensated for by an increased blood flow, tissues with lowest access to blood could become anoxic and die or become functionally impaired.

For example, Israel and co-workers[32] administered alcohol to rats and then subjected them to hypoxia, as would occur following respiratory depression. (The latter is not uncommonly associated with heavy drinking.) As a result of the low oxygen tensions, liver damage and degeneration occurred. Similar kinds of changes occured in alcohol-treated animals when they were made anemic or their hepatic arteries were ligated.[33,34] As previously noted, anemia is associated with chronic drinking in pregnant women. Likewise, alcohol ingestion reduces blood flow by causing vasoconstriction due to release of catecholamines from the adrenals.[35,36] Liver tissue from animals given alcohol also exhibits an increased sensitivity to anoxia,[37] even after a single exposure.[38]

In addition to producing necrosis, which in the developing embryo/fetus might result in spontaneous abortion or congenital malformations, alcohol-related hypoxia could also produce intrauterine growth retardation through inhibition of ATP activity.

Fetal growth retardation is a well-known consequence of long-term hypoxia, such as that which occurs among infants who are born to mothers living at high altitudes.[30,38,39] As a result of such long-term hypoxia, blood flow is redistributed within the fetus so that oxygen and nutrients are shunted to the brain. As a result, the brain is "spared" compared to other fetal organs.[40,41] When fetal hypoxia is especially severe, brain growth is also reduced.

References

1. Véghelyi, P. V., Osztovics, M., Kardos, G., Leisztner, L., Szaszovsky, E., Igali, S., and Imrei, J. The fetal alcohol syndrome: Symptoms and pathogenesis. *Acta Paediatrica Academiae Scientiarum Hungaricae*, 1978, *19*, 171–189.
2. Majewski, F. Alcohol embryopathy: Some facts and speculations about pathogenesis. *Neurobehavioral Toxicology and Teratology*, 1981, *3*, 129–144.
3. Weiner, H. Acetaldehyde metabolism. In E. Majchrowica and E. P. Noble (Eds.), *Biochemistry and pharmacology of ethanol*. New York: Plenum Press, 1979. pp. 125–144.
4. O'Shea, K. S., and Kaufman, M. H. The teratogenic effect of acetaldehyde. *Journal of Anatomy*, 1979, *128*, 65–76.
5. Popov, V. B., Vaisman, B. L., Puchkov, V. F., and Ignat'eva, T. V. Toxic action of ethanol and its biotransformation products on postimplantation rat embryos in culture. *Byulleten Eksperimental'noi Biologii i Meditsiny*, 1981, *92*, 725–728.
6. Brown, N. A., Goulding, E. H., and Fabro, S. Ethanol embryotoxicity: Direct effects on mammalian embryos *in vitro*. *Science*, 1979, *206*, 573–575.
7. Daniels, M., and Evans, M. A. Effect of maternal alcohol consumption on fetal and newborn development. *Federation Proceedings*, 1980, *39*, 766.
8. Grant, K. A., and Samson, H. H. Ethanol and tertiary butanol induced microcephaly in the neonatal rat: Comparison of brain growth parameters. *Neurobehavioral Toxicology and Teratology*, 1982, *4*, 315–321.
9. Wood, J. M., and Laverty, R. Physical dependence following prolonged ethanol or t-butanol administration to rats. *Pharmacology, Biochemistry and Behavior*, 1979, *10*, 113–119.
10. Fox, H. E., Steinbrecher, M., Pessel, D., Inglis, J., Medvid, L., and Angel, E. Maternal ethanol ingestion and the occurrence of human fetal breathing movements. *American Journal of Obstetrics and Gyneacology*, 1978, *132*, 354–358.
11. Lewis, P., and Boylan, P. Alcohol and fetal breathing. *Lancet*, 1977, *1*, 388.
12. Chapman, E. R., and Williams, P. T. Intravenous alcohol an an obstetrical analgesia. *American Journal of Obstetrics and Gynecology*, 1951, *61*, 676–679.
13. Cook, L. N., Schott, R. J., and Andrews, B. F. Acute transplacental ethanol intoxication. *American Journal of Diseases of Children*, 1975, *129*, 1075–1076.
14. Belinkoff, S., and Hall, O. W. Intravenous alcohol during labor. *American Journal of Obstetrics and Gynecology*, 1950, *59*, 429–432.

15. Jung, A. I., Roan, Y., and Temple, A. R. Neonatal death associated with acute transplacental ethanol intoxication. *American Journal of Diseases of Children,* 1980, *134,* 419–420.
16. Zervoudakis, I. A., Krauss, A. A., and Fuchs, F. Infants of mothers treated with ethanol for premature labor. *American Journal of Obstetrics and Gynecology,* 1980, *137,* 713–718.
17. Streissguth, A. P., Barr, H. M., and Martin, D. C. Offspring effects and pregnancy complications related to self-reported maternal alcohol use. *Developmental Pharmacology and Therapeutics,* 1982, *5,* 21–32.
18. Mann, L. I., Bhakthavathsalan, A., Liu, M., and Makowski, P. Placental transport of alcohol and its effect on maternal and fetal acid-base balance. *American Journal of Obstetrics and Gynecology,* 1975, *122,* 837–844.
19. Horiguchi, T., Suzuki, K., Comas-Urrutia, A. C., Mueller-Heubach, E., Boyer-Milic, A. M., Baratz, R. A., Morishima, H. O., James, L. S., and Adamsons, K. Effect of ethanol upon uterine activity and fetal acid-base state in the rhesus monkey. *American Journal of Obstetrics and Gynecology,* 1971, *109,* 910–917.
20. Greenhouse, B. S., Hook, R., and Hehre, R. W. Aspiration pneumonia following intravenous administration of alcohol during labor. *Journal of the American Medical Association,* 1969, *210,* 168–171.
21. Ott, A., Hayes, J., and Polin, J. Severe lactic acidosis associated with intravenous alcohol for premature labor. *Obstetrics and Gynecology,* 1976, *48,* 362–364.
22. Lumpkin, J. R., Baker, F. J., and Franaszek, F. B. Alcoholic ketoacidosis in a pregnant woman. *Journal of the American College of Emergency Physicians,* 1979, *8,* 21–23.
23. Cooperman, M. T., Davidoff, F., Spark, R., and Pallotta, J. Clinical studies of alcoholic ketoacidosis. *Diabetes,* 1974, *23,* 133–139.
24. Sokol, R. J., Miller, S. I., and Reed, G. Alcohol abuse during pregnancy: An epidemiologic study. *Alcoholism: Clinical and Experimental Research,* 1980, *4,* 135–145.
25. Starko, G. C. Correlation of meconium-stained amniotic fluid, early intrapartum fetal pH, and Apgar scores as predictors of prenatal outcome. *Obstetrics and Gynecology,* 1980, *56,* 604–609.
26. Figgs, G. W., and Peachey, M. J. Meconium staining. *Arizona Medicine,* 1980, *37,* 415–416.
27. Kaminski, M., Rumeau-Rouquett, C., and Schwartz, D. Consommation d'alcool chez les femmes enceintes et issue de la grossesse. *Revue d'Épidémiologie, Médicine Sociale et Santé Publique,* 1976, *24,* 27–40.
28. Olegård, R., Sabel, K. G., Aronsson, M., Sandin, B., Johansson, P. R., Carlsson, C., Kyllerman, M., Iversen, K., and Hrbek, A. Effects on the child of alcohol abuse during pregnancy: Retrospective and prospective studies. *Acta Paediatrica Scandinavica, Supplement,* 1979, *175,* 112–121.
29. Mukherjee, A. B., and Hodgen, G. D. Maternal ethanol exposure induces transient impairment of umbilical circulation and fetal hypoxia in monkeys. *Science,* 1982, *218,* 700–702.
30. Abel, E. L. Smoking during pregnancy: Effects on growth and development of offspring. *Human Biology,* 1980, *52,* 593–625.
31. Ugarte, G., and Valenzuela, J. Mechanisms of liver and pancreas damage in man. In Y. Israel and J. Mardones (Eds.), *Biological basis of alcoholism.* New York: Wiley, 1971. pp. 133–161.
32. Israel, Y., Kalanat, H., Orrego, H., Khanna, J. M., Videla, L., and Phillips, M. J. Experimental alcohol-induced hepatic necrosis: Suppression by propylthioural. *Proceedings of the National Academy of Sciences,* 1975, *72,* 1137–1141.
33. Isarel, Y., Orrego, H., Khanna, J. M., Stewart, D. J., Phillips, M. J., and Kalant, H. Alcohol-induced susceptibility to hypoxic liver damage: Possible role in the pathogenesis of alcoholic liver disease. In M. M. Fisher and J. R. Rankin (Eds.), *Alcohol and the liver.* New York: Plenum, 1977. pp. 323–346.
34. Kalant, H., Israel, Y., Phillips, M. J., Woo, N., Khanna, J. M., and Orrego, H. Necrosis produced by hepatic arterial ligation in alcohol fed rat. *Federation Proceedings,* 1975, *34,* 719.

35. Anton, A. H. Ethanol and urinary catecholamines in man. *Clinical Pharmacology and Therapeutics,* 1965, *6,* 462–469.
36. Klingman, G. I., and Goodall, M. Urinary epinephrine and levarterenal excretion during sublethal intoxication in dogs. *Journal of Pharmacology and Experimental Therapeutics,* 1957, *121,* 313–318.
37. Britton, R. S., Koves, G., Orrego, H., Kalant, H., Phillips, M. J., Khanna, J. M., and Israel, Y. Suppression by antithyroid drugs of experimental hepatic necrosis after ethanol treatment: Effect on thyroid gland or on peripheral deiodination. *Toxicology and Applied Pharmacology,* 1979, *51,* 145–155.
38. Kruger, H., and Arias-Stella, J. The placenta and the newborn infant at high altitudes. *American Journal of Obstetrics and Gynecology,* 1970, *106,* 586–591.
39. Lichty, J. A., Ting, R. Y., Bruns, P. D., and Dyer, E. Studies of babies born at high altitude. *American Journal of Diseases of Children,* 1957, *93,* 666–678.
40. Assali, N. S., and Brinkman, C. R. The role of circulatory buffers in fetal tolerance to stress. *American Journal of Obstetrics and Gynecology,* 1973, *117,* 643–653.
41. Warshaw, J. B. The growth retarded fetus. *Clinical Perinatology,* 1979, *6,* 353–363.
42. Jones, D. P. Hypoxia and drug metabolism. *Biochemical Pharmacology,* 1981, *30,* 1019–1023.
43. Israel, Y., Salazar, I., and Rosemann, E. Inhibitory effects of alcohol on intestinal amino acid transport in vivo and in vitro. *Journal of Nutrition,* 1968, *96,* 499–504.
44. Rawat, A. K. Ribosomal protein synthesis in the fetal and neonatal rat brain as influenced by maternal ethanol consumption. *Research Communications in Chemical Pathology and Pharmacology,* 1975, *12,* 723–732.
45. Rawat, A. K. Effect of maternal ethanol consumption on foetal and neonatal rat hepatic protein synthesis. *Biochemical Journal, 1976, 160,* 653–661.
46. Rawat, A. K. Derangement in cardiac protein metabolism in fetal alcohol syndrome. *Research Communications in Chemical Pathology and Pharmacology,* 1979, *25,* 365–375.

CHAPTER 14

Fetal Alcohol Syndrome
A Case of Prenatal Child Abuse?

Recognition and acceptance of fetal alcohol syndrome and fetal alcohol effects raises a number of legal questions that are fast becoming of more than academic interest.

For example, might a parent sue a physician if the birth of a fetal alcohol syndrome child could have been prevented if the mother had been counseled to stop drinking? Might a person who is stigmatized by fetal alcohol effects that cause suffering or disability claim damages against his or her mother's doctor—or against the mother herself—for such disfigurement or disability? Could a mother be charged with prenatal child abuse if her drinking poses a threat to her unborn child's welfare?

Comparable cases with respect to these issues have already been adjudicated, and the findings in these cases have a direct bearing on the future disposition of cases involving fetal alcohol effects. While no cases have yet been heard in United States courts involving fetal alcohol syndrome, one such case has occurred in Canada. In this chapter, the details of this Canadian case, in which a a charge of prenatal child abuse was brought against the mother of a fetal alcohol syndrome child, will first be examined. The general area of "diminished life"—a legal issue involving children born with birth defects in the United States—will then be examined, and the possible implications of the findings in these litigations for fetal alcohol syndrome will be discussed.

Fetal Alcohol Syndrome in the Canadian Courts

In 1981 a child abuse suit was brought against the mother of an infant girl born with fetal alcohol syndrome in Kenora, Ontario.*

*I thank Mr. D. Novak for providing me with a transcript of the hearing for this case. Details are from this hearing.

213

Prior to the birth of this child, the mother had been involved in 15 alcohol-related incidents with the police. One of her previous children had been born prematurely and intoxicated in 1977. Apgar scores for that child had been 3 at 1 minute and 7 at 5 minutes. Its birth weight was 1960 grams, and the child had gone through withdrawal. When it was 1 year old, the child was diagnosed as having fetal alcohol syndrome.

In 1980, when this same woman became pregnant again, her physician wrote to the Kenora Children's Aid Society expressing his concerns about the amount of drinking the mother was doing during her pregnancy. He also suggested that the unborn child's rights were being violated and that the mother refused to stop drinking.

In 1981 the infant was born while the mother was intoxicated. The baby was jittery and restless and experienced alcohol withdrawal, and it was diagnosed as having fetal alcohol syndrome.

At the hearings concerning this case, the woman was charged with willfully inflicting fetal alcohol syndrome upon her child by her refusal to seek help for her alcohol problem despite being so urged by her doctor. As a result, the child was removed from the mother under the Child Welfare Act by reason of her physical abuse of her child. This abuse, the court ruled, occurred by her excessive drinking of alcohol during pregnancy, which endangered her unborn child's health, and by her neglect or refusal to get remedial care or treatment for the child's health, as urged by a legally qualified doctor.

Could anything comparable occur in the United States?

"Diminished Life"

The grounds for legal confrontation in conjunction with birth defects is encompassed in the legal categories of "wrongful life" and "diminished life." The former refers to claims in which an impaired child charges negligence on the part of a physician—usually an obstetrician—or a medical laboratory. "Diminished life" is an extension of the "wrongful life" suit, in which the parents of an impaired child are the plaintiffs, rather than the child per se. [1–3]

Prior to 1975, most courts refused to award damages for either situation on the basis of a precedent established in 1884. [4] In this case, a pregnant woman fell on a sidewalk that had not been properly maintained, and a miscarriage occurred. Justice Oliver Wendell Holmes ruled that a fetus was part of a mother and could not independently sue for damages. Holmes also implied that even if the child had lived, it could not have sued for injuries.

In 1946 the courts began to move away from this view in the case of Bonbrest v. Kotz. [5] In this case, the court ruled that a physician was liable for injuring a child during birth. Since the child was alive, the court argued, it had a legitimate grievance against the doctor. In 1956, in the case of *Hornbuckle v. the Plantation Pipe Line,*[6] the court once again eroded Justic Holmes's decision by ruling that fetal viability at the time of injury was not relevant so long as the child was born alive.

In 1960, in *Smith v. Brennan,*[7] a New Jersey court ruled that "A child has a legal right to begin life with a sound mind and body." Previous arguments that the fetus did not exist independently of its mother and therefore was not an independent individual, the court said, were invalid. Instead, the court maintained that an individual was in existence from the moment of conception and was not just a part of its mother's body.

The area of law in which such cases are heard is torts—wrongs done by one person to another—and these confrontations are normally settled in terms of monetary compensation. The amount of damages is awarded so as to restore the plaintiff theoretically to where he would be had the defendant not been negligent. The defendent is usually an obstetrician or a medical laboratory, and medical malpractice is charged when the defendent is negligent in diagnosing or anticipating the risk of a birth defect when this is well within the defendent's realm of knowledge. Failure to tell a prospective mother about likely defects deprives her of her legal rights to abort defective children. As a result, the child is born physically or mentally impaired.

In general, the courts have ruled that parents could not sue for damages on behalf of their impaired children when the course of action by the parents would have been abortion. The premise for this ruling is that damages in such cases would be theoretically given to restore the child to where he would have been had no negligence occurred, i.e., nonexistence. One cannot claim damages for nonexistence.

In contrast to the "wrongful life" suit, the "diminished life" suit is one in which a child or his parents ask for past and future expenses in caring for an impaired child or for emotional suffering in giving birth to or in raising an impaired child. The landmark case in which parents were awarded such damages occurred in 1975 in the case of *Jacobs v. Theimer.*[8] In this case, the parents sued their obstetrician, a Dr. Theimer, on the grounds that he had been negligent in not diagnosing *rubella* in the mother while she was pregnant and had not informed her of the possibility that her child would be born with *rubella*-related birth defects. The basis of the award to the parents was that the physician was negligent in not informing the parents and thereby allowing them the option of having the child aborted. The damages in this case were not for "wrongful birth" but for "diminished birth." The subtlety involves the plaintiff. In the "wrongful life" claim, the child, as represented by his parents, asks for damages. In the "diminished life" claim, the parents of an impaired child seek the damages.

In deciding the case of *Jacobs v. Theimer* in favor of the parents, the

Supreme Court of Texas claimed that a physician was "under a duty to make reasonable disclosure" of *rubella* and its potential risks to the unborn child. This decision established the precedent that a physician is obligated to inform a woman of a risk to her unborn child and that failure to do so constitutes neglect. A major question left unanswered by this decision, however, concerns how recognizable a risk there must be before the physician can be considered negligent for not recognizing it.

Fetal Alcohol Syndrome and Negligence

Following *Jacobs v. Theimer,* several other related cases have been adjudicated, and the courts have expressed the opinion that doctors are "bound to keep abreast of the times" and that "if a physician, as an aid to diagnosis, i.e., his judgment, does not avail himself of the scientific means and facilities open to him for the collection of the best factual data upon which to arrive at his diagnosis, the result is not an error of judgment but negligence in failing to secure an adequate factual basis upon which to support his diagnosis or judgment."

In deciding whether negligence has occurred, a primary issue confronting the courts is whether or not medical knowledge at the time of the alleged injury was such that the physician could have anticipated the birth of an impaired child.

In this context, what is the status of the fetal alcohol syndrome?

The existence of the fetal alcohol syndrome has now been clearly established. There have been literally hundreds of case studies reported in the medical literature.[8] Does this mean that an obstetrician is obliged to advise pregnant patients not to drink or to reduce their drinking if he suspects they are alcoholics? Can he be charged with negligence if he does not?

This will be a very difficult issue to decide since there are no clear-cut diagnostic tools available, such as in genetic screening, upon which the physician may rely for his prediction of impairment. Indeed, only a very small proportion of women with alcohol problems give birth to children with fetal alcohol syndrome. (However, not all children whose mothers have *rubella* are born impaired, yet obstetricians have been found negligent when such impairments have occurred. The same may be the ruling in the case of maternal alcoholism.)

More problematical—how great must the risk appear before a physician feels it necessary to warn a woman of the dangers of her drinking? Should a warning be given if a woman has only two drinks a day during pregnancy?

Another problem concerns how aggressive a physician must be in issuing such warnings. Must he volunteer this information or should he be required to offer it only in response to questions from a patient?

While no comparable instance of prenatal child abuse has yet occurred in the United States in conjunction with drinking during pregnancy, a case filed in connection with maternal heroin abuse indicates that such an occurrence is not out of the realm of possibility.

There are also other indications that fetal rights may take precedence over maternal rights. Bowes and Selgestad,[10] for example, describe a recent case in which a pregnant woman refused a Cesarean section although her unborn child was clearly experiencing fetal distress during labor. At the hastily convened hearing that took place in the patient's room, arguments for both the mother and the child were heard. The court decided that the unborn child was suffering from neglect and ordered a Cesarean section to be performed to safeguard its life. In other words, the court ruled that medical treatment could be administered to the woman even against her will, the principle being that the court had a right to protect the interests of the unborn child.

Similar instances of the court acting to protect an unborn child against the wishes of a parent have occurred in conjunction with blood transfusions that have been refused by mothers on the basis of religious convictions (see, e.g., reference 11).

The implications of various decisions suggest that the courts may indeed become the arbiters of what prenatal care should, or should not, consist of. There is also the possibility that children may one day be filing lawsuits against their parents for alleged damage they suffered while in the womb. In the case of fetal alcohol effects, for example, a child may one day ask for damages because of facial disfigurement.

The ramifications of such a possibility can only be guessed. For example, if such damages are claimed, what criteria will be accepted for "partial fetal alcohol syndrome?" What will be the position of parents with regard to drinking at all? If "social" drinking is indeed found to be a contributor to subsequent behavioral problems in offspring, will a woman who has a glass of wine at dinner, or an occasional cocktail while pregnant, be guilty of child abuse?

References

1. Furrow, B. J. Diminished lives and malpractice: Courts stalled in transition. *Law, Medicine and Health Care,* 1982, *10,* 100–107, 114.
2. Trotzig, M. The defective child and the actions for wrongful life and wrongful birth. *Family Law Quarterly,* 1980, *14,* 15–18.
3. Furrow, B. J. The causes of "wrongful life" suits: Ruminations on the diffusion of medical technologies. *Law, Medicine and Health Care,* 1982, *10, 11–14, 47.*
4. *Dietrich v. Inhabitants of Northampton, 138 Mass. 14, 52 Am. R. 242 (1884).*
5. *Bonbrest v. Kotz, 65 F. Supp. 138 (D.C. D.C. 1946).*

6. *Hornbuckle v. Plantation Pipe Line, 93 S.E. 2d. 727 (Ga. 1956).*

7. *Smith v. Brennan, 157 a. 2d. 497 (N.J., 1960).*

8. Abel, E. L. *Marihuana, tobacco, alcohol and reproduction.* Boca Raton, Fla.: CRC Press, 1983.

9. *The Journal,* July 1977, 6, p. 1.

10. Bowes, W. A., and Selgestad, B. Fetal versus maternal rights: Medical and legal perspectives. *Obstetrics and Gynecology,* 1981, *58,* 209–214.

11. *Raleigh Fitkin-Paul Morgan Memorial Hospital v. Anderson, 42 N.J. 421, 201 A 2d. 537 (N.J. S. Ct. 1964).*

Prevention of Fetal Alcohol Syndrome

Prevention of health hazards such as fetal alcohol syndrome can take many forms. One form involves basic research into the ways in which an agent produces a disorder or into the risk factors that predispose an individual to be affected by an agent. Such information may eventually be used to prevent the disorder.

In the case of fetal alcohol syndrome, there is no longer any doubt that alcohol is the primary agent responsible for the syndrome. However, since not all alcoholic women give birth to children with the syndrome, there are obviously associated risk factors that contribute to the syndrome's occurrence. Some of these potential risk factors have been summarized in Chapter 11. Thus far, a primary risk factor appears to be, not surprisingly, maternal blood alcohol levels. The reason not all alcoholic women give birth to children with fetal alcohol syndrome, despite consuming about equal amounts of alcohol, is that some women achieve higher blood alcohol levels due to constitutional or genetic factors. A second major factor, evident from twin studies, is that genetically, some conceptuses are more or less susceptible to the effects of *in utero* alcohol exposure.

Since there is now little doubt that alcohol can act as a teratogen, and since there is no way as yet of determining *a priori* which women are at risk for fetal alcohol syndrome, the most simple course of action vis-à-vis prevention would appear to be abstinence or, at the very least, a reduction in drinking during pregnancy. Efforts to achieve such goals have already been attempted at the national, state, and local levels—with mixed results.

The Labeling Issue

The Jurisdictional Dispute

In protecting people against health hazards, the federal government can regulate the availability of a suspected health hazard and it can also educate the public about the dangers of exposure to such an agent.

In the case of alcohol, regulation of alcohol's availability in the United States is related to alcohol's widespread acceptance and usage, and its status as a billion-dollar tax revenue generator. Administratively, the two main federal agencies responsible for its regulation are the Bureau of Alcohol, Tobacco and Firearms (BATF) of the Department of the Treasury and the Food and Drug Administration (FDA) of the Department of Health and Human Services. The BATF oversees trade practices in the sale of alcohol and collects alcohol-related taxes. The FDA is responsible for monitoring the contents of alcoholic beverages since alcohol can be considered a food or a drug.

Under the Food, Drug and Cosmetic Act of 1938, all food and drug labels are required to list their ingredients, and the FDA was supposed to monitor such listing. This should have placed authority for the labeling of alcoholic beverages under FDA, but it maintained such jurisdiction only when alcohol was used as a medicinal agent. When alcohol was regarded as a food, the BATF was left with authority over labeling of alcoholic beverages as part of its mandate to prevent fraud and deception to purchasers of such beverages.

Although the FDA felt that it had authority over the labelling of alcoholic beverages as well as medicinal labels, it did not challenge the BATF's prerogative on this issue until 1975. Believing that ingredient listing was essential to informing the public about health hazards, e.g., possible ingredients in alcoholic beverages that could cause allergic reactions, the FDA sought official recognition for such a prerogative. The distilled spirits and wine industries balked at this effort, preferring regulation by the BATF, which was a tax-collecting agency, rather than the FDA, which was a health agency, and it challenged the FDA's actions in the courts.

In 1976 the Federal District Court for Western Kentucky ruled in favor of the alcohol industry. Although acknowledging that alcoholic beverages were a food as defined in the Food, Drug and Cosmetic Act, it nevertheless left authority for labeling of such beverages in the hands of the BATF (*Brown-Forman Distillers v. Matthews,*[1] a ruling subsequently described as a "sweetheart" decision rendered "in the heart of Bourbon County [by] a Kentucky judge. . ."[2]).

Although the FDA wanted to appeal the decision, it was dissuaded from doing so by the administration,[3] and instead, it was ordered to come to some understanding with the BATF, possibly in an advisory capacity.[3]

Donald Kennedy, then commissioner of the FDA, subsequently wrote to the director of the BATF, Rex Davis, urging him to seriously consider a warning label on alcoholic beverages in light of the growing concern being expressed about the fetal alcohol syndrome. In this letter, quoted by Ernest Noble, former director of the National Institute on Alcoholism and Alcohol Abuse, Kennedy wrote: "Quite frankly, if the FDA [had] jurisdiction over the labeling of alcoholic beverages, it would waste no time in commencing proceedings to require a labeling warning; I hope that [your agency] which now has exclusive responsibility for such labeling, will move promptly to address this serious health risk."[3]

In the meantime, pressure for such warning labels began to be felt from other directions, and this pressure has not yet been dissipated.

Pressure from Congress

The first attempt to introduce federal legislation requiring alcoholic beverages to carry warning labels occurred in 1972 under the sponsorship of Strom Thurmond, senator from South Carolina. Thurmond proposed that all alcoholic beverages containing 24% alcohol by volume carry a label reading, "Caution: Consumption of alcoholic beverages may be hazardous to your health and may be habit forming." This legislation did not get out of committee and was reintroduced annually with the same degree of success, until 1978.

In January 1978 hearings on the issue were finally held in the Senate, due to a newly felt urgency precipitated by the increasing coverage given to the fetal alcohol syndrome. During the hearings, Thurmond again proposed that alcoholic beverages carry a warning label but extended his proposal to all alcoholic beverages, regardless of alcohol content, and made the warning more specific. His revised suggestion for such a label was "Caution: Consumption of alcoholic beverages may be hazardous to your health, may be habit forming, and may cause serious birth defects when consumed during pregnancy."

In May 1979 Thurmond was finally able to bring his proposal up for vote in the Senate by a subterfuge. Instead of relying on the committee process, which could quash such a proposal so that it could not be voted upon, Thurmond had his proposal amended to S.440, the renewal legislation for the National Institute on Alcoholism and Alcohol Abuse (NIAAA). This maneuver apparently caught the beverage alcohol industry off guard since there was no prior lobbying against the bill containing the amendment.[2] Subsequent lobbying efforts to persuade the legislators not to vote for the bill were too little and too late. In the debate centering on the bill itself, Michigan Senator Donald Riegle, who supported the Thurmond amendment, commented, "When the nation is losing $43 billion a year because of alcohol abuse and when at least 1,500 babies annually may suffer birth defects because of their mothers' drinking, health warning labels to alert consumers to the risk of alcohol abuse are long overdue." His colleagues in the Senate agreed, and the bill passed 68 to 21.

Table 42. Summary of Arguments for and against Placing Health Warnings on Alcoholic Beverages vis-à-vis Drinking during Pregnancy

For	Against
Government has a responsibility to inform its citizens of possible health hazards so that they can make informed choices.	Overuse of health alerts causes the public to become bewildered, apathetic, and indifferent about such warnings.
Labels will raise public awareness of health hazards of excessive drinking.	Moderate drinking has not been shown to be hazardous for most people. Therefore, unlike the case with cigarettes, it would be misleading to state that alcohol was hazardous to health.
	Most of the people who drink to excess are probably dependent and therefore would not be deterred by warning labels.
	It is overly simplistic. All products are dangerous if used to excess.
Even though labels are aimed at a minority (i.e., problem drinkers), this minority numbers in the millions.	Minority of problem drinkers already know the risks of excessive drinking but are unable to control drinking and would not be influenced by labels.
Even if very few people paid attention, if only one baby was kept from suffering alcohol-related birth defects, labels would be worth while.	There is no scientific evidence that warning labels would deter drinking.
Labels will not do any harm.	Warning labels could lead to increased drinking for some through use of alcohol to overcome fear and guilt.

(continued)

When the bill came to the House, however, the lobbyists were prepared, and in the debate that ensued, the NIAAA renewal bill that finally emerged did not contain a labeling requirement. In the final compromise between the Senate and the House, the NIAAA renewal did not contain a requirement for a health warning, but the Secretary of Health and Human Services and the Secretary of the Treasury were told to report jointly to the President and to Congress, no later than June 1, 1980, about the dangers of drinking during pregnancy, the extent of such drinking, and what measures should be taken to alert the public about such dangers.

Table 42. (*Continued*)

For	Against
Labels could alert potential problem drinkers about dangers of excessive drinking before problem begins.	This practice might make drinking more glamorous to young people by creating an opportunity for bravado to be publicly displayed.
Warnings could act as support systems for short-term behavior required to stop drinking during pregnancy.	
Labels would be an incentive for further positive actions in public education.	If labels are adopted, other efforts may not be federally supported because of the feeling that the problem has been dealt with.
	This would undermine efforts to change public image of the alcoholic back to someone whose problem is due to "weak willpower" to abstain.
	It might lead to a neo-Prohibition mentality.
	New regulations for protection would increase the already overbearing federal bureaucracy.
	Labels would cause costly overregulation of business, and costs would be borne by public eventually.
	The alcohol industry would be faced with having its product considered "dangerous."

In the joint report that followed in November 1980[4] (5 months after the deadline date), the two departments indicated that they had given serious consideration to specific warning labels about the dangers of drinking during pregnancy but considered such measures "premature," and listed various reasons for this conclusion. (These, and other reasons from concerned agencies are summarized in Table 42.)

Although the two departments had not come out in favor of labels, President Carter issued a press release on the same day as the report was submitted to Congress, claiming, "The rationale [for the report] does not represent the position of the Administration on the general issue of health warning labels, which can be a useful and cost-effective means of informing the public. . . ."[5]

Despite the president's interest in seeing such a warning, Congress did not appear to be persuaded to be interested in legislating such a measure after receiving the November 1980 report. However, a new source of support for labeling appeared the following year.

Although the Food and Drug Administration had been denied authority over labeling, its powers to inform the public by other means about the dangers of drinking during pregnancy had not been curtailed. On July 16, 1981, the *FDA Drug Bulletin* carried a statement from the Surgeon General about drinking during pregnancy. This caution was based on information from the *Health Hazards Report*[4] and said, "The Surgeon General advises women who are pregnant (or considering pregnancy) not to drink alcoholic beverages and to be aware of the alcoholic content of food and drugs."[6]

About 2 weeks later, on July 30, Senator Thurmond once again introduced legislation (known as S. 1543) requiring a health warning on alcoholic beverages that contained more than 24% alcohol by volume. The legislation, which had bipartisan support, was to require the following message to appear on such containers: "CAUTION: The Surgeon General has determined that consumption of alcoholic beverages during pregnancy can cause serious birth defects. Alcohol can also impair driving ability, create dependency or addiction, and can contribute to other major serious health hazards."

The following day, Senator Jepsen of Idaho announced that he would support the labeling measure but added that he was going to propose an amendment that would widen the legislation to cover all alcoholic beverages, including beer and wine.

Senate hearings on the labeling issue were once again heard in September 1982. The chairman of the Alcoholism and Drug Abuse Subcommittee, Senatory Humphrey, who had previously been opposed to warning labels, stated that he was now in favor, giving as his reason for this change: "I find that there is a very low perception and awareness of the likely effects on unborn children of alcohol consumption by the mothers."[7]

As of September, 1982, the legislation (S. 1543) requiring labeling of alcoholic beverages is still pending. A comparable bill (H.R. 2251) has also been introduced in the House of Representatives.

National Education Efforts

As part of its recommendations to Congress and the president, the 1980 *Health Hazards Report* advised practitioners to contact the NIAAA's National Clearinghouse for Alcohol Information for various brochures it had published on the fetal alcohol syndrome and for materials on how to interview patients about their drinking habits.

The National Institute on Alcohol Abuse and Alcoholism is the main agency within the federal government responsible for public information about alcohol. It is also concerned with prevention, treatment, and rehabilitation programs for alcoholism and with evaluating scientific evidence about alcohol and its effects. As part of its activities in scientific evaluation, the NIAAA, under Ernest Noble, its director at that time, organized a workshop in 1977 to examine the evidence to date on alcohol and the fetus. On the basis of the information presented at that workshop, the NIAAA concluded that the fetal alcohol syndrome did exist as a distinct clinical entity in humans, and the kinds of malformations seen in animals prenatally exposed to large amounts of alcohol were very similar to those occuring in humans. On the basis of these conclusions, the scientists present at the workshop recommended the issuance of a public statement by the NIAAA about the dangers of drinking during pregnancy.

This recommendation was forwarded to the Secretary of Health, Education and Welfare and was approved. On June 1, 1977, Dr. Noble issued the following "health caution" at a press conference held at HEW in Washington:

> Recent research reports indicate that heavy use of alcohol by women during pregnancy may result in a pattern of abnormalities in the offspring, termed the Fetal Alcohol Syndrome, which consists of specific congenital and behavioral abnormalities. Studies undertaken in animals corroborate the initial observations in humans and indicate as well an increased incidence of stillbirths, resorptions and spontaneous abortions. Both the risks and the extent of abnormalities appear to be dose-related, increasing with higher alcohol intake during the pregnancy period. In human studies, alcohol is an unequivocal factor when the full pattern of the Fetal Alcohol Syndrome is present. In cases where all the characteristics are not present, the correlations between alcohol and the adverse effects are complicated by such factors as nutrition, smoking, caffeine and other drug consumption.
>
> Given the total evidence available at this time, pregnant women should be particularly conscious of the extent of their drinking. While safe levels of drinking are unknown, it appears that a risk is established with ingestion above 3 ounces of absolute alcohol or 6 drinks per day. Between one and three ounces, there is still uncertainty but caution is advised. Therefore, pregnant women and those likely to become pregnant should discuss their drinking habits and the potential dangers with their physicians.[8]

This health caution was printed in the FDA *Drug Bulletin,* which is regularly mailed to practicing physicians, and was also sent to all professional medical societies with a request that they help disseminate the information concerning drinking and pregnancy.

In 1978 NIAAA also issued a brochure, entitled "Alcohol and Your Unborn Baby," containing information about drinking during pregnancy and how it affects the fetus. Several millions of these brochures were distributed to physicians' offices and various health agencies as well as supermarkets and community meeting areas. This was followed by various other related public information materials. In 1981 NIAAA issued a special guide to help obstetricians determine if their patients had an alcohol-related problem. The guide, entitled "Preventing Fetal Alcohol Effects: A Practical Guide for Ob/Gyn Physicians and Nurses," was prepared by Drs. R. J. Sokol and S. I. Miller, with S. S. Martier. The following year NIAAA launched an extensive public education campaign about alcohol at the national, state, and local levels aimed at three specific target audiences: youth, pregnant women, and adult women. As part of its program, NIAAA offered to provide various TV and radio public service announcements to both national and local outlets, as well as magazine ads, posters, and brochures to interested parties. State and local organizations participating in the campaign were offered the cooperation of a film and advertising production company.

A nationwide campaign has also been launched by the Bureau of Alcohol, Tobacco and Firearms. Part of the BATF's efforts are a 16-page comic book entitled "Rex Morgan, M.D., Talks About Your Unborn Child." In this comic book, Dr. Morgan treats a pregnant woman who has cut her hand while she was drunk. In the course of attending his patient, Morgan discusses the dangers of drinking during pregnancy and offers advice to readers on what to do if they have any questions about drinking during pregnancy.

The second thrust of its education campaign involved distribution of a public service announcement entitled, "Two Tummies," which the BATF distributed to 720 TV stations across the country in cooperation with state prevention offices, which in turn were encouraged to add local referral information at broadcast time.

Other National Efforts

A number of nationally based organizations have prepared their own materials and media campaigns to alert the public about drinking during pregnancy. Some of these efforts merely duplicate programs and materials already in place, although in some cases the approach and the messages are somewhat different.

In some instances, there have been rivalries reminiscent of the interdepartmental squabbling between the BATF and the FDA noted above. For example, on the day prior to NIAAA's "health caution" warning, the National Council on Alcoholism held its own press conference on the dangers of drinking during pregnancy. Like the NIAAA, the NCA acknowledged the dangers of such drinking, but in contrast to the NIAAA's advice to limit drinking to two drinks a day, the NCA advised total abstention during pregnancy.

The fact that the NCA news conference came 1 day before the NIAAA conference was seen by some as more than a coincidence. Dr. Noble, director of the NIAAA, stated that George Dimas, executive director of NCA, knew about NIAAA's plans to hold its conference 10 days beforehand. Some officials at NIAAA consequently regarded the NCA press conference as ''a cheap attempt to upstage them.''[9]

This was not the first time the NIAAA and the NCA had publicly disagreed. In the previous year the two agencies had argued over the merits of an NIAAA-funded study, conducted by the Rand Corporation, intimating that alcoholics could drink moderately. The NCA contested such a conclusion, considering it ''misleading, inaccurate, and dangerous.''[9] The dispute between the NIAAA and the NCA over the ''controlled drinking'' question may thus in fact have been a factor in the coincidental timing of the two news conferences.[9]

In any case, the squabble between the two agencies did not detract from the campaigns each subsequently engaged in, and in a letter written several months later, NCA's executive director congratulated NIAAA's director for his presentation of the facts about fetal alcohol syndrome on national TV and assured him that NCA ''would support any efforts to obtain increased funds from Congress [for research on fetal alcohol syndrome].''[10] The NCA director also assured Noble that ''we will continue our efforts to increase the private sector funding to add to and complement the Government's support of Fetal Alcohol Syndrome research.''[10]

NCA's public education efforts have involved publication of its own pamphlet, entitled ''What You Need to Know About You, Your Baby and Drinking.'' It has also provided information to various health-related agencies, and for the past several years, it has supported research into fetal alcohol syndrome by its Research Society on Alcoholism and by its American Medical Society on Alcoholism. NCA has also provided facilities for meetings of the Study Section on Fetal Alcohol Syndrome at its annual NCA forum.

In response to the Bureau of Alcohol, Tobacco and Firearms report in February 1979, indicating the advisability of the private sector to conduct a public awareness campaign to educate the public about the dangers of drinking during pregnancy, 10 representatives of the alcohol beverage industry formed the Beverage Alcohol Information Council (BAIC) to produce such a campaign.

In June 1979 the BAIC presented its plans to the BATF and was encouraged to carry out its plans. The thrust of this campaign was: ''What you do makes a difference. You owe it to yourself and your unborn child to be informed about drinking during pregnancy and to avoid excessive or abuse drinking.''

Two main groups were targeted. The first was women of childbearing age, e.g., women under the care of a physician, teenagers, minority/poverty women, and alcoholic or problem drinkers. The second group were health care professionals—including physicians, nurses, social workers, alcoholism counselors, teachers, and health educators—as well as clergy.

As part of its campaign aimed at women of childbearing age, the BAIC placed public service ads in magazines such as *Baby Talk* and *American Baby*, which are distributed by mail to pregnant women and are also sent to obstetricians' offices. Posters were also distributed to over 4000 health clinics containing a similar public service notice about drinking and pregnancy. Public service TV messages were likewise developed under sponsorship of the BAIC for distribution across the country.

As part of its campaign aimed at health care providers, the BAIC distributed to 26,000 physicians across the country a review article on the fetal alcohol syndrome by Dr. J. H. Mendelson.[11] Support was also provided to Dr. H. Rosett, to develop materials on prevention of fetal alcohol syndrome to be presented to various professional groups such as the American College of Obstetrics and Gynecology, the American Academy of Pediatrics, and the Academy of Family Physicians. In 1980 Rosett's exhibit received an award from the American College of Obstetricians and Gynecologists.

In 1978 the March of Dimes Birth Defects Foundation issued a pamphlet entitled "When You Drink, Your Unborn Baby Does, Too!" However, this pamphlet was subsequently withdrawn and replaced in 1979 by another pamphlet entitled "Pregnant? Before You Drink, Think . . . " (based on information provided by the BAIC). The change was highlighted by a shift in message from one endorsing abstinence from alcohol, in the first pamphlet, to one suggesting caution about drinking during pregnancy. The reason given for the change was the desire to avoid "overkill."[12] The March of Dimes has also produced a film, *Crisis for the Unborn,* dealing with drinking during pregnancy.

In 1981 the American Council on Science and Health, an independent educational association concerned with promotion of scientific evaluations of health concerns, published an 18-page booklet entitled "Alcohol Use During Pregnancy," which summarized evidence to date on fetal alcohol syndrome. On the basis of this evidence, the ACSH felt that abstinence from alcohol was not necessary for protecting the health of the fetus since there was no evidence that drinking less than two drinks per day has been proven dangerous to fetal development.

A final national effort worth noting is the one by the Education Commission of the States, an organization made up of 47 state organizations concerned with student education. In 1980 it issued a pamphlet entitled "What Students Should Know About Drinking and Pregnancy," outlining ways in which alcohol abuse programs should be presented to students, including information about drinking during pregnancy. Although the text is seemingly about drinking during pregnancy, relatively little information is provided on the subject. Instead, the emphasis is on encouraging responsible drinking. In this sense, the title is somewhat misleading.

Besides the written materials that have been produced, four films dealing with fetal alcohol syndrome have also been released. The film produced by the

March of Dimes has already been mentioned. In 1980 the National Broadcasting Company released a film titled *Fetal Alcohol Syndrome*, which is alarmist in content. It contains interviews with parents of children diagnosed as "alcohol syndrome children" and contrasts them with normal children. At the end of the film, which runs for 14 minutes, one mother of an FAS child says, "If I had only been told what my drinking would do to my child. . . ." The film is said to be aimed at an audience ranging from children at the Grade 10 level to adults.

In 1981 Peter Glaws Productions released an hour-long film entitled *Pregnancy on the Rocks: The Fetal Alcohol Syndrome*, which contains interviews with leading clinicians and researchers in the field and shows a mother and her FAS child.

Public Information at the State Level

Several states have produced various informational campaigns of their own, some with the help of federal agencies and some independently of federal aid. These campaigns include the production of pamphlets, posters, public service radio and TV announcements, bumper stickers, and buttons.

In 1978 Wisconsin became the first of many states to initiate such activities. Beginning with a symposium on fetal alcohol syndrome in which various aspects of the problem were discussed, the Wisconsin State Bureau for Alcohol and Other Drug Abuse prepared a packet of materials including in-depth reviews of information about drinking during pregnancy, along with posters and a brochure. The theme of this program was the slogan for the original March of Dimes pamphlet, "When You Drink, Your Unborn Baby Does, Too!" In 1980 the governor of Wisconsin designated an "FAS Awareness Month," and the materials prepared by the Bureau of Alcohol were sent out statewide to various health agencies and public media offices.

In 1979 the governor of Texas declared the week of January 21–27 "Fetal Alcohol Syndrome Awareness Week." A statewide campaign under the Texas Commission on Alcoholism mailed relevant materials to physicians and other health care providers about the dangers of drinking during pregnancy. Many of the materials used in the Texas campaign were adapted from the Wisconsin program and were duly credited.

In 1980 the New York State Division of Alcoholism and Alcohol Abuse initiated a statewide effort to inform the public and especially pregnant women about the dangers of drinking during pregnancy. This effort grew out of the recommendations offered by the Governor's Task Force on the Fetal Alcohol Syndrome the previous year. The slogan for the New York State campaign is "WARNING: Alcohol can be hazardous to your unborn baby's health."

**Table 43. Survey of Public Health Message concerning Drinking during
Pregnancy Produced by National and State Agencies**

Agency	Public health message	Abstinence recommended
American Council on Science and Health (ACSH)	. . . women [should] be cautious about alcohol use during pregnancy. For those women who choose to drink during pregnancy, ACSH advises that they limit their daily intake to two drinks or less of beer, wine, or liquor. . . . Although no absolutely safe level of alcohol ingestion has been defined or probably ever will be, the health risks associated with the above level of consumption are apparently low, if they exist at all. These recommendations are intended only as guidelines, as there are substantial differences among women in their ability to tolerate alcohol. ("Alcohol Use During Pregnancy," 1981)	No
Beverage Alcohol Information Council (BAIC)	What you do during pregnancy makes all the difference . . . for one little reason. You owe it to your unborn baby to find out all you can about drinking and other health habits, before and during pregnancy. The steps you take now to avoid excessive or abuse drinking can help insure better health for you and your child. If you are pregnant, or considering having a baby, we urge you to follow your doctor's advice on all drinking, nutrition and health matters. It does make a difference. (BAIC poster, 1980)	No
Bureau of Alcohol, Tobacco and Fire-arms (BATF)	Fetal alcohol syndrome is the most severe form of alcohol damage to the fetus. . . . And it is the third most common birth defect with mental retardation! Here's some practical advice on how to give your baby the best chance for a healthy start in life! 1. See your family doctor or go to a maternity clinic when you learn that you are pregnant. Early prenatal care pays off in healthier babies. 2. Think before you drink! If you have any questions about drinking beer, wine or liquor during pregnancy, discuss them with your doctor . . . and follow his advice.	No

Table 43. (*Continued*)

Agency	Public health message	Abstinence recommended
	3. If you can't control your drinking, get help. 4. Take pride in your personal health to better insure your baby's good health. ("Rex Morgan, M.D. Talks . . . About Your Unborn Child." 1980)	
Do It Now Foundation	When you consider that excessive use of alcohol not only endangers the fetus, but can cause problems which will affect him or her all their lives, it seems well worth the effort to stop drinking. ("Smoking, Drinking and Pregnancy," 1978)	Yes
Education Commission of the States (ECS)	1. Assume personal responsibility for your health status. 2. Consult your physician about diet, exercise and the use of alcohol and other drugs during pregnancy. 3. Recognize that alcohol is a drug and be aware of its effects. 6. Recognize that an individual's tolerance for alcohol varies from time to time, and set limits on your consumption accordingly. Pregnancy may make it necessary to set a lower limit or abstain entirely. ("What Students Should Know About Drinking and Pregnancy," 1980)	No
Hazelden Foundation	How much is too much, then? If you're pregnant, any alcohol is too much. To fully protect your baby, you should completely abstain from alcohol and eat a nutritionally balanced diet daily . . . (*Fetal Alcohol Syndrome,* 1980)	Yes
March of Dimes	If you are a woman of childbearing age, you can prevent birth defects caused by excessive use of alcohol. If you're pregnant, don't drink. If you drink heavily, don't become pregnant. If you can't stop drinking on your own, seek help before you become pregnant. (When you Drink, Your Unborn Baby Does, Too!" 1978)	Yes

(*continued*)

Table 43. (*Continued*)

Agency	Public health message	Abstinence recommended
	If you are a woman of childbearing age, you can prevent birth defects caused by excessive use of alcohol. If you can't stop drinking on your own, seek help before you become pregnant. ("Pregnant? Before You Drink, Think . . . ," 1979)	No
National Council on Alcoholism (NCA)	The less you drink, the better your chance of having a healthy baby. The safest decision is not to drink at all. ("What You Need to Know About You, Your Baby and Drinking," 1978)	Yes
National Institute on Alcohol Abuse and Alcoholism (NIAAA)	We really don't know at what level alcohol begins to harm the fetus, but there is evidence that a risk is established if you drink six drinks a day or more. Between two and six drinks, the risk factor is uncertain. However, minimum risk is involved if you limit your drinking to two drinks a say or less. ("Alcohol and Your Unborn Baby," 1978)	No
	We really don't know at what level alcohol begins to harm the fetus. At the lowest doses, the risks from alcohol are probably very small, but as alcohol consumption increases, so does the risk. Of course, there is no possibility of fetal damage from alcohol if the mother doesn't drink at all. And until all the facts are in, this seems the safest and wisest course to follow to ensure the best possible outcome of pregnancy. ("Alcohol and Your Unborn Baby," 1981)	Yes
Massachusetts—Eunice Kennedy Shriver Center	All the evidence at this point indicates that heavy drinking women who stop drinking during pregnancy can have normal, healthy babies. But the best advice for any women who plans to have a baby is to stop drinking before becoming pregnant.	Yes
New York State Division of Alcoholism and Alcohol Abuse	We do not know how much is too much. Research scientists across the country are actively studying this problem, but it may take years before all the answers are in.	Yes

Table 43. (*Continued*)

Agency	Public health message	Abstinence recommended
	We *do* know, however, that the more a pregnant woman drinks, the greater the risk of having a baby with FAS or ARBD (alcohol-related birth defects). Women who take two drinks a day or more run a risk of losing the pregnancy. The baby may be born smaller and not develop as well. . . . One thing is certain, FAS can not happen if you do not drink when you are pregnant. ("WARNING: Alcohol can be hazardous to your unborn baby's health," 1980)	
Wisconsin Clearinghouse for Alcohol and Other Drug Information	If you choose to drink alcohol: Then be careful not to get pregnant. Sometimes people forget to be careful when they are drinking. So think clearly before drinking about the kinds of choices you are prepared to make. . . . If you become pregnant (or if there is a chance that you might): You can decide not to have any alcoholic drinks at all. Many experts advise this, since the risks may be even greater than what we already know. . . . If you become pregnant and do choose to drink: You will be exposing your baby to added risk. There is no guarantee that any amount of alcohol is "safe." If you are going to drink on a certain occasion, we suggest you only have one drink. ("Choices for the Future: Alcohol and Pregnancy," 1979)	No
Washington—Pregnancy and Health Program, University of Washington	Plan your pregnancy. Try not to drink for at least a month before you conceive, so your baby has a good start. Have an alcohol-free pregnancy. That means beer and wine too! . . . No one knows how much a woman can drink safely during pregnancy. Until we do, remember, Alcohol and Pregnancy Don't Mix. ("Mothering Begins Before Birth. How Alcohol May Affect Your Unborn Baby," 1980)	Yes

(*continued*)

Table 43. (*Continued*)

Agency	Public health message	Abstinence recommended
Texas Commission on Alcoholism	There are a lot of ''dos'' and don'ts'' associated with pregnancy, and sometimes you may feel a bit overwhelmed by them. It often seems there is so much to suspect, reject and avoid! But underlying all the advice and recommendations you receive is the important message that *what you do makes a difference.* By making informed, intelligent choices about alcohol use during pregnancy you can increase your chances of bearing a healthy, normal baby. (''Alcohol and Your Unborn Baby,'' n.d.)	No
Missouri Department of Mental Health	Like smoking and the use of any psychoactive drug, alcohol can be a serious threat to the health of our unborn. When you see a mother-to-be enjoying a drink, mention Fetal Alcohol Syndrome to her, or hand her this pamphlet. She may not know. (''Fetal Alcohol Syndrome. . . .'' n.d.)	Yes
New Mexico Substance Abuse Bureau	No one knows how much a woman can drink safely during pregnancy. Until we do, remember, Alcohol and Pregnancy Don't Mix. (''A Pregnant Woman Never Drinks Alone,'' n.d.).	Yes
Georgia Department of Human Resources	FAS is a tragedy that doesn't have to happen. If you are a woman of childbearing age, you can prevent birth defects caused by drinking. (''If you drink, your unborn baby does, too., n.d.)	Yes
Colorado Department of Health	For those children already affected by Fetal Alcohol Syndrome, reversal is impossible. However, it is vital to note that Fetal Alcohol Syndrome is preventable.	No
California Department of Alcohol and Drug Abuse	The few months of not drinking alcohol will go by fast enough, with all the things there are to prepare for a baby . . . a beautiful healthy baby . . . without a fetal alcohol syndrome. (''Our Children Deserve the Best,'' n.d.).	No

Table 43. (*Continued*)

Agency	Public health message	Abstinence recommended
Canada—Alberta Alcoholism and Drug Abuse Commission	We know that women who drink heavily, more than 5 drinks a day, run a serious risk of giving birth to alcohol-damaged children. Binge drinking, occasional drunkenness by a pregnant woman who otherwise does not drink regularly, may hurt the fetus, if it takes place at critical periods of fetal development. New research, however, indicates that a pregnant woman who drinks any amount of alcohol may risk damaging her unborn child—there is no safe limit. ("Alcohol and Your Unborn Baby," n.d.)	Yes
England—All Faiths World Alcohol Project (AlFAWAP)	What should you do about drinking during your pregnancy? Don't drink beer, wine, or liquor. As you increase the number of drinks per day, you also increase the risk to your unborn baby.	Yes

Various other states have also implemented information campaigns along similar lines.

Evaluation of Information/Education Campaigns

Many agencies, public and private, national and state, have produced and distributed materials about drinking during pregnancy. There is obviously a considerable duplication of the basic information being disseminated. Where the various agencies differ is in the directness with which the subject of drinking during pregnancy is approached and in the recommendations for abstention. Basically, the approaches can be divided into two main categories. One approach directly cautions women not to drink while they are pregnant or, at the very least, to reduce their drinking. This is the position taken by many health and alcoholism service agencies. The other approach, followed by industry-related groups and those supported by them, has been to advise women to see their physicians if they are concerned about drinking during pregnancy. These messages and their impact have previously been examined by Robe[12–14] and by Maloney and her co-workers[15] and are summarized in Table 43.

In evaluating the impact of these effects at public education there are two main issues to consider. These concern whether or not the public has been made aware of the possible dangers of drinking during pregnancy and whether such information has had any impact on drinking practices during pregnancy.

In surveys conducted on a national level,[16–18] about 54% to 66% of the people interviewed said that they had heard something about drinking during pregnancy. When aided recall on these surveys was given, awareness level was over 80%.[16,18] In a regional survey conducted in Oregon, 90% of those contacted said that they had heard something about the dangers of drinking during pregnancy.[19] These results are summarized in Table 44. In some instances, the question concerning awareness has been rather pointed, such as that initially asked by the Opinion Research Corporation.[16] However, even when the questions have been phrased in an open-ended format, the results have been similar.[17,18]

In the most recent survey, conducted in 1980 for the FDA,[18] awareness of the potential dangers of drinking during pregnancy was highest among women of childbearing age (77%), compared to that of men (59%). Level of education was another important variable, with 65% of the college graduates indicating awareness of the dangers without any prompting, compared to 46% of respondents with less than high school education.

The FDA survey also indicated that very few people could recall anything specific about the warnings they had heard. About 28% of the respodents said that drinking during pregnancy should be avoided because "it harms the unborn child." About 17% stated "birth defects" as a cause for avoiding alcohol, but could recall no specific defects. About 10% said a baby could be born "alcoholic," about 9% cited brain damage, about 7% cited deformity, 5% cited growth retardation, 3% cited miscarriage, and only 2% cited "fetal alcohol syndrome."

Awareness of the problem of drinking during pregnancy was clearly related to the seriousness with which people rated the issue. About 49% of those who said they had not heard anything about fetal alcohol syndrome did not consider it a serious problem, compared to 88% of those who had heard about it previously. This difference is regarded as reflecting "media impact." As noted in the report, "even though people exhibited relatively little recall of message content . . . the mere fact that they were aware that such messages existed and had been carried by the media served to intensify their concern with these issues."

The final aspect of the FDA survey asked for public opinion about what should be done at the federal level about the problem. Only 27% of those regarding fetal alcohol syndrome as a serious problem felt that the federal government should somehow become involved (although no options for involvement, such as warning labels, were offered). Among those who were favorably inclined toward federal action, only 10% suggested warning labels as a way of informing the public about the dangers of drinking during pregnancy. Among those who did not urge federal involvement, 39% said that the best way of

Table 44. Level of Public Awareness Concerning Possible Dangers of Drinking during Pregnancy

Study site	Source	Question asked	N	Total awareness (%)	Awareness among women
National	BATF[16]	"Are you aware that substantial alcohol drinking by a pregnant woman or by a woman of child-bearing age may cause birth defects, which are referred to as Fetal Alcohol Syndrome?"	2083	82	86
National	BATF[17]	"Have you read or heard anything about the effects of alcohol on a fetus?"	2054	66	73
National	FDA[18]	"Have you recently read or heard anything about things that a pregnant women should not eat or drink, or that they should not eat or drink too much of?"	1499	54%	55
		"Have your read or heard anything about the dangers to pregnant women of drinking alcoholic beverages?" (Question asked of those not naming alcohol in previous question)		32%	33%
			(Total)	86%	88%
Oregon	Washington State Alcoholism and Drug Abuse Institute[19]	"Can you name any foods which a pregnant woman might eat that could have an undesirable effect on her unborn child?"	430	90%	N.A.

informing women about the problem is via their doctors, compared to only 9% who were in favor of federal action.

Unfortunately, the FDA survey did not ask about the drinking habits of those who were aware and not aware of the dangers of drinking during pregnancy. However, one such question was asked in the regional study by Little and her co-workers:[19] Among those women who regarded drinking during pregnancy as harmful, only 25% felt that abstaining from alcohol during pregnancy was the best course. Among those not recommending abstinence, the remaining 85% considered up to three drinks a day as safe.

Evaluation of Efforts

There is no shortage of materials or public media messages available concerning drinking during pregnancy. These materials have been produced by federal, state, and local agencies, and much of the material is redundant. The main differences concern the advice to abstain during pregnancy and the way in which the issue is presented. Various surveys indicate that these information campaigns have been very successful in informing the public about the possible dangers of drinking during pregnancy.

As previously pointed out, however, awareness does not necessarily indicate changes in behavior. Thus far, there does not appear to be an indication that these media efforts have caused women to stop drinking during pregnancy to any important extent. There also seems to be a reluctance to have the federal government intervene in this issue. The evidence thus far seems to indicate that only a small proportion of those feeling that drinking during pregnancy is a serious issue would like to see warning labels about the problem. Most people, it appears, prefer having the information come from their physicians.

Thus three possibilities exist: (1) that the position adopted by the BATF and the alcohol industry has had more of an impact than that promulgated by the FDA and other public groups, (2) that this may indeed have been the attitude of the general public to begin with and that it continues to represent public opinion, or (3) that the surveys conducted thus far have been biased in such a way as not to reflect public opinion on the issue. If the latter is true, the onus of proof is now on those who advocate such issues as warning labels and other federal intervention.

Identification and Treatment of Alcohol-Related
Problems in Prenatal Clinics

Another strategy for prevention of fetal alcohol effects that differs from the mass media public education effort involves counseling of pregnant women about alcohol in prenatal clinics.

The first such program was initated at Boston City Hospital in 1974 by Rosett and his co-workers.[20] Women who attended the prenatal clinic were interviewed during their first visit and were asked about their diet, smoking habits, and use of alcohol and other drugs. As a result of this interview, women were classified as heavy, moderate, or rare drinkers on the basis of the Cahalan volume-variability index. Women who were considered moderate drinkers were informed about the risks of drinking during pregnancy and were advised to reduce their consumption.

Women classified as heavy drinkers were encouraged to return to the clinic for counseling. These counseling sessions consisted of meetings with a psychiatrist and a counselor for about 20 minutes, during which these women were told of the benefits of reducing their drinking as far as their unborn child was concerned. The general approach stressed the positive side of abstinence or reduced drinking rather than emphasizing the problem in a negative or alarmist format.

This program (now suspended) was moderately successful in reducing drinking among some women, and this in turn had a beneficial effect on their pregnancies. For example, in the pilot study[20] involving 322 women, 42 (13%) were heavy-drinking mothers and 34 agreed to counseling sessions. Of these 34, 15 were able to reduce their drinking prior to their third trimester of pregnancy. These women had fewer children with growth retardation below the 10th percentile than the 19 women who also underwent counseling but did not reduce their drinking, or the 8 women who did not agree to counseling and continued drinking heavily throughout their pregnancies. This study also found that children born to previously heavy drinkers slept more than those born to women who did not modify their drinking. Children born to the latter were more restless and "jittery" as well.[21]

In a second study, involving 27 additional heavy-drinking women, similar results were obtained.[22]

As part of the Boston City Hospital's identification and treatment program of drinking problems during pregnancy, Rosett and his co-workers initiated efforts aimed at educating physicians and other health professionals about fetal alcohol syndrome and about procedures for obtaining drinking histories.[23] Similar instruments for routine history-taking about alcohol consumption have also been developed in Cleveland[24] and in Buffalo.[25] To motivate physicians to use this questionnaire, Rosett and his co-workers have conducted workshops for the obstetrical staff. Various aspects of drinking, including its impact on the fetus, are discussed.

Assessment of this program[26] indicated that, prior to its implementation, few patient charts contained drinking histories. After the program was initiated, drinking histories were recorded for 77% to 92% of all patients from 1978 to 1979. When the researchers were no longer present at the clinic on a regular basis, the percentage of patients for whom drinking histories were recorded dropped to 59% during the first 6 months thereafter, and to less than 40% in the second 6 months. After the chairman of the Department of Obstetrics and Gynecology issued a directive that all prenatal charts contain drinking histories, drinking histories increased to 59%.

As noted by the authors of this study, attitudes are not necessarily related to behavior, so that even though this program increased awareness of alcohol-related problems among pregnant women, this does not necessarily mean that the professionals in charge of women with such problems changed their behavior toward them or referred them to other professionals for help. The authors also note that without continued education and support, health care providers may lose interest in efforts to identify possible drinking problems among their pregnant patients.

References

1. Brown-Forman Distillers Corp. v. Mathews, 435 F. Supp. 5 (W.D. Kentucky 1976).
2. American Business Men's Research Foundation. The great debate. Health warnings for alcoholic beverages. *The Bottom Line on Alcohol in Society*, 1980, *3*, 3–5.
3. Randall, C. L., and Noble, E. P. Alcohol abuse and fetal growth and development. In N. K. Mello (Ed.), *Advances in substance abuse*. Greenwich, Conn.: Aijai Press, 1980. pp. 327–367.
4. U.S. Department of the Treasury and U.S. Department of Health and Human Services. *Report to the President and the Congress on health hazards associated with alcohol and methods to inform the general public of these hazards*. Washington, D.C.: U.S. Government Printing Office, 1980.
5. Presidential press release, November 25, 1980.
6. Federal Drug Administration. Surgeon general's advisory on alcohol and pregnancy. *FDA Drug Bulletin*, 1981, *11*, 1.
7. *The Alcoholism Report*, 1982, *10*(23), 4.
8. Noble, E. P. Health caution. *NIAAA Information and Feature Service*, September 8, 1977, IFS No. *39*, 1.
9. Must pregnant women stop drinking? *Medical World News*, June 17, 1977, p. 9.
10. Dimas, G. C. Letter to Ernest P. Noble, June 9, 1977.
11. Mendelson, J. H. The fetal alcohol syndrome. *Advances in Alcoholism*, 1979, *1*, 1–4.
12. Robe, L. B. MOD modifies FAS advice. *The Journal*, April 1, 1980, p. 5.
12. Robe, L. B. What they're saying about FAS. *The Journal*, October 1, 1980, p. 9.
13. Robe, L. B. *FAS education campaign comparisons reveal varied attitudes*. Paper presented at the National Council on Alcoholism Forum, New Orleans, 1981.
14. Robe, L. B. Drinking during pregnancy: Straight talk or double-talk. *Alcoholism*, September 1982, pp. 33–34.
15. Maloney, S. K., Bast, R. J., and O'Gorman, P. Perspectives on prevention of fetal alcohol effects. *Neurobehavioral Toxicology*, 1980, *2*, 271–276.
16. Opinion Research Corporation. *Fetal alcohol syndrome. A nationwide survey conducted for Bureau of Alcohol, Tobacco and Firearms*, February 1979.
17. Opinion Research Corporation. *Public perceptions of alcohol consumption and pregnancy. A nationwide survey conducted for Bureau of Alcohol, Tobacco and Firearms* (ORC Study #33710), September 1979.
18. Louis Harris and Associates. *Alcohol, caffeine and pregnancy: The public view* (prepared as part of 1980 Multipurpose Survey for Division of Consumer Studies, Bureau of Foods.) (PB-80-106750), May 1981.

19. Little, R. E., Grathwohl, H. L., Streissguth, A. P., and McIntyre, C. Public awareness and knowledge about the risks of drinking during pregnancy in Multnomah County, Oregon. *American Journal of Public Health,* 1981, *71,* 312–314.

20. Rosett, H. L., Ouellette, E. M., Weiner, L., and Owens, E. Therapy of heavy drinking during pregnancy. *Obstetrics and Gynecology,* 1978, *51,* 41–46.

21. Rosett, H. L., Snyder, P. A., Sander, L. W., Lee, A., Cook, P., Weiner, L., and Gould, J. Effects of maternal drinking on neonate state regulation. *Developmental Medicine and Child Neurology,* 1979, *21,* 464–473.

22. Rosett, H. L., Weiner, L., Zuckerman, B., McKinlay, S., and Edelin, K. C. Reduction of alcohol consumption during pregnancy with benefits to the newborn. *Alcoholism: Clinical and Experimental Research,* 1980, *4,* 178–184.

23. Rosett, H. L., Weiner, L., and Edelin, K. C. Strategies for prevention of fetal alcohol effects. *Obstetrics and Gynecology,* 1981, *57,* 1–7.

24. Sokol, R. J., Miller, S. I., and Martier, S. *Identifying the alcohol-abusing obstetric/gynecologic patient: A practical approach* (DHHS Publication No. (ADM) 81-1163). Washington, D.C.: U.S. Government Printing Office, 1981.

25. Blume, S. B. Drinking and pregnancy. *New York State Journal of Medicine,* 1981, *81,* 95–98.

26. Weiner, L., Rosett, H. L., and Edelin, K. C. Behavioral evaluation of fetal alcohol education for physicians. *Alcoholism: Clinical and Experimental Research,* 1982, *6,* 230–233.

Index